Prophetic TIMELINE of Revelation Comprehensive study and how to understand Prophecy

These Prophecies are occurring current in our timeline
We are in the last of the Last Days

The Four Horseman of the Apocalypse

A must read if you wish to understand current world events and
The Identity of America and England in End Time Prophecy

Jesse R. Cox

WORKBOOK PRESS LLC
187 E Warm Springs Rd,
Suite B285 Las Vegas NV 89119 USA

Website: https://workbookpress.com/
Hotline: 1-888-818-4856
Email: admin@workbookpress.com

Ordering Information:
Quantity sales. Special discounts are available on quantity purchases by corporations, associations, and others. For details, contact the publisher at the address above.

ISBN-13: 978-1-963718-92-8 Paperback Version
          978-1-963718-93-5 Digital Version

REV. DATE: 03/22/2024

TABLE OF CONTENTS

Introduction

The modern Church no longer teach Bible Prophecy as a whole except a hand full throughout this country. This is a shame for they will miss a great blessing from God, *"Blessed is he that readeth, and they that bear the words of his prophecy"* (Rev 1:3) and *"blessed is he that keepeth the sayings of the prophecy of this book"* (Rev 22:7). God tells us to watch and be ready for Rev 3:2-5 gives a dire warning in verse three *"If therefore thou shalt not watch, I will come on thee as a thief"* and Luke 21:36, *"Watch ye therefore, and pray always, that ye may be accounted worthy to escape"* for Luke is speaking of the day of Trouble called Tribulation as John the Revelator lays out.

This Author will outline, given by the Spirit, the Key Secrets hidden within the Book of Revelation that baffle most Christian. Pastors do not want to touch Prophecy for they do not see or understand the timeline. This book will help the reader to understand God's chronological, sequential unbroken timeline as laid out in this book but the reader must ask the Lord for Spiritual guidance. First, we must understand the dispensations of time. Gen 1:1 **"In the beginning God created the heaven and the earth"**, meaning it was perfect. This verse covers pre-adamic age when the dinosaurs roamed the earth that could have been millions of years before Adam and Eve. Gen 1:2 **"and the earth was without form and void"** for Satan destroyed the earth due to rage when God kicked him out of Heaven. From Gen 1:3 is when it took God seven days to rebuild the Earth and created man. From Gen 1:3 till Rev 16:17 there has been an absolute unbroken timeline of the history of man. Rev 16:17-21 when it says "it is done", meaning, the seven-year Tribulation is done/over/ complete. The Gospel is "finished" on earth in Rev 10:7, 11:7 and Dan 12:7 in the middle of the Tribulation at the 3½ year mark. Rev chapter 17-22 is only John's commentary that can be placed from the time Satan was kicked out of Heaven prior to Gen 1:1 up to the New Heaven and Earth descending down engulfing millions of years.

It is extremely critical for the reader to understand that there is an unbroken timeline from Rev 1:1, at the beginning of the Church age in the book of Acts, till the pouring of the 7th Vial in Rev 16:17-21 where **"It is done"**. The advancement of time does not change in any way as laid out within this book. During this period of time, there is certain unwritten or proven synopsis that should be considered that clarifies several unsolved questions. The first question is, why does many Christian websites, videos and talking heads say that Russia wins the up-coming Ezekiel 38 and 39 war when Ezekiel 39 clearly states the Russia Islamic confederation as Magog having 5/6th of their armies, destroyed in Eze 39:2,6,9&11. These verses clearly state that it will take seven years to burn their weapons proving that the Tribulation Period last for seven years and

1

not just 42 months. Satan has three goals to complete in the Ezekiel 38 and 39 war and they are: 1. Destroy both USA/UK and Russia to clear the way for implementing his New World Order. 2. The Christian and Muslim religions must be destroyed and will be along with Christian America and Muslims with Russia and the Middle East so that he can declare himself god. 3. To usher in the Anti-Christ when Satan is released from the bottomless pit in Rev 9:1 blowing of the 5th Trumpet at the two-year mark of the 1st half of the Trib. This subject brings up a dilemma for the Christian talking heads all say that America and NATO are twenty years behind Russia and China in technology of Nukes and hypersonic weapons where America is destroyed! Is that true? This is the scenario that no one is discussing: Satan will not allow Russia, China and the Arab States to destroy his plans for a NWO developing through the Deep State of the Western Nations. For more than fifty years, Satan's Black Projects has developed secret weapons that no one in this world knows about and this Author believes it to be lazar weapon systems. Lazers are far quicker and more accurate than any hypersonic weapons for they are located on space-based platforms, ships, aircraft, hand held and ground vehicles. The Deep State has allowed their enemies to believe that America and NATO are week and far behind in their weapons technology that puts a hook into Magog's jaws. This lures Russia and the Arab nations into WWIII which is the Ezekiel 38 war that takes place at the beginning of the seven-year period of Tribulation. The Scriptures clearly state that it takes Israel seven years to burn their weapons prior to the so-called second coming of Jesus.

Final Scenario: Yes, America and Russia are destroyed during WWIII according to Dan 7:4-5 and Eze 38-39 but the Deep State of Babylon is not destroyed for it is the platform for the coming of the Anti-Christ paid for by the American dollar. America as head of NATO is the rider of the white horse in Rev 6:2-3 representing the lion with eagle's wings in Dan 7:3. Note that the Lion is England and the Wings are the Eagle of America. Russia is the red horse in Rev 6:3-4 where they plucked off the wings of the white horse of America prior to their destruction in Daniel's vision in Dan 7:4-5. Rev 6:2-4 and Dan 7:3-4 are the same war which is the world war of Ezekiel 38 and 39 that again occurs at the beginning of the seven-year Tribulation. When the rider of the white horse is plucked off in the war of Rev 6:3-4 and Dan 7:5, it is the wounded head of the Anti-Christ government system mentioned in Rev 13:3. This is the destruction of America but the system survives through the Deep State of Babylon rooted in America and Europe. The military head is revived through European NATO and becomes the 3rd and 4th beast of Dan 7:6-7 as the mightiest army in the history of the world controlled by the Anti-Christ as stated in Rev 13:4. We must remember that Christian America as the West and Muslim Russia has to be destroyed prior to the coming of the Anti-Christ and Rev 6:2-4 and Dan 7:3-4 accomplishes this fact. How does this happen? America is only a small portion of the Deep State and is allowed to control military power due to the American tax dollar and military power that has paid for the Beast System. When WWIII starts in Rev 6:4 and Dan 7:4, God allows Satan through Russia to bring judgment and destroys America with a nuke first strike. The moment America is destroyed, the Anti-Christ Deep State activates their land/space Lazer systems and destroys Russia along with their Arab coalition. Zechariah 14:12 states, **"all the people that have fought against Jerusalem; Their flesh shall consume away while they stand upon their feet, and their eyes shall consume away in their holes, and their tongue shall consume away in their mouth"**. This verse sure sounds like a Lazer weapon to me! China betrays Russia and the Muslims by laying back and allowing the Beast Deep State to destroy Russia in the WWIII scenario. China become a part of the Anti-Christ Beast System during the seven-year Tribulation period.

Ladies and Gentlemen, we must be very careful when studying the Scriptures and writing about God's Word! There is only one true interpolation and we must discern the spirit of God from Satan's influence for the Serpent the Devil is very powerful and Christians can be deceived. Rev 22:18-19 gives us a dire warning that if we change or add to his Word, we will receive the plagues of his Book, Hell Fire. This calls for deep study, research and prayer given by the Holy Spirit to ward off Satan as we write about Prophecy based on the Scriptures. To a Christian writer, this is terrifying, for the consequences are great to maintain Scripture integrity and truth of the Holy Spirit. There is a false teaching on some Conservative Christian Talk Shows that there are no Pre-Tribulation Rapture or taking of the Church prior to the seven-year Tribulation that they believe to last for only 42 months. The hypothesis of the Church being Raptured prior to the Tribulation is proven by Scripture, confirmed within this book, to be correct if you truly believe the Prophetic Scriptures and the timeline that is specifically laid out. This book is based solely on God given personal inspiration given to this Author based on great study, research and prayer within the King James Bible, the Apocrypha and the book of Jasher to include other supporting inspired books all proven to be of God's Word. Closely study the layout of this book which is based only on the Scriptures, not from man's books or the writer's personal thoughts. If we fail to truly understand the timeline as the sequence of events listed within this book solely based on the Scriptures, we completely miss the meaning of the book of Revelation. The truth is within the unbroken TIMELINE of the whole book of Revelation that many Christians fail to study. We only need to identify the continual sequence of events from John's commentary's that seems to divide the Chapters into different times and events. In reality, John's commentary and the sequence of events are within an unbroken timeline that this book will prove by Scripture. This lesson is a hard read for it is based on deep study and research into God's Word. Without the help of the Holy Spirit, you cannot understand the events that I lay out in this book.

Gods Master Time Clock

The book of Revelation, Daniel and all Prophetic
Books of the Bible represent a constant unbroken timeline
evident if the reader is willing to
Study the Scriptures

The Secret Keys

This book gives a panoramic view of the book of Revelation

Can you find the Keys within?

There are secret key verses that unlocks the timeline suppressed deep within the Book of Revelation found in the opening of the 5th and 6th Trumpets. You cannot understand the timeline unless you unlock the key! This book will guide you to open the key to help understand all the prophetic Books of the Bible. During my fifty years of Bible study, this Author has missed the understanding of this KEY till now, and the Holy Spirit has prompted me to write this book to show its SECRETS.

Revelation is the most mis-understood Book in the Bible simply because Christians do not understand the timeline. For some reason, the Church cannot see that from Rev chapters 1 thru 22, all events of the 7 Seals, Trumpets and Vials occur in sequential order just as a time clock that never stops. Each event can be placed within the Seals, Trumpets and Vials in sequence of the timeline but John's commentary places some events out of order. With study, we can place them in their proper order.

This book is a hard read for it is a deep study that compiles verses from almost every book in the Old and New Testaments to include supporting books such as Jasher, I&II Enoch, Apocalypse of Baruch, the Apocrypha and others. The Scriptures are fascinating for it ties all the Bible Prophetic books together into the book of Revelations. Prophetic events fit together perfectly like a million-peace jigsaw puzzle. There are certain KEYS that unlock the Secrets. The Apostle John was chosen by God to compile end-time prophecy into one book that correlates perfectly with all Biblical writings so that the Church could understand in the last days. One third of all Scripture is Prophetic and we must "study to show thyself approved", II Tim 2:15. Daniel 12:9 states, *"And he said, Go thy way, Daniel: for the words are closed up and sealed till the time of the end"*. It is now time to unseal the Keys and understand the Prophetic truths that has now been released. God is currently revealing these hidden secrets of Prophecy to his chosen ones and he, for some reason, has chosen me to unlock his prophetic secrets to you. By guidance of the Holy Spirit, deep study and prayer, Jesus has given me the secrets of the book of Revelation to tell the world. Are you willing to take the same sacrifice and seek the Truth? This, is my mission in life, to present the Reader these secrets in dedication to my Lord Jesus Christ.

4

Preface

Christians that study prophecy in the book of Revelation and all prophetic books of the Bible will receive a great blessing according to these Scriptures, Rev 1:3, **"Blessed is he that readeth, and they that hear the words of this prophecy"**, Rev 22:7, **"Behold, I come quickly: blessed is he that keepeth the sayings of the prophecy of this book"**. God takes great pleasure when his children read and study his mysteries and secrets of his Gospel and Prophecies. If we lack knowledge II Tim 2:15 tells us to **"Study to show thyself approved unto God, a workman that needeth not to be ashamed, rightly dividing the word of truth"**. If we lack wisdom James 1:5 states, **"If any of you lack wisdom, let him ask of God, that giveth to all men liberally, and upbraideth not; and it shall be given him"**. Apply these two Scriptures to James 5:16, **"The effectual fervent prayer of a righteous man availeth much"**. Closely study these verses prior to reading this book or the Revelation of John. With these Scriptures in mind, this writer must make a very true statement. From the age of thirteen when I was born into Gods family till the age of fifty, I longed for the knowledge of Bible Prophecy by reading many Christian books on the subject and diligently studied the Scriptures. According to my Scriptural study and what the Churches and Prophetic teachers taught in books did not match. Something was very wrong for it was different from what the Scriptures state! I got on my knees for almost a year in fervent prayer for Jesus to give me guidance and understanding of the truth of the Scriptures. In my heart, I knew that the truth of Prophecy had to come from the Holy Bible and not from the teachings of Christian men. It took a year of study and prayer with tears for God to show and anoint me with his truth. With a flash of light and a breeze of a warm spring day, God opened my eyes to his Holy Word from the Old to the New Testament and it all made perfect since. No, he did not pour it into me, but, now when I study, he shows me his mysteries of the Gospel and the secrets of his Prophecies when I read Scripture. I had to earn the right to know God's Secrets through deep study and prayer for his knowledge of spiritual guidance. A Christian has to work diligently in praying, studying, and researching word studies for God to reveal his truth, it takes hard work. From the age of fifty-two till now, the secrets that God has shown me in his Word, I can now share those mysteries given by the Holy Spirit to you.

The timeline of Bible Prophecy is the key in understanding all prophecy. To better understand the timeframe of prophetic events prophesied within the prophetic books, we must comprehend one key verse, Mark 13:32, **"But of that day and that hour knoweth no man, no not the angels which are in heaven, neither the Son, but the Father"**. This verse cannot be speaking of Jesus coming in power and glory with fire at the end of the Tribulation but of the coming in the clouds to take his Church in I Thessalonians that clearly indicate an upward movement, **"Then we which are alive and remain shall be caught up together with them in the clouds, to meet the Lord in the air",** I Thess 4:17. Why would Jesus come for his Church and immediately take them back to earth when II Thess 1:7 tells us that the Church is resting with him in Heaven when he comes in power and glory, **"And to you who are troubled rest with us, when the Lord Jesus shall be revealed from heaven with his mighty angels".** Christ coming in power and glory is mentioned in II Thessalonians indicating a downward movement from Heaven to Earth with his Saints the Church with him "rest with us". Study I&II Thessalonians carefully and you will see that I Thess is a coming in the clouds indicating an upward movement and II Thess indicate a downward movement when Jesus comes in Power and Glory to destroy ungodly man. If you closely study you will see that I (*upward movement*) and II Thessalonians (*downward movement*) speak of two different and distinct comings of Jesus. Most Christians either fail or refuse to study the difference between the two books for each is speaking of a completely different coming of Jesus, one with an upward and one with a downward movement. All through the Old Testament God planed major events to occur on feast days, blood moons, the Passover or other special Jewish Holidays but if we closely study this coming, it is different. Let's not make the mistake and think that the coming in Mark 13:32 is Christ's second coming where no man knows the day or hour to include Jesus and the angels. If this verse is speaking of the second coming then we could figure out the exact day of his coming. According to these verses, there has to be three comings of Jesus, one at his birth (Matt, Mark, Luke and John), one to take his Church (I Thess 4:14-17 & I Cor 15:51) and one at the end of the Tribulation as stated in II Thess 1:7-9 and Rev 1:7. Mark 13:32 is speaking of Gods coming in the clouds as a secret that not even Christ knows. This coming is in direct relation to the parable of the fig tree in Mark 13:28, just three verses prior, when the Master of the vineyard comes in secret. The coming at the end of the Tribulation can almost be planned to the day according to stated Scripture so it cannot be a Secret. The coming that Apostle Mark is speaking of is associated to Christ coming in the clouds to take his Church (his vineyard servants) just as his parable in Matt 21:33-34 and his coming in the clouds spoken of in I Cor 15:51-52, I Thess 4:14-18 and Dan 12:1-2. He does not set foot on earth at this coming. By Scripture, there are three comings of Jesus, 1st at birth establishing the Gospel on earth, 2nd coming in the clouds as an upward movement taking his Church and 3rd coming with clouds as a downward movement in power with fire and glory on a white horse.

Do not fall for the false teaching of the Mid or Post Tribulation for the Bible clearly lays out three different comings of Christ. Again, the **1st** when he was born into the world in the flesh as a child to establish his ministry as laid out in the Gospels. The **2nd** when he comes in the clouds in the air to take his Church as spoken in I Thessalonians and the **3rd** when he comes at the end of the Tribulation *"with clouds"* in II Thess and Rev 1:7 in power and glory with his Heavenly Kingdom to reign for one thousand years. Closely study the difference between I and II Thessalonians for it is key in understanding the Pre-Tribulation rapture. We must not confuse the word clouds mentioned in I Thess 4:17 and Rev 1:7 for each verse has a completely different meaning. I Thess 4:17 states, **"Then we which are alive and remain shall be caught up together with them in the clouds, to meet the Lord in the air: and so shall we ever be with the Lord"**. This verse clearly indicates an upward movement from the earth to the clouds, *"caught up together with them in the clouds, to meet the Lord in the air"* representing that they are normal every day clouds that are in the atmosphere. Now let's review Rev 1:7, **"Behold, he cometh with clouds; and every eye shall see him, and they also which pierced him: and all kindreds of the earth shall wail because of him"**. This verse indicates a downward movement not with the normal clouds in the air but with clouds of smoke and fire around him, *"he cometh with* [fire] *clouds;"* from Heaven to earth bringing judgment with fire. There is a distinct difference between the meaning of clouds in these two verses if we review objectively.

Another point that makes this event different is that God will not come till mans cup of iniquity is full for God has to fully justify the ending of mans self-rule and to bring judgment upon evil humankind. The destruction of Nineveh, Jonah 3:10, is an example of Gods mercy and judgment where the time of judgment can be changed if a nation repents. We live in an extreme time of evil and God wants the world to repent just as he sent Noah and his Patriarchs preaching prior to judgment of the Flood. The same is true today. God would love to change or extend the time of judgment, just as in the days of Nineveh where he deferred the hour and date of judgment due to repentance. This is why the Angels and Christ do not know the hour and date of his coming for this event has an open date depending on international, national and individual repentance. Only God knows when and only he has the power to change the date of judgment depending on mans hearts of repentance. If the "last day" Christians try to plan his coming around Jewish Holidays, that will be a mistake for we are no longer under the Law but the age of grace, II Esdras 1:31, **"When ye offer unto me, I will turn my face from you: for your solemn feast-days, your new moons, and your circumcisions, have I forsaken"**. This verse is speaking of Israel being under judgment after the Babylonian captivity just as the Church is under judgment today for his coming will not be judged on Jewish Holidays. This verse also applies to the Church Age. The date of his coming is an open date that only God, in his omnipotent power can make and he is anxious to change that date if only man repents. It cannot be based upon a Jewish Holiday! Therefore, the date of Christ to take his Church into the clouds and Gods coming in judgment will be based upon man's decision to repent of his evil sins.

There is an aspect that most theologians do not consider. The Scriptures are clear that there will be seven years between the beginning of the Tribulation Period and the ending when Christ comes in power and glory found in Dan 9:24-27 as the 70th week prophecy of seven years. Rev 11:1-2 and 13:5 divides the seven years into two separate halves by indicating two numbers of time as **"forty and two months"** (42 mo.) representing the newly built Temple in the last half of the Tribulation and 42 months given as a time of rule to the Anti-Christ. The time period given in Rev 11:3 of **"thousand two hundred and threescore days"** or 1260 days represents the time period for the two Witnesses. Both of these separate periods represent 3½ years of time equaling seven years total. Rev 11:3 gives the two witnesses 1260 days or 3½ years in the 1st half and verse two gives the Anti-Christ 3½ years or 42 months to tread the Temple under foot in the 2nd half. We must note the reason God divides one as days (1260) and one as months (42). Each number is to specifically identify two separate time periods dividing the seven years into two halves as two distinct periods of time. Rev 11:2, 13:5 and Dan 7:25 allots the Anti-Christ 42 months in the 2nd half where Rev 11:3 allots the two witnesses 1260 days in the 1st half of the Tribulation. Be assured that the beginning of the Tribulation will be marked by a great event that will be very clear by date and time which is the taking of the Church into the clouds separating a dispensation of time between the Church Age and the seven years of wrath. Simply mark off seven years and you will know the date of the ending of the Tribulation. Therefore, how can his coming be a secret as a thief in the night. For some odd reason, theologians cannot comprehend that there are three comings of Christ where his second coming is in the clouds and air. I Thess 4:17 clearly stating that he does not set his foot on earth during this coming for it is clearly an upward movement when taking his Spiritual Church. Christ's first coming at birth to establish his Church and Gospel was prophesied but the season was not known. The only other coming that is secret is his second coming in the clouds at the beginning of the Tribulation where even Christ and his angels do not know the hour and day. We as Christians were to only know the season of his coming as a thief in the night. If Christ comes in the middle or at the end of the Tribulation, it could be figured almost to the day of his coming due to calculation of known events given by Scripture. Therefore, a mid or pre-Tribulation taking of the Church is out of the question for it could not be as a thief in the night.

The following two verses are critical in understanding Bible Prophecies for without the guidance of the Holy Spirit, it is impossible to comprehend. If Christians apply James 1:5 and II Tim 2:15 as quoted above, God will show you his biblical mysteries but only with diligent prayer and study. If we as Christians work hard with study and prayer by abiding by these two scriptures, we will stand tall before God but will be an outcast in the End Time Church and Society itself. God never fails on a promise. The Prophet Daniel, in Dan 12:4 is told to shut up the book till the time of the end. We know that we are currently in the end days. Therefore, if we do not have an open mind in prayer with James 1:5 and II Tim 2:15 in mind seeking wisdom through study on a daily bases, God cannot and will not show us his end time prophecy through the Holy Spirit. God is only now revealing the Prophet's secrets through daily current events so we have to be ready to receive his fulfillments as they occur with study and prayer through the Holy Spirit as a guide. If we as Christians are close minded and refuse guidance from the Spirit, God will not show us his truths. During our studies, if we try to interject our own thoughts and beliefs, how can God give us the truth through the Spirit, he cannot? We must lay aside our own personal thoughts, knowledge and pride for Gods Spirit to work with us each day with a truthful open heart. Otherwise, he will ignore our prayers seeking prophetic knowledge. Do not be afraid of Satan's influence if you truly have a close relationship with the Holy Spirit, for he will protect you.

Authors Note
Which Bible is God's True Word?

Before I go into this lesson, the Author would like to made a personal statement to the reader. It is very important to understand how to pray, read and study the Holy Scriptures if we are to properly learn how to recognize God's whisper of inspiration. All Christians are different and God inspires each individual in a unique way. It took years of prayer to learn in how God personally communicates to me and to truly know his voice. He knows our voice when we pray, therefore, we must know his absolute pure voice when he talks to us in Spirit. If we fail to recognize his spiritual voice as a whisper, dream or a Spirit given thought, he cannot show us the meaning of his Holy Word in wisdom and knowledge. We must maintain an open mind to God without preconceived thoughts or ideas to distinguish the difference between the Spirit voice of Jesus and the evil enticing voice of Satan. Even pets and farm animals recognize the voice of the master that feeds them and Christians must do the same.

With this thought in mind, this Author would like to share, with the reader, an unbelievable inspiration that came from the Master Lord Jesus! Yes, I know his voice clearly! I was listening to a Christian video speaking of the early Hebrew Jewish feast's holidays in Old Testiment Scriptures and a thought from God clearly came into my mind. Most Christians know that the ancient writings of all of Gods Patriarchs and Prophets culminated into the ancient Scriptures now called the Old and New Testaments. From Adam to Jesus, the Scriptures were transcribed many times over from stone or brass tablets to parchment due to destruction of time down through the ages. God inspired Priests, Scribes and Holy Men to transcribe Scripture through time for the purpose to be given to the end time Church. He also gave us a promise that his Holy Word would be properly and correctly preserved throughout all generations in I Pet 1:25, John 1:1-2&14, Matt 24:35 and II Tim 3:16. History tells us that there are many new modern words today that was not written in the old Scriptures of ancient languages in Latin, Hebrew and Greek from Adam to Christ establishing his Church all the way up to the translation of the ancient manuscripts into the King James Version Bible by 47 Scholers in 1611AD. History proves to us that the KJV Bible was used by God to evangelize the world to common man. That is a fact that cannot be disputed by true history. The translators had an almost impossible job to transcribe ancient Scripture and maintain its pure meaning into new words of the modern English language. Early Galic of Britania is based on Hebrew words and letters that evolved into the English language. Slowly English was adopted by the world due to world shipping, business, economics, banking and aviation as a common world language. Due to the power of world trade of the British Empire, English was chosen to be the world's language for global trade, business, shipping and aviation. This brings up a very important question! How and why has God preserved the promise to maintain his true unchanged Holy Word into the English language? This is the inspiration that God gave me as his Servant to pass to you. To establish his Church worldwide, God needed his Holy Bible to be compiled into one book for the purpose of evangelizing the world through the Church. God personally chose King James of England for the purpose of gathering all known inspired manuscripts to be compiled into one single book for the salvation of common man. *My inspired thought is this: FACT- The King James Version is the only Bible in history that was chosen and inspired by God to be printed into one single language. Since the 1611 King James Version, there has been hundreds of other bibles translated into modern thought, in many different languages, where words and whole sentience's has been changed by Religious University Professors and Theologians for the supposedly purpose of better understanding in modern thought. There is a belief that the old English is too hard to read so, with the help of Satan, uninspired men changed the wording and meaning of the Scriptures. The only Bible inspired by God with the guidance of his hand is the King James Version in 1611AD and this is an absolute fact weather Christians believe it or not. All modern versions of the Bible, except the original KJV, is not inspired by God but printed by unholy University Professors and organizations, follow the money. We must recognize that Satan is trying to destroy God's Word through modern translations for Many Christians follow after these modern bibles thinking it is Gods true Scripture when it is not inspired by God.* The history listed below will help the reader to better understand this fact. Only God has the power to translate ancient manuscripts into a modern language with thousands of new words that did not exist in early history and maintain the true inspired meaning of the ancient texts. Not one "jot" was changed from ancient to modern texts according to Matt 5:18. In the Greek ref 2503, "jot" means *the tenth letter of the Hebrew alphabet and the 8th of the Greek alphabet, a very small part of anything*. The word Law in this scripture means in Greek 3551, *law of Moses or also of the Gospel*. By these definitions, not **"one jot or one tittle shall in**

no wise pass from the law, till all be fulfilled" speaking directly of the Law of Moses incorporated into the Gospel of Christ. Not one letter or period was to be changed in anyway by promise of God.

Key Secrets in understanding the book of Revelation:

1st Key: The Reader must believe that the King Jamse Authorized Version 1611 Bible is true and infallible as God's Holy Word.

2nd Key: Christians must believe that the Tribulation Period last for seven-years broken down into two 3½ year periods by Scripture or we cannot understand the prophetic timeline. This fact is proven in Dan 9:27 and the Apocalypse of Baruch 26:1 (XXVI), 27:1-13 XXVIII), 28:1-2, and 30:1. We must rely on what the Scripture actually say and not read into it. Don't maintain your old way of thinking.

3rd Key: The key in unlocking the timeline of the book of Revelation is found in the blowing of the 5th and 6th Trumpets in Rev 9:1 and 9:13.

4th Key: Understanding the sequential events that occur within the unbroken timeline verses John's commentary given in chapters 17-22. Each commentary can be chronologically placed within one of the Seals, Trumpets or Vials maintaining all events listed from chapter four through sixteen within the unbroken timeline.

Biblical History

Why did God choose the English language to establish his only inspired Bible to evangelize the world by his Church? Who is the Church? The following Scriptures will identify the Church and its language used to evangelized the world.

1. The Birthright Tribe of Israel- Joseph inherited the family birthright from Jacob, the father of Israel, to be named Israel found in Gen 48:15-22 to be a multitude of nations. Jacob clearly gave his name Israel only to the two lads of Ephraim and Manasseh directly through Joseph with the symbol of the "unicorn" in Duet 33:17. By Scripture, Ephraim and Manasseh were to be called Israel not the Jews of Jerusalem as clearly stated in Gen 48:13-16. These two lads were to be leaders of the ten northern tribes called the house of Israel confirmed in I Kings 11:26&28 as the house of Joseph. They were the northern kingdom of ten tribes in I Kings 11:30-37 to be called the Children or the house of Israel in I Kings 12:19-24. After their Assyrian captivity, they dispersed into the wilderness documented in II Esdras 13:40-46 of the Apocrypha to wait for the coming of Christ's Gospel. Their world blessing was to be fulfilled **"in the**

last days" according to Gen 49:1.

2. Ephriam and Manasseh as the house of Israel is given the Church to be God's *"peculiar people"* **called** *"a living stone"*, *"Sion a chief corner stone"* **in I Peter 2:4-9, Matt 10:6, 15:24, Acts 10:36 and Eze 3:1-5** *"of a strange speech and of an hard language, but to the house of Israel"*: By Scripture, the house of Israel is called the "lost sheep" in Jerm 50:17 **"Israel is a scattered sheep"**, Eze 34:12 **"I seek out my sheep"**, Zec 13:7 **"and the sheep shall be scattered"**, I Peter 1:1 **"to the strangers scattered abroad"**, James 1:1 **"to the twelve tribes which are scattered abroad"**, Mark 14:27 **"and the sheep shall be scattered"**.

3. We must identify the modern language of the inheritance tribes of Ephraim and Manassehas as God's scattered sheep: The house of Israel was to be named after Isaac in Gen 21:12, **"for in Isaac shall thy seed be called"**. Paul in Rom 9:7 was speaking directly to Israel as Israelites, **"but in Isaac shall thy seed be called"**. Paul in Heb 11:18 was speaking of the linage of Abraham through Isaac to be given to Jacob and his son Joseph to pass directly to Joseph's two sons Ephraim and Manasseh in Heb 11:21-22, **"That in Isaac shall thy seed be called"**. Clearly by these scriptures, the seed of Joseph that received the family name ISRAEL and birthright was to be called after Isaac as his lineage, identity and language to be called Saxon as laid out within this book. Isaiah 3:5 speak of a language that is not strange or hard for Galic is the basic language of the British People. The English language is based on Hebrew characters where the house of Israel was scattered abroad into the wilderness of Europe and Britania according to, I Peter 1:1 and James 1:1. The British People is called "barbarians" in Acts 28:4 and Rom 1:14 where the Romans called Scottish warriors barbarians for their ferociousness during the Roman invasion of England in 54BC. In Greek barbarian means *a foreigner*.

4. Who were to receive the Gospel to be leader of the Church: To absolutely confirm this fact, Jesus personally gave his Church directly to the lost sheep of the house of Israel in Matt 10:6, 15:24, Rev 2:14, where Jesus states, **"I am not sent but unto the lost sheep of the house of Israel"**. Eze 3:1-5 and Rev 10:9-10 are almost identical verses and calls the Gospel a "roll" and "little book" where God sent his Gospel to the house of Israel. The house of Joseph which was given to Ephraim and Manasseh as the Birthright inheritance tribes were to be many nations as the shepherd of the Church clearly stated in Gen 49:24, **"(from thence is the shepherd, the stone** [or Church] **of Israel)"**. According to Moses, the house of Israel was to be identified throughout the world in the end days as Unicorns and Bullocks symbols of the UK as the Unicorn and USA as the bull of Wall Street. According to Duet 33:17, **"His glory is like the firstling of his bullock and his horns are like the horns of unicorns, with them he shall push the people together to the ends of the earth: and they are the ten thousands of Ephraim and they are the thousands of Manasseh"**. The only nation in world history to carry the symbol of the unicorn of Ephraim is England as the British Empire of 46 Commonwealth nations fulfilling Duet 33:17 and Gen 48:19. They were to be many nations **"he shall push the people together to the ends of the earth"** in Duet 33:17 through world trade by shipping and banking. Manasseh were to be one single nation as the Bullocks which is America, Ephraim's brother both receiving the family birthright inheritance as tribes.

Common man has no way to verify if these new translations have been properly transcribed from the King James Version unless we trust University Leaders and Theologians. Are they men of God? We, as the common man, have no way in knowing if they were true men of God for God did not inspire their translations. The only translations authorized by a Commission by King or Government authority was the KJV for by history all other Bible translations were authorized only by their own volition, not by Spiritual authority. By verified history, the linage of the Throne of England can be traced back to King David for England and America are the descendants of the house of Israel. This fact can be easily researched in ancient English history. Christians must depend only on the KJV as the inspired Cannon and as proof, initially, only the KJV evangelized the world. God has the power to preserve all his manuscripts down through ancient times and translations from Latin, Hebrew and Greek into the English King James Version. God's inspiration ends at the KJV for it is his final draft to be given to common man. God gave man grade schools, Colleges and Universities to promote his Scriptures to teach man how to read and study his Word. The early Fathers of Christ's original Church was given guidance by the Holy Spirit to conduct councils to establish and compile the books of the Holy Scriptures at the Council of Maratorian Canon in 170AD, the Council of Laodicea in 393AD, Council of Hippo in 393AD and the council of Carth in 397AD. We must note that the early Church of Christ and the Roman Catholic Church was two separate and different religious systems and Churches. The council of Rome in 382AD, Ecumenical Council of Florence in 1442AD and the Council of Trent in 1546AD formulated the Roman Catholic Bible of 73 books. Christ's early Church had a serious problem with the Catholic Church trying to infiltrate with Catholic doctrine. The sixty-six books of the Bible were formulated but was still not translated into one inspired language. The following inspired early Church Fathers are only a few that established these Councils and compiled the Holy Scriptures that we have today: The early Fathers of Christ's Church were Clement of Rome 95AD, Ploycarp a Disciple of John 108AD, Ignatius of Antioch 115AD, Irenaeus 185AD and Hippolytus in 170-235AD. The Holy Spirit overcame this problem and God preserved his inspired Word through the 1611AD King James Version. Note: no other major religion in the world followed after the KJV except Christ's original Church, not even the Roman Catholic Church proving its authenticity.

How do we know which Bible in this world is God's True WORD for he says in John 1:1-2&14, **"In the beginning was the Word, and the Word was with God, and the Word was God. The same was in the beginning with God."** **"And the Word was made flesh, and dwelt among us, (and we beheld his glory, the glory as of the only begotten of the Father) full of grace and truth."** According to these verses, the Holy Bible is Christ, therefore, there was only one Christ so there can be only one true Holy Bible. Matt 5:18 tells us that his Word is the Law of his Gospel, **"For verily I say unto you, Till heaven and earth pass, one jot or one tittle shall in no wise pass from the law, till all be fulfilled"**. This verse flat tells us that from the original writings of his Patriarchs, Prophets, Apostles and Holy Men that wrote the sixty-six books of the KJV Bible, not one jot or tittle meaning not one comma, period, word or sentence that he approves will be changed. Finally, II Timothy 3:16 tells us, **"All scripture is given by inspiration of God, and is profitable for doctrine, for reproof, for correction, for instruction in righteousness"**. With all these scriptures said, God gives man a dire warning in Rev 22:18, **"For I testify unto every man that heareth the words of the prophecy of this book, If any man shall add unto these things, God shall add unto him the plagues that are written in this book:"**. If man changes one jot or tittle of God's Word, he will see the judgment of Hell. The only inspired Bible in modern times is the King James Version 1611AD for all revised Bibles after the KJV were not inspired by God but by men and so-called Christian Organizations given no Spiritual Authority from God. If the reader does not believe that the Bible is true and inspired, you need not read this book any farther.

Identifying Gods Earthly Kingdom as the Church

To better understand the book of Revelation, we must first recognize the creation of God's earthly kingdom and why. By comprehending God's Kingdom in ancient and modern times, it can help Christians apply it to end time Prophecy!

As Christians, we need to understand the correlation between Gods ancient kingdom verses the pledged Heavenly Kingdom to include David's Throne promised to Christ's Church. This lesson will help us to understand the difference between the two and how Gods ancient kingdom of Israel (the old lion) and his modern kingdom of his Church as the house of Israel (the young lions) are one and the same. David's throne and Kingdom as the Church and Gospel was taken from the old lion (house of Judah) and given to the young lions (house of Israel Matt 10:6&15:24) in Matt 21:42-44 as his stone Kingdom in Dan 2:35&44-45). He promises that his Word, the Scriptures, would never change or ever will in Malachi 3:6, **"For I am the Lord, I change not:"**. His ancient temple and modern kingdom of salvation through Christ's Gospel has to maintain the same elements throughout time which are the 12 Tribes, the Throne of David and the Temple/Church. All three elements of his kingdom have to be currently present on this Earth to include the Throne of King David. It is currently found in the Throne of England carrying the symbol of the Lion and Unicorn as a national symbol and three crouched lions on the flag of the King representing the linage of the Tribe of Judah.

Let's review the **Hebrew** meaning of Kingdom as relating to Gods plan of salvation for man in ancient verses modern times. A plan of Salvation to save humanity was the purpose of his earthly Kingdom. Has his Kingdom changed over time, not according to his promise? The Hebrew meaning of kingdom: (4467, II Sam 7:13-16 **"of thy kingdom upon Israel for ever"**) *dominion, the estate rule or the country realm of a kingdom, king's reign, royal* (4427) *to reign, to ascend the throne, to induct into royalty hence to take counsel, be Queen* (4410, Ps 22:28 **"for the kingdom is the Lord's"**) *something ruled as a realm, kingdom, king's as royal* (4437, Dan 2:44, 4:3&17) *dominion, kingdom, kingly, realm, reign* same as (4438) *a rule dominion empire, kingdom, realm, reign, royal.* The **Greek** meaning of Kingdom: (932, Matt 3:2) *royalty, rule or a realm, kingdom, reign,* same as (935) *through the notion of a foundation of power, a sovereign king* same as (939) *to walk, a pace by the foot.* According to these definitions, Gods earthly kingdom was to be a physical sovereign king as a man reigning on a throne in a realm of an earthly nation of people and this kingdom was to travel by foot. Clearly by Scripture, King David's throne was to always have a man sitting upon it through all generations as stated in Jerm 33:14-17, I Kings 9:5, II Chron 7:18 and rule during all generations in Ps 89:4&145:13, **"There shall not fail thee a man upon the throne of Israel"**. By Scripture, King David's throne has to exist today, so, where is it, the throne of England as the Unicorn of Ephraim, Duet 33:17 with his brother the Bull of the USA? If we apply the Hebrew and Greek meaning of Israel to these definitions, we can see that the word Israel is the key. In Hebrew Israel means ref # 3478, *he will rule as God, a symbol name of Jacob and of his posterity, Israel.* In Greek 2474, *the adopted name of Jacob or his descendants, Israel, 2475, an Israelite or descendant of Israel.* By these definitions and the following listed Scripture, Israel or the house of Israel were to rule the world through Christ's Gospel as a direct inheritance. Gen 48:16 is absolutely clear that the name Jacob changed to Israel were to be given only

15

to the two sons of Joseph named Ephraim and Manasseh not to the Jews. The Scriptures further explains that God's earthly realm or kingdom were to be ruled by Gods people of Israel as a special people as a stone kingdom stated in Daniel 2:34 and 44-45, **"and the kingdom shall not be left to other people"** and **"the stone was cut out of the mountain without hands"**. This verse is speaking of Christ's Church with Jesus as its chief corner stone which is his stone kingdom mentioned in, I Peter 2:4-9 as his stone Church, **"a royal priesthood, and holy nation, a peculiar people"**. This verse is calling his Church a holy nation of peculiar people called Israel as spoken of in Duet 14:2 and 26:18-19 as a direct reference to God's Chosen People as the nation of Israel. These verses are confirmed in Matt 10:6, 15:24, Acts 10:36 and Eze 3:1-5 where Jesus personally gave his earthly kingdom as his Church only to the lost sheep of the house of Israel, again, not to the Jews.

As we review the Hebrew and Greek meaning of kingdom as related to Gods Heavenly Kingdom in ancient times verses modern times, we see that both are a physical country, nation or realm that is ruled by a royal male King or female Queen through dominion as a sovereign leader. When we go to the Scriptures two different kingdoms are mentioned. We see the earthly human kingdoms by evil kings such as the kingdom of Og, Sihon, Babel etc. The first kingdom mentioned in the Bible is in Gen 10:10 where it speaks of the kingdom of Babel ruled by Nimrod as the kingdom of men. Gods' kingdom is not mentioned till I Samuel 13:13 where his Kingdom is placed upon Israel where their first king is King Saul, an evil king. This verse states; **"for now would the Lord have established thy kingdom upon Israel for ever."** This is the first establishment of Gods kingdom in the Scriptures and note "for ever" for his kingdom was not only to be a throne with a king but his people lead by his commandments by faith under the Old Covenant Temple and the New Covenant Church. Let's see what are the elements of his kingdom. We know that King Saul was the first king that sat on the throne of Israel so the **Throne** is the first element. Who did King Saul rule over? We are told by Scripture that he ruled over the twelve tribes of Israel so the second element of Gods kingdom has to be the twelve tribes of Israel called the house of Israel. What were the religion of Gods people of Israel and why did God establish Judaism as the faith of his people? We know that the Hebrew religion was Judaism under the Law of Moses as the Old Covenant consisting of the Tabernacle or Temple where the Holy of Holies of Gods Spirit administered by the High Priests of the tribe of Levi. The Temple is the heart of Gods Kingdom making the **Temple/Church** the third element of his kingdom. The Temple/Church represents the Holy Spirit of God being physically with his people where a believer in God/Christ inherits the birthright name of Israel, *he will rule as God*. Therefore, the three elements of Gods Kingdom have to be the **Throne**, the **twelve tribes of Israel** and the **Temple/Church**, ancient and modern, maintaining Gods Spirit with the people. With this in mind, let's review I Sam

13:13 above where God absolutely stated that his kingdom will be forever meaning that the Throne, Israel and the Temple as the end time Church will be forever. This means, the modern Kingdom of Gods Church has to maintain King David's Throne, the house of Israel as the twelve tribes and the Church as his Kingdom mentioned in I Sam 13:13. The books of I and II Samuel establish Gods earthly kingdom where we know that Saul was Israel's first King but was evil. I Samuel 13:13 and II Sam 3:10 translates Gods Kingdom from Saul to King David as a righteous man of God where he wanted to build God a house or Temple. II Samuel 7:1-17 establishes Gods Kingdom on earth where he gave it to King David and in verse 13 promise his Kingdom to King David forever, **"and I will stablish the throne of his kingdom for ever"**. The word "ever" is mentioned again in II Chronicles 13:5 where it also stated: **"Ought ye not to know that the Lord God of Israel gave the kingdom over Israel to David for ever, even to him and to his sons by a covenant of salt?"**. King David's Throne was promised to Jesus in Luke 1:32-33, **"and the Lord God shall give unto him the throne of his father David: And he shall reign over the house of Jacob for ever; and of his kingdom there shall be no end."** We must note that the term *"for ever"* and *"there shall be no end"* means that King David's Throne will be given to Christ as the Church at his coming, therefore, it has to currently exist on earth today. As a fact of Scripture, the Church today has to maintain all three elements of Gods ancient kingdom of Israel which is the Throne, the twelve tribes and the Temple/Church. The Throne of King David has to exist somewhere in the modern world today and that is the Throne of England. David's throne is the Unicorn of Ephraim and the Bull of Manasseh (England & USA) in Duet 33:17 given to the lost sheep of the end time Church by Christ himself.

This is proven in Matt 10:6, 15:24, Act 10:36 and Eze 3:1-5 where Christ personally gave responsibility and authority to his twelve Apostles to take his Gospel and Church to the house of Israel, **"But go rather to the lost sheep of the house of Israel, And as ye go, preach, saying, The kingdom of heaven is at hand"**. Clearly in these verses during the last days, the house of Israel was to evangelize the world with Christ's Gospel. Rev 10:10 and Eze 3:1-5 speak of **"the little book"** and **"eat this roll"** which means Christ's Gospel as God's Word for the house of Israel to preach and teach to the world. Both Scriptures say that it was sweet in the mouth but bitter in the belly proving that it is speaking of the Gospel of Christ to be given to the house of Israel. Ezekiel 3:1-5 mentions "the house of Israel" three times in speaking of this subject and Matt 10:6 and 15:24 proves that the Gospel was given only to the *"lost sheep of the house of Israel"*. The identity of the children of Israel as the house of Israel is proven in I Kings 12:19-24 where they were given King David's throne to be **"over all Israel"** in verse 20. As these verses state, the ten northern tribes are the house of Israel as the children of Israel (the Church in Rev 3:14 & Act 10:36) in verses 21&24. Revelation chapter 4 will prove that God's Earthly

17

Kingdom of King David's Throne, the twelve tribes of Israel and his Temple/
Church is taken to Heaven where Christ sets upon his promised throne prior to
the beginning of the seven years of Tribulation.

Chapter One

The seven-years of Tribulation and Daniel's 70th week are one and the Same in the relationship of the Timeline of the Book of Revelation

How can we know that the Tribulation Period within the book of Revelation and Daniel's 70th week prophecy is speaking of the same time period of seven years? It is simple, for Dan 8:11 speak of the **"daily sacrifice was taken away"** and Dan 9:27, **"And he shall confirm the covenant with many for one week: and in the midst of the week** [seven years] **he shall cause the sacrifice and the oblation to cease"**. This verse proves that Daniel's 70th week or seven years are broken into two separate parts divided by 1260 days or 42 months which is also 1260 days totaling seven years as listed in the above paragraph. The book of the Apocalypse of Baruch 28:1-2 confirms Dan 9:27 for it states, *"For the measure and reckoning of that time are two parts weeks of seven week"*. The Anti-Christ in the middle of the week or seven-year period will stop blood sacrificing and Dan 8:17&19 places Daniel's vision **"at the time of the end shall be the vision"** and **"for at the time appointed the end shall be"** which is the last days during the **"time of trouble"** in Dan 12:1. Dan 2:28 clearly places all of Daniel's prophecies to take place in the last days for it states, **"know to the king Nebuchadnezzar what shall be in the latter days"**. This verse pertains to the whole book of Daniel. The Church as Christ's Bride will not see wrath but escapes and be delivered as clearly stated in, Luke 21:36 (escape all these things), Dan 12:1 (deliver from trouble), I Thess 1:10 (delivered from wrath), 2:16 (saved from wrath), 5:9 and II Esdras 9:7-9 (escape perils) as a few verses that state this fact. II Esdras 8:63 clearly places this timeframe in the *"begin to do in the last times* [days]*"*. The key words and definitions of <u>escape, delivered</u> and <u>saved</u> tells us that the Church will be taken by *fleeing out of place or time, escape by slipperiness* and *to save, deliver, protect and save self* by being taken to Heaven in the clouds in I Thess 4:14-17 and I Cor 15:51 for Rev 13:15 state that all that do not worship the Beast will be killed at the 3½ year mark of the seven years of Tribulation. God is not going to allow his Church as a Bride to be killed! It is also clear that Daniel's 70th week is called **"a time of trouble"** in Dan 12:1 and Jerm 30:7 where Jeremiah clearly states in this verse that Jacob's trouble, his people the Church will escape, **"he shall be saved out of it"** just as Luke 21:36 states, **"Watch ye therefore, and pray always, that ye may be accounted worthy to escape all these things that shall come to pass, and to stand before the Son of man"**. Rom 5:9 confirms, **"we shall be saved from wrath through him"**. Study the definitions of *"Jacob's trouble"*, *"time of trouble"* and *"days of trouble"* in the paragraphs below for the full seven years of the Tribulation is wrath.

Over View and Order of Wrath

The Rapture takes place at the beginning of the first 3½ years of the Tribulation Period consisting of seven total years. John being in the Spirit and taken into heaven in Rev 4:1-2 is symbolic to the Rapture or "Taking" of the Church. Further proof that the Church is in Heaven at the beginning of the seven-year Tribulation Period is found in Rev 4:7 where the four beasts represent the four brigades of Israel as the lion, calf, man and eagle. They are called the stone of the house of Israel in Gen 49:22-26 and Duet 33:13-17 given to Joseph passed to Ephraim (modern UK with symbol as the Unicorn) and Manasseh (USA with symbol of the Eagle, Bull or Ox) as the lost sheep of the house of Israel called the Church in Matt 10:6, 15:24, Acts 10:36 and Eze 3:1-5. The four brigades of Israel are the Lion, Calf, Man and Eagle mentioned in Rev 4:7, Eze 1:5, 10:12-14 as travelling like a wheel to spread the Gospel as Christ's Church. Revelation chapter five gives the account of who was authorized to open the seven seals and only the Lamb or Christ with his Church has that right, therefore, the Church has to be in Heaven prior to the opening of the seven Seals, Trumpets and Vials of wrath. Christ do not receive his authority to begin wrath till he inherits his earthly Kingdom of David's Throne promised in Luke 1:31-33 and given in Rev 4:1-2. The Throne is set, his people called the lost sheep of the twelve tribes and his Temple/Church is now in Heaven at the very beginning of the seven years of Tribulation. Rev 5:6 proves it even further for the seven Spirits of the Churches is in Heaven with Christ prior to opening the seals and this verse states; **"And I beheld, and, lo, in the midst of the throne** [King David's] **and of the four beasts** [house of Israel], **and in the midst of the elders, stood a Lamb as it had been slain, having seven horns and seven eyes, which are the seven Spirits of God** [Christ's Church] **sent forth into all the earth"**. This verse proves that the seven spirits of the Church spoken if in the first three chapters of Revelation being on earth is now in Heaven with the completion of Rev 4:1-2 **"a throne was set in heaven"**. John being taken into Heaven is a symbol of the Church being raptured. This verse clearly states that Christ the Lamb and his Church, the four beasts are the four brigades of the house of Israel, and the seven Spirits of the Church that was *"sent forth into all the earth"* is now in Heaven prior to the beginning of wrath at the opening of the 1st Seal. The seven Spirits are the seven Churches as stated in Rev 1:4&20 as the seven stars, seven golden candlesticks and the angels of the seven Churches. Rev 4:5 places the seven stars, candlesticks and angels in Heaven as the Seven Spirits of God as the Church. Clearly, Revelation chapter four places the Throne of King David that Christ sets upon, the 24 Elders of ancient Israel, the seven Spirits of God as the spiritual Church, and the four beasts representing the four brigades of the lost sheep of the house of Israel as the physical Church in Ezekiel 1:10, 10:14 and Rev 4:7 are now in

20

Heaven. This completes all three elements of Gods earthly Kingdom, 1st King David's Throne, 2nd the Temple/Church and 3rd the twelve tribes of Israel all being in Heaven prior to the opening of the seven Seals that begin the seven-year Tribulation Period of wrath.

The Taking/Rapture within God's timeline This event begins the seven-year Tribulation Period called Daniel's 70th week by first placing Christ's Kingdom, Church, house/children of Israel and King David's Throne in Heaven prior to the opening the **Seven Seals**, the blowing of the **Seven Trumpets** and finally the pouring out of the **Seven Vials of Wrath** completing a total of seven years or the 70th week of Daniel's prophecy as recorded in Daniel 9:24-27. There is an unbroken constant timeline from Rev 1:1 to Rev 16:17 at the opening of the 7th Vial. What is very confusing is that John describes certain events in commentary such as the destruction of Babylon the Great, sealing of the 144,000 and Marriage Supper of the Lamb taking place at different times described within this unbroken timeline. It would appear that the timeline is broken but in reality, it is not for John is simply describing events that take place at different times within this seven-year period. It is also very important to understand that Daniel's 70th week or seven-year period of Wrath is under the Old Covenant Law dealing with wrath of the wickedness of man and the Tribe of Judah as the Jews of Jerusalem by bringing Wrath upon the wicked. Seventy weeks or 490 years, 70 weeks Times 7 weeks or 7 years equals 490 years for the prophecy of Jerusalem to be complete under blood sacrifice. Dan 9:25 is clear, only 69 weeks **"seven weeks, and threescore and two weeks"** which is 7 weeks plus 60 weeks plus 2 weeks equals 69 weeks total that has been completed by this verse. The 70th week under blood sacrificing is still to be fulfill in the seven-year Tribulation. By Jewish law, the Church under Christ's blood is not acceptable during these seven years of blood sacrificing but has to fulfill prophecy for Daniel clearly states that the 70th week are **"upon thy people and upon thy holy city to finish the transgression"** to apply only to Jerusalem. The two Witnesses are to preach the Gospel of Jesus to not only the Gentiles but also to the Jews for their last chance to accept Jesus as their Messiah that they rejected causing the Prophecy to stop at 69-weeks. The completion of the 70th week of Daniel's prophecy is for the Jews of Jerusalem and Orthodox Judaism around the world for the Church cannot be present under Christ's blood if the Jews are to reestablish blood sacrificing. Millions upon millions of people will be saved under the blood or Jesus during the 1st half of the seven-year Tribulation period to include the Jews that realize Christ is the true Messiah. The blood sacrificing will only apply to the Jews of Jerusalem and Orthodox Judaism around the world. The 69-week prophecy stopped when the Jews of Jerusalem rejected Jesus when he entered Jerusalem on an ass (colt) in Matt 21:2-5 stopping the 70th week prophecy at 69 weeks or 483 years from the time that the 2nd Temple was built during the time of Nehemiah, Ne 2:1-9 and Dan 9:24-27. The 70th week or seven years under the Old Covenant blood sacrifice is not complete but will be fulfilled during Daniel's 70th week or seven years of Tribulation. At our current time, there are one week or seven years of the Old Law of Moses under the Old Covenant that has to be fulfilled called Daniel's 70th week. It is logical by God's Law that the last week or Daniel's 70th week cannot be completed till the New Covenant of the Church is taken out. The Rapture ends the Church period of Grace under Christ's Gospel as the New Covenant covered by the shed blood of Jesus. II Thess 2:7 states that the Anti-Christ cannot take power till the Holy Spirit of the Church, as the salt of the earth, is taken away in the middle of the seven-years of Tribulation, **"only he who now letteth will let, until he be taken out of the way"** as the seven Spirits [Holy Spirit] of God as the Church. We must note that when the Church is taken in Rev 4:1-2 the Holy Spirit remains on earth to finish Christ's Gospel **"the mystery of God should be finished"** in the middle of the Trib. when the two witnesses are killed in Rev 11:7. The Gospel is finished in Dan 12:7, (times time and half or 3½ years when "to scatter the power of the holy people", Rev 10:7 (at the blowing of the 7th Trump) and 11:7-9 (when the 2 witnesses are killed) all marking the middle of the Trib according to these verses. Daniel's 70th week consisting of the seven years of the Tribulation Period under the Old Covenant and our current period of the Church age under the New Covenant cannot overlap. If God is to complete the sins and prophecy of Jerusalem of the Jews that were under the Old Law of blood sacrificing, the 490-year prophecy has to be completed under the blood of animals. One week or 7 years of the Old Covenant animal sacrificing by the Jews is not complete. Why can't Christians see this fact and understand that the Church has to be taken prior to the seven years of Daniel's 70th week prophecy for the Old [blood sacrificing] and New Covenants [Christ's Church] cannot overlap? The Rapture or taking of the Church has to occur prior to the seven-year Tribulation of Wrath as spoken of in the Book of Revelation for the Church cannot be present under the completion of the last seven years of the Old Covenant Law of Moses under blood sacrifice. Keep in mind that the taking of the Church does not complete the Gospel for the two witnesses with candlesticks takes the place of the Church with its candlesticks that has been taken (raptured) during the first half of the Tribulation Period. This is why each Witness is given a candlestick with supernatural powers for they represent the Church under the power of the Holy Spirit, Rev 1:20. The Gospel is not finished till Rev 10:7, 11:7 and Dan 12:7 is fulfilled when the two witnesses are killed in the middle of the Tribulation. Rev 11:3&7&12 occurs in the middle of the Trib immediately after the blowing of the 7th Trumpet ending the Gospel. There are no more candlesticks [representing the Holy Spirit] left in the world for the two witnesses and all people that refuse the Anti-Christ are killed in Rev 13:15 soon after the Anti-Christ receives his power in the middle of the Trib. This killing event occurs at the beginning of his 42-month reign as stated in Rev 13:5 and 13:15 **"cause that as many as would not worship the image of the beast should be killed"** at the beginning of his 42-month reign.

22

There is no one else to be saved for the sealed 144,000 flee into the wilderness in Dan 12:7 *"to scatter the poser of the holy people, all these things shall be finished"* to hide for all other people worship the Beast. All others are killed leaving only the 144,000 and the Beast worshipers.

Extreme Important Note: Why is Daniel's 70th week Prophecy called the seven-year Tribulation given only to the Jews of Jerusalem in Dan 9:24? We have already explained that the Old and New Covenants of animal blood and the blood of Jesus cannot overlap. There is another very important reason in why the seven years of wrath pertain only to the Jews of Jerusalem and Jews scattered throughout the world. I Kings chapter eleven and twelve clearly tells us that God's earthly kingdom was divided into two parts, the southern kingdom of Judah (Jerusalem) and Benjamin and the northern kingdom of the other ten tribes of the house of Israel called the lost sheep scattered into the wilderness of Europe to wait for his Gospel. Clearly, Jesus himself gave the Gospel as his Church to the ten tribes of Israel in Matt 10:6, 15:24, Acts 10:36 and Eze 3:1-5. When the lost sheep of Israel as Christ's Church is taken or raptured at the beginning of the 7 years of Tribulation, it leaves the southern kingdom of Judah of Jerusalem on earth. The Jews of Jerusalem is one twelfth of his earthly kingdom on earth for they rejected Jesus as the Messiah two thousand years ago and still reject him to this day. God has to deal only with the Jews during the seven years of WRATH for the house of Israel as the Church has been taken to Heaven. God's kingdom is now separated where the physical tribe of Judah is on earth and the ten northern tribes of the spiritual house of Israel as his Church is in Heaven. The sealed 144,000, 12,000 from each tribe of Israel represent the physical house of Israel during the Tribulation. Daniel's seven-year prophecy gives the Jews one last chance on earth to accept Jesus as their Messiah through the preaching and teaching of the two Witnesses during the first half of the Trib. The seven-years fulfills the 490-year prophecy of the Jewish people under blood sacrifice of the Old Law of Moses for seven years has not been completed. We must understand that a large portion of the Jewish faith accepted Jesus as the Messiah over the past two thousand years. This completes God's earthly kingdom when the house of Israel along with David's Throne (I Kings 12:19-20 and Luke 1:31-33) is taken into Heaven at the beginning of the Tribulation. That gave Christ the authority to set upon his throne in Rev 4:1-2 so Daniel's 70th week Prophecy could be fulfilled for only Jesus as the Lamb of Judah can open the seven Seals, Trumpets and Vials.

Chapter Two

Understanding the unbroken Timeline of Revelation
Tribulation timeline: by 42 mo, "time, times an half or 1260 days all representing 3 ½ years

The Apostle John gives a time guideline in Rev 1:4, **"from him which is** [Present]**, and which was** [Past] **and which is to come** [Future]**"**, Rev 1:8, **"I am Alpha and Omega the beginning and the ending, saith the Lord, which is** [Present]**, and which was** [Past]**, and which is to come** [Future]**, the Almighty"**, Rev 4:8, in reference to the Lord God Almighty, **"which was** [Past]**, and is** [Present]**, and is to come** [Future]**"**, and Rev 11:17, **"which art** [Present]**, and wast** [Past]**, and art to come** [Future]**"**. We must understand that from the creation of Adam out of the dust (the past) to our current date in time (present) till the time God destroys the old earth and heaven (future), there is a constant unbroken timeline of the *past*, *present* and *future*. These verses state that Almighty God, Jesus and his Church exists in ancient and modern time periods in a constant unbroken time line of Past, Present and Future. This is proven in I Enoch chapter 69:20 for it clearly states, **"And through that oath the sun and moon complete their courses, and deviate not from their ordinance from eternity to eternity"**. Only once in the Scriptures does time either stop or altered and that is found in Joshua 10:13, Habakkuk 3:11 and Jasher LXXVIII 63-64 which is chapter 83:63-64 when Joshua prayed for God to stop the sun and moon for a day, 24 hours, to finish the battle with the Amorites. Other than this event, the book of Revelation is a continuous unbroken timeline divided by commentary by Apostle John. Each of John's commentaries that seem to bounce through time can be properly placed into one of the Seals, Trumpets or Vials. This is why the book of Revelation is so misunderstood, for, if you do not understand the timeline, you will not understand the order of events within this book. The inspiration in this book was given to this Author by the Holy Spirit himself through deep prayer, study and research with guidance. It did not come from other men's writings but directly from the Holy Spirit.

Clearly by Scripture the seven-year Tribulation Period is broken up into two half's both representing a different time period of Vengeance and Wrath. The 1st half is Vengeance on the nations of Babylon the Great Whore lead by America. The Old Baal religion came out of Egypt created by the Canaanites that came from the seed of Satan given to Eve in the Garden and later to Cain her son. The progression of evil on earth came first from Satan passed to Eve and then to Cain where his descendance became the Canaanites, Palestinians that became ancient and modern Palestine, an evil race of people. This is why God commanded Judah to kill all that breathed, man, woman/children and animals to eradicate evil so it would not spread into the end times. The Israelite Priest mingled with the bloodline of Cain establishing their religion through the Kabbalah during their captivity of four hundred years in Egypt. These Jewish BAAL Priest are the vipers that Christ spoke of as the Synagogue of Satan in Rev 2:9&3:9 for they were of the Serpents bloodline as vipers. How do we know that the Kabbalah is Satanist, simply through the four levels of the Kabbalah:

1ˢᵗ level Peshat, *"the plan or literal meaning of the text"*.

2ⁿᵈ level Remez, "hint" *refers to interpretation of the Torah that are not stated explicitly but hinted at in the text.*

3ʳᵈ level Drash, *homiletics of Midrash which is Jewish fantastical stories related to the Bible considered a deeper meaning, a form of allegory.*

4ᵗʰ level Sod, the 4ᵗʰ and highest level of the Torah knowledge meaning *"Secret"*. Sod has the Esoteric meaning; *understood by a select few or belonging to a select few as Secret Societies.*

The Kabbalah is all the secret societies of today such as the Masons, Illuminati, Jesuits, Knights of Malt, Knights Templars and all the others have merged into the Great Whore of Babylon as our end time system that God will destroy. Masonry has adopted all these Secret Societies into their ranked order of 33 degrees. Do not believe this Author but research these facts for yourselves.

The Bible warns Christians to not have or be in organizations that are based on secrets sworn in dark forbidden rooms, Mark 4:22, Luke 8:17, John 7:4, 18:20 and Eph 5:12 are very clear, **"For there is no man that doeth anything in secret, and he himself seeketh to be known openly"**, **"For it is a shame even to speak of those things which are done of them in secret"**. This verse is directed at Masonry of the Masonic Order demanding their secrecy in which many Christians are members believing it is a benign family-oriented society. During the Egyptian captivity, the Jewish Kabbalah was written and established under secrecy into the Jewish faith. Satan tried to pervert God's word from its beginning. We must remember that the true Jewish Faith under the Old Law of Moses was not recognized by God until Moses established it during the forty years in the wilderness with the tribe of Levi as Priests and the Tabernacle was built for sacrificing for the sins of the people in Exo 25:1-9. They will try to tell you that the Kabbalah was the verbal spiritual version God gave Moses on Mount Sinai where the Ten Commandments were the physical form given to man but the Kabbalah is the higher level of secrecy. When Babylon took Israel into captivity in approx. 586BC, during their 70 years, they reestablished the old Baal religion of the Cabbala/Kabbala. The verbal secrets of Masonry and Illuminati began as old secret societies where they dominate today in every level of our communities where almost every small town in the world has a Masonic Lodge which is Satan's religion.

The calculated Timeline
Very Important to understand

This subject is very detailed and takes prayer with a deep desire to comprehend and even so, it may take the reader several times to read and grasp with clarity. It took 59 years for the Holy Spirit to show this author but now I truly believe it's time for God to show all of us his mystery of the timeline. **The 5th Seal in Rev 6:9, the 6th Seal in Rev 6:12 and the 7th Seal in Rev 8:1&10:7 are the only verses that gives us a clue to a specific timeframe in the 1st half of the Tribulation. From these verses, we can calculate a timeline which is simple if we are willing to comprehend.** If we closely study the 7th Seal, we can see that it marks the middle of the seven-year Tribulation which is the first major key. The Gospel is clearly finished after the two witnesses are killed in Rev 11:7 after 1260 days or 3½ years of preaching to the world which would be at the middle of the Tribulation. The word "finished" is the next key and confirmed in Rev 10:7 *"the mysteries of God* [Gospel] *shall be finished"*, 11:7 *"and when they shall have finished their testimony"* and Dan 12:7 *"all these things shall be finished* [Dan 9:24, 70 weeks to "finish" sin and prophecy]*"*. Clearly, the Gospel is finished in the middle of the Tribulation by these four verses for the two witnesses are killed at the blowing of the 7th Trumpet marking the end of 42 months or 3 ½ years. The next key is found in the 5th Trumpet that last <u>five months</u> in Rev 9:5 and the 6th Trumpet that last for *"an hour, and a day, and a month and a year"* which represent <u>13 months</u>. If we add 5 months for the 5th Trumpet and 13 months for the 6th Trumpet where we know that the 7th Trumpet is at the very end of the 3½ year mark or at the exact middle of the seven years, we get 18 months total or 1 and ½ years. We can now place the 5th Trumpet occurring at the two-year mark of the 1st half of the Tribulation by subtracting 1.5 years from 3.5 years which is at the two-year mark of the seven-years of Tribulation. **This is critical in understanding the timeline of John's Tribulation.** We can now place all events that occurred to a specific period of time by simply interpolating each event by knowing when the 5th Seal took place in the seven-years of time. We can now calculate each of the seven Seals, Trumpets and Vials by knowing the timeline. Now, we know that the 7 Seals and the first 4 Trumpets occurred in the first two years of the 1st half of the Tribulation period totaling 11 events. If we divided 11 events into 24 months, we get the 7 Seals and first four Trumpets lasting approx. 2.2 months each. Now we also know that the 7 Vials all occur within 42 months during the 2nd Half of the Tribulation so we can interpolate that each last for approx. six months for there is no other Scripture to indicate a timeframe. Note that 6 months or 6 is the number of man, 666, the number of ungodly man.

The next major key is found in Revelation chapter fourteen where approx. seven events take place in constant sequential quick order one after the other with no break in time. The 1st event in chapter 14 is the Sealing of the 144,000 Saints that we know occurred in Rev 7:4-8 at the opening of the 6th Seal marking the 13th month of the 1st half. The 6th Seal is the 6th event, so, if we multiplying 6 times 2.2, the 6th Seal occurred at approx. the 13th month mark. This event also begins wrath in Rev 6:17 **"his wrath is come"** releasing the Saints under the Alter mentioned in the 5th Seal where they are released in the 6th Seal.

Many Christians believe the Tribulation Period is for only 42 months. This cannot be true for Daniel's 70th week prophecy is clear that the 70th week last seven years in Dan 9:24-27. The following verse also makes it clear that the Tribulation last more than 42 months or 1260 days. If this is true, how can you explain Dan 8:14 that last for 2300 days or 76.6 months, Dan 12:11 for 1290 days or 43 months and Dan 12:12 that last for 1335 days or 44.5 months all in accordance with Daniel's 70th week or seven-year prophecy. Note the time chart #3 on page 29.

(Time Chart #1)
1st Half of the Tribulation Major Events

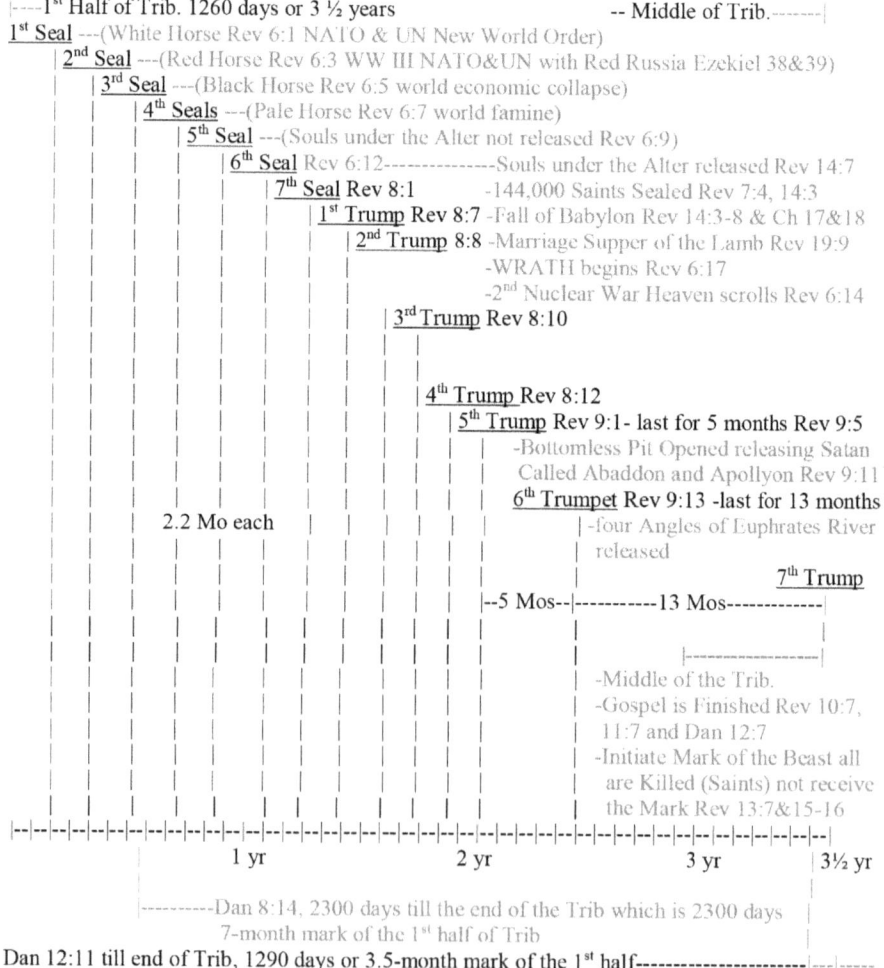

28

(Time Chart #2)
2nd Half of the Tribulation Major Event
Rule of the Anti-Christ for 42 months

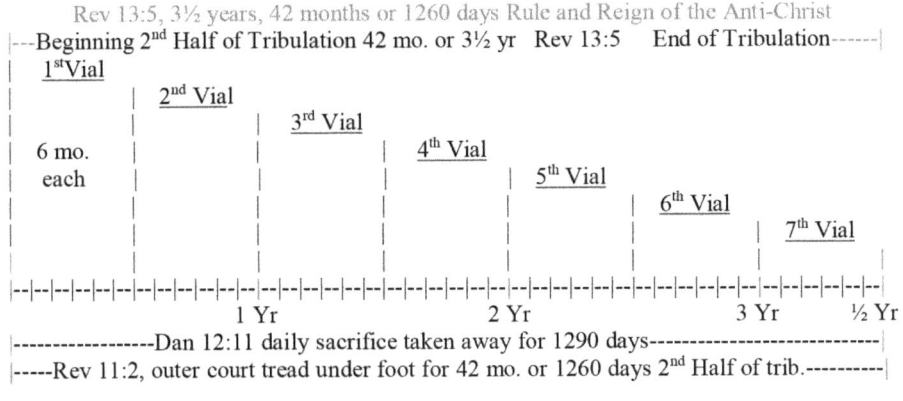

Rev 13:5, 3½ years, 42 months or 1260 days Rule and Reign of the Anti-Christ
|---Beginning 2nd Half of Tribulation 42 mo. or 3½ yr   Rev 13:5   End of Tribulation------|
| 1stVial
| | 2nd Vial
| | | 3rd Vial
| 6 mo. | | | 4th Vial
| each | | | | 5th Vial
| | | | | | 6th Vial
| | | | | | | 7th Vial
1 Yr   2 Yr   3 Yr   ½ Yr
------------------Dan 12:11 daily sacrifice taken away for 1290 days----------------------
------Rev 11:2, outer court tread under foot for 42 mo. or 1260 days 2nd Half of trib.----------

---

(Time Chart #3)
Full Seven Year Tribulation of Major/Special Events listed by
Scripture in time of Days, Months or Years

Beginning of Trib	Middle of Trib	**End of Trib**
Day Zero	1260 Days, 42 Mo., 31/2 yrs.	2520 Days or 7 Yrs.

|--|
|----------------------------------Dan 9:27 covenant for one week 7 years------------------|
--Rev 11:3 Two Witnessed preach 1260days---	---
------**1st**	--Dan 8:14 vision of daily sacrifice taken away for 2300 day----------------
	at the 7th month mark of the 1st half----------------------------------
	2nd |---Satan released from the bottomless pit at the sounding------
		of the 5th Trump at two-year mark of the 1st half has 1½ yr--
		to build Power---
		3rd	|---Dan 12:12, 144000 flee to wilderness for-
76.6	60		|---1335 days or 44.5 months in 2nd half------
mo.	mo.		|-----Dan 12:11 sacrifice taken for 1290 days--
			|-----Rev 13:5 Anti-Christ's rule-----------------
		44.5	|----at the 3.5 months mark of 1st half----------
		mo.	|----Dan 9:27 Med week daily sacrifice ends--
			|-----Rev 11:2 outer court & Jerusalem----------
			|----trodden 42 mos.---------------------------------
			|--Rev 11:3 Two Witness for 1260 days.----
				--Satan in power Rev 13:5 for 42 mo.------
        1 yr   2 yr   3 yr   Mid   4 yr   5 yr   6 yr   7 yr
                                                   Trib

Note: Three events last more than 42 months or 3½ years as listed within this time chart meaning that the Tribulation Period runs for a full seven-years just

29

as Dan 9:27 states. Many Christians believe the Tribulation last for only 42 months which is not true according to these Scriptures. The last half or 42 months is Wrath upon ungodly man that take the Mark of the Beast in Rev 16:1 where all people that do not worship the beast and take his mark are killed in the middle of the Trib. No man can be saved during the 2nd half for the Gospel is finished in Rev 11:7 where the Holy Spirit is taken out in II Thess 2:7 clearing the way for the Anti-Christ. Note, this occurs in the middle of the Tribulation and Christ's so called second coming does not happen till the end of the seven years. There has to be three comings of Christ, 1st at birth to establish his gospel, 2nd to take his Church at the beginning of the seven years and 3rd his coming in power and glory with fire at the end of the seven years of Tribulation.

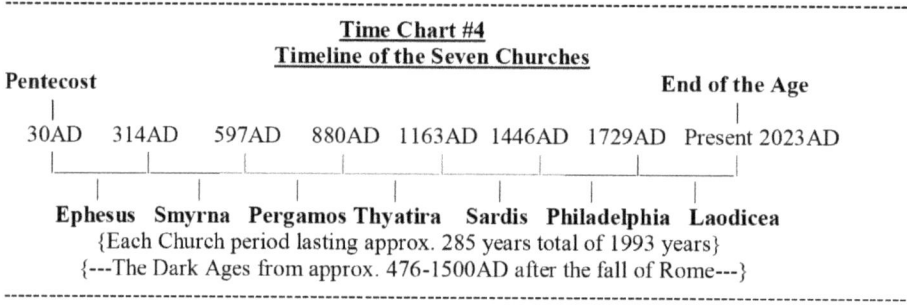

Time Chart #4
Timeline of the Seven Churches

Pentecost   End of the Age

30AD   314AD   597AD   880AD   1163AD 1446AD 1729AD Present 2023AD

Ephesus Smyrna Pergamos Thyatira Sardis Philadelphia Laodicea
{Each Church period lasting approx. 285 years total of 1993 years}
{---The Dark Ages from approx. 476-1500AD after the fall of Rome---}

30

TIME CHART
God's Time Clock of Revelation

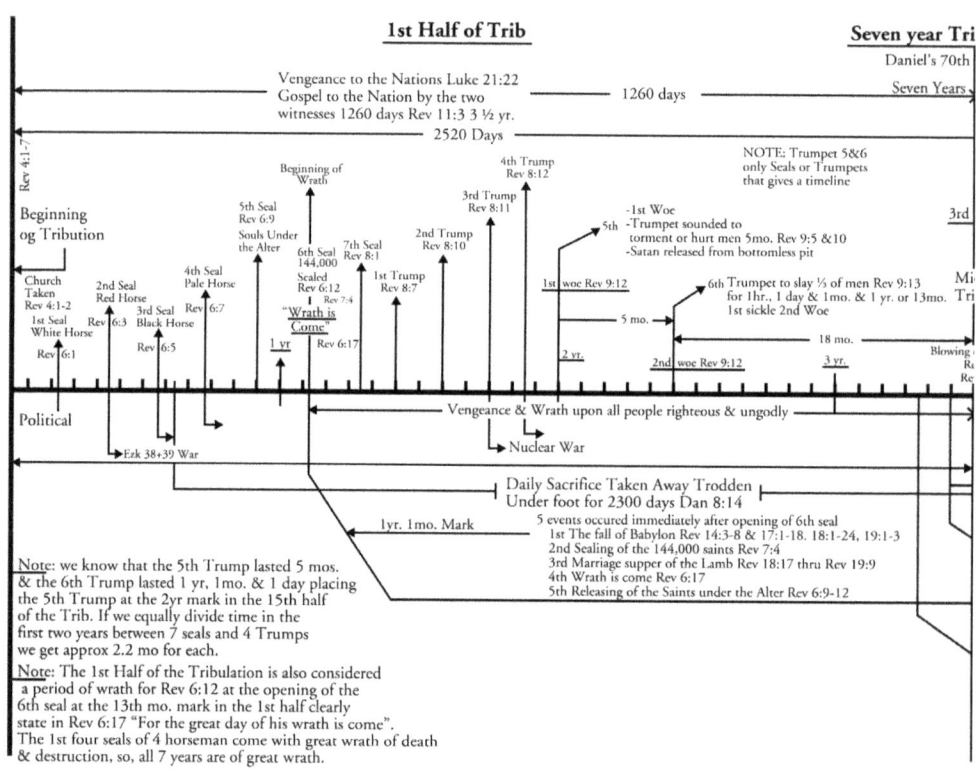

Note: we know that the 5th Trump lasted 5 mos.
& the 6th Trump lasted 1 yr, 1mo. & 1 day placing
the 5th Trump at the 2yr mark in the 15th half
of the Trib. If we equally divide time in the
first two years between 7 seals and 4 Trumps
we get approx 2.2 mo for each.

Note: The 1st Half of the Tribulation is also considered
a period of wrath for Rev 6:12 at the opening of the
6th seal at the 13th mo. mark in the 1st half clearly
state in Rev 6:17 "For the great day of his wrath is come".
The 1st four seals of 4 horseman come with great wrath of death
& destruction, so, all 7 years are of great wrath.

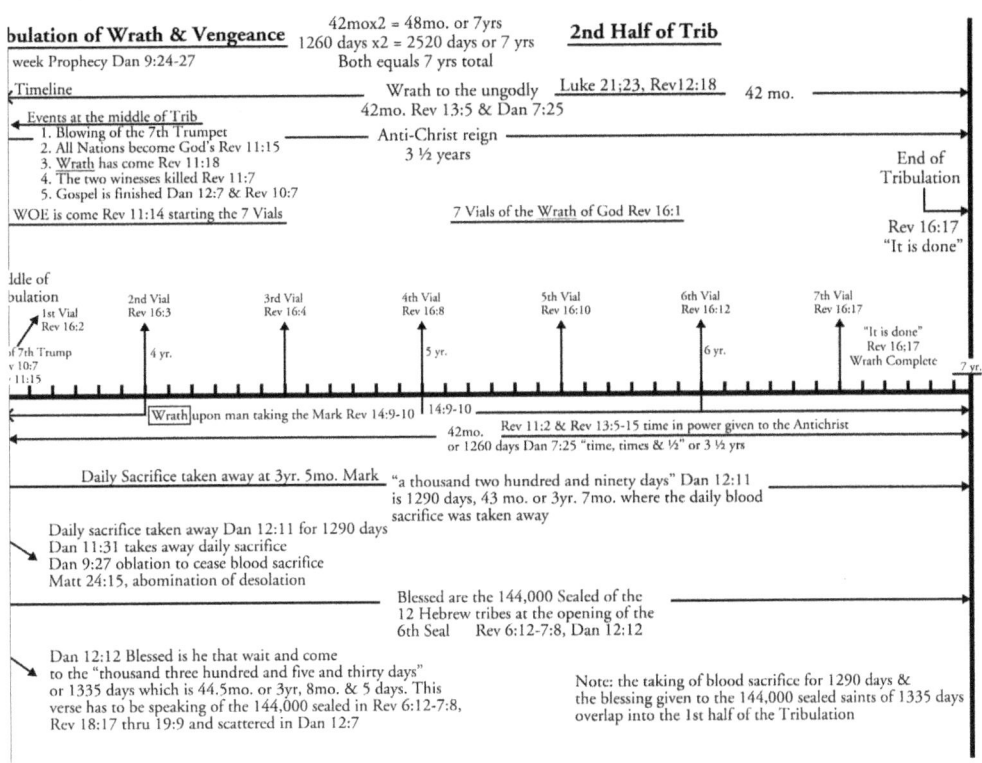

bulation of **Wrath & Vengeance**
week Prophecy Dan 9:24-27

42mox2 = 48mo. or 7yrs
1260 days x2 = 2520 days or 7 yrs
Both equals 7 yrs total

2nd Half of Trib

Timeline — Wrath to the ungodly Luke 21;23, Rev12:18 42 mo.
42mo. Rev 13:5 & Dan 7:25

Events at the middle of Trib
1. Blowing of the 7th Trumpet
2. All Nations become God's Rev 11:15 — Anti-Christ reign
3. Wrath has come Rev 11:18   3 ½ years
4. The two winesses killed Rev 11:7
5. Gospel is finished Dan 12:7 & Rev 10:7
WOE is come Rev 11:14 starting the 7 Vials

End of
Tribulation

7 Vials of the Wrath of God Rev 16:1

Rev 16:17
"It is done"

Idle of
bulation

2nd Vial   3rd Vial   4th Vial   5th Vial   6th Vial   7th Vial
Rev 16:3   Rev 16:4   Rev 16:8   Rev 16:10   Rev 16:12   Rev 16:17

1st Vial
Rev 16:2

"It is done"
Rev 16:17
Wrath Complete

f 7th Trump   4 yr.   5 yr.   6 yr.   7 yr.
v 10:7
11:15

Wrath upon man taking the Mark Rev 14:9-10   14:9-10
Rev 11:2 & Rev 13:5-15 time in power given to the Antichrist
42mo.
or 1260 days Dan 7:25 "time, times & ½" or 3 ½ yrs

Daily Sacrifice taken away at 3yr. 5mo. Mark   "a thousand two hundred and ninety days" Dan 12:11
is 1290 days, 43 mo. or 3yr. 7mo. where the daily blood
sacrifice was taken away

Daily sacrifice taken away Dan 12:11 for 1290 days
Dan 11:31 takes away daily sacrifice
Dan 9:27 oblation to cease blood sacrifice
Matt 24:15, abomination of desolation

Blessed are the 144,000 Sealed of the
12 Hebrew tribes at the opening of the
6th Seal   Rev 6:12-7:8, Dan 12:12

Dan 12:12 Blessed is he that wait and come
to the "thousand three hundred and five and thirty days"
or 1335 which is 44.5mo. or 3yr, 8mo. & 5 days. This
verse has to be speaking of the 144,000 sealed in Rev 6:12-7:8,
Rev 18:17 thru 19:9 and scattered in Dan 12:7

Note: the taking of blood sacrifice for 1290 days &
the blessing given to the 144,000 sealed saints of 1335 days
overlap into the 1st half of the Tribulation

33

Five events occur in immediate order with the opening of the **6th Seal** at the 13th month mark of the 1st half. The first event sets the timeline, **1st Event**, the Sealing of the 144,000 Hebrews, 12,000 from each tribe in Rev 7:3-8 immediately after the opening of the 6th Seal in Rev 6:12. **2nd Event** in Rev 14:6-7 refer to the Saints under the Alter takes place in the 5th Seal and not released till the 6th Seal in Rev 6:12 where the Saints cannot be released till "judgment" and "wrath" has come which occurs in Rev 6:17, **"day of his wrath is come"** and "Rev 14:7, **"for the hour of his judgment is come"** and 14:10, **"the wrath of God"**. Note, all of these verses speaking of God's wrath begins in the 6th Seal at the 13th month mark of the 1st half of the Trib. The Saints are released as recorded in Rev 7:13-14. **3rd Event**, the fall of Babylon occurs in the opening of the 6th Seal according to verse one in Rev 14:1-8 immediately after the sealing of the 144,000. The sealing of the Saints in Rev 7:4-7 and Rev 14:1 is the same event immediately after the opening of the 6th Seal for this sets the timeline for the fall of Babylon. John's commentary on the fall of Babylon in chapters 17 thru 18 and Rev 19:2 all occur immediately after the Sealing of the 144,000 in the 6th Seal proven by the sequential order listed in Revelation chapter 14. Ezekiel 24:8, 25:12-15 and Jerm 50:33-39 gives this account of the fall of Mystery Babylon in the Old Testament to take place in the last days as stated in Jerm 49:39, **"come to pass in the later days"**. **4rth Event**, Marriage Supper of the Lamb in Rev 19:7-10 is placed to occur immediately after the fall of Babylon for Rev 19:1-9 clearly link these two events to occur immediately after each other at the opening of the 6th Seal. According to these Scriptures, the sealing of the 144,000, fall of Babylon and the Marriage Supper all occurred in immediate sequential order as proven in Revelation chapter 14. The **5th Event**, at the opening of the 6th Seal is WRATH upon ungodly men in Rev 6:16-17, 14:7&10 and 18:3. Note that the Saints under the alter in the 5th Seal could not be released till the WRATH of man began, giving authority to be released. The fall of Babylon is the beginning of his VENGEANCE/WRATH. These verses prove that the 1st half of the Tribulation is considered vengeance as listed in the Old and New Testaments for Luke 21:22 calls it **"the days of vengeance"** where Eze 25:17 calls it **"great vengeance"**. If we closely study the different meanings of vengeance and wrath between the Hebrew and Greek, they mean basically the same for punishment. There is one difference that I can see; VENGEANCE is a punishment of LOVE as punishing a child and WATH is a punishment of a HATE crime or justifiable abhorrence of *anger* and *rage*. This means that the 1st half of the Tribulation is punishment from God to the nations out of love due to Christians being present within the world as you would punish your child. The 2nd Half is justified punishment to hateful ungodly man as a hard-core criminal.

According to the commentary of Rev 14:1-5, 144,000 Saints are sealed immediately after Rev 6:12 at the opening of the 6th Seal at the 13th month mark of the 1st half of the Trib. Instantaneously, another Angel sounds and the one hour of destruction of Babylon takes place in Rev 14:7-8. This same occurrence brings wrath in Rev 6:16-17. At this moment in time, at the opening of the 6th Seal the five events listed above occurs in quick chronological succession at the one year and one month mark in the 1st half of the Tribulation period. We can set the timeline by these events. Revelation chapter fourteen list seven events repeating some events listed above:

1. **Rev 14:1-5** (opened by Christ himself standing on mount Sion (Christ's Church) Sealing of the 144,000 where we know by Scripture occurred in Rev 7:4-8 immediately after the opening of the 6th Seal in Rev 6:12 as listed above.

2. **Rev 14:6-7** (1st Angel or another Angel) preaching the Gospel and begins *"judgment"* or *"wrath"* releasing the Saints that were under the Alter in Rev 6:9-12 but are now released in Rev 7:13-14 directly connected to the opening of the 6th Seal in Rev 6:12&17 also listed above.

3. **Rev 14:8** (by a 2st Angel or another Angel) states that *"Babylon is fallen, is fallen"* meaning it had to occur in succession at the blowing of the 6th Trumpet also immediately after the sealing of the 144,000 Saints, again as listed above.

4. **Rev 14:9-11** (by a 3nd Angel) warning to people that *"receive his mark"* the Mark of the Beast.

5. **Rev14:12-13** (a loud voice from Heaven speaks) blessed are they that keep Gods Commandments and faith in Jesus *"Blessed are the dead which die in the Lord from henceforth"*. These Saints mentioned receive a mercy death so they will not see the wrath to come just as Noah and Lot's family and the Church all taken out of the earth prior to Gods wrath.

6. **Rev 14:14-16** (Jesus sitting on a white cloud having the **1st Sickle** in his hand) these verses are a continuation of verses 12-13 in how Jesus reaped the earth and took his Saints through a mercy death to prevent them from seeing his wrath to come, *blessed are they which die in the Lord* just as he took his faithful prior to the flood in Jasher 4:20-21 and 5:5 *"And all men who walked in the ways of the Lord, died in those days, before the Lord brought the evil upon man* [the Flood]*"*.

7. **Rev 14:17-20** (Angel came out of the Temple having a sharp sickle which is the 2nd Sickle of death). The Angel thrust in his sickle **"and reaped the earth with death and cast it into the great winepress of the wrath of God"**, where blood came up to the horse bridles for a thousand and six hundred furlongs. This is the second death into hell. This is the same wrath and judgment mentioned in Rev 6:17, 14:7 and 14:10.

Important Note: Revelation chapter 6, 7 and 14 sets the timeline and commentary that occurs in a continuing timeline in sequential order at the 13th month mark of the seven-year Tribulation. This chapter sets in time all seven events that occur in immediate succession one after another in quick order. Each of the seven events in Revelation chapter six, seven and fourteen is first opened by Jesus standing on Mount Sion which is the Church in Heaven during the first half of the Trib. This gives the authority for the next three events for they are opened by Angels and the 5th event is opened by a voice from Heaven, could be Christ or God himself. The 6th event is opened by Jesus sitting on a white cloud with the 1st Sickle of death and the 7th event is opened by an Angel having the 2nd Sickle of death that came out of the Temple in Heaven. This confirms Rev 5:5 that only the Lamb as the Lion of Judah which is Christ and his Church has the authority to open the Seals, Trumpets and Vials.

Chapter Three

God's Kingdom Temple and Church within the unbroken timeline

These verses are referring to a continual timeline of the past, present and future in reference to the Kingdom of Jesus Christ in ancient and modern times. The main subject of his creation is his peculiar people as the twelve tribes of Israel, the Temple/Church and King David's throne where John is speaking directly to his seven Churches existing throughout an unbroken timeline. Each Church represent a certain distinct time period by being in the past, present and future. There is an unbroken timeline from the time God created Adam till the New Heaven and New Earth descend down from the Heavens ending God's earthly creation with man. To understand the book of Revelation, we must identify the correct timeline for it is based on his creation. John specifically identifies seven different Church periods that chronologically, without a break in time, runs from Rev 1:1 through Rev 3:22 where Rev 4:1-2 is the taking or Rapture of the Church into Heaven ending the Church Age. This is only the end of the Church period where the timeline begins the Tribulation into another dispensation of time but the sequential timeline continues unbroken. The Revelation timeline is constant from Rev 1:1 through Rev 10:7 and 11:15 at the blowing of the 7th Trumpet marking the 3½ year time mark or middle of the Tribulation finishing the Gospel and continues uninterrupted through the pouring of the 7th Vial in Rev 16:17 finishing seven years of vengeance/wrath during the last half of the Trib. God gave each Church a separate candlestick and star or Spirit totaling seven from Rev 1:1 through Rev 4:2 and each of the two Witnesses one candlestick each from Rev 4:2 when the Church is taken to Rev 11:15 at the blowing of the 7th Trumpet marking the middle of the first half of the Trib. Rev 1:20 clearly identifies a candlestick given to each Church with a star assigned an Angel or Spirit of each Church period which is completely different in name, nature and time. Clearly there are seven distance diverse Church periods with a different Candlestick and Spirit identified by distinctive names, each representing a given time period by definition and meaning. The time period can be identified by the Greek meaning of the name of each Church period from the 1st Church of Ephesus to the 7th called Laodicea. All seven Churches were located in western central Turkey within a hundred miles of Smyrna as modern Izmir Turkey where the map below shows. The following is the timeline for each Church time period and is approximant:

The names of each Church period were given as a symbol of how the Church was to go worldwide into Europe to expand into all nations of the world to spread Christ's Gospel as the twelve tribes of Israel. They were given the Great Commission in Matt 28:19-20, 10:6, 15:24, Acts 10:36, and Eze 3:1-5. Israels encampment in the wilderness was laid out in the shape of a wheel in Numbers chapter two to take place in ancient verses modern times. Each tribe encamped on the north, south, east and west representing the spokes of a wheel with the Tabernacle and the tribe of Levi as Preast in the middle as its hub. The wheel is a mode of travel where they are called a "living creature and wheel" in Eze 3:13 as they traveled into the Promised Land and as the Church evangelizing the world in modern times. The four brigades of Israel as the twelve tribes is called a <u>Cherub/Ox/Calf</u>, <u>man</u>, <u>lion</u> and <u>eagle</u> in Eze 1:10, 10:14 and Rev 4:7. These four living creatures are mentioned 12 times as a wheel in Ezekiel chapter ten indicating worldwide travel after the shape of their encampment. They were to traveled as a wheel into the wilderness to spread Christ's Gospel by the wheel of a ship, horse and wagon and wheels of a car and airplane. All travel is by some kind of a wheel. The twelve tribes are the spokes of the wheel and the Tabernacle and Priests represent the hub in the middle of their encampment shaped as a wheel. They are called the lost sheep of the house of Israel commanded by Jesus himself. These Hebrew nations as Christ's Church is called "mountains of Israel" in Eze 38:8 where they are called nations in Hebrew. The word mountain can be exchanged for nation or an actual mountain but in this verse, it is clear that mountain is called nations. These verses clearly gave responsibility to evangelize the world as Christ's Church to the lost sheep of the house of Israel called **"the children of Israel"** as Christ's Church in Acts 10:36 and Rev 2:14. The account of the lost tribes is given in II Esdras 13:40-46 of the Apocrypha where they departed the Promised Land and proceeded over the Euphrates River into Europe across the Caucasus Mountains where they are called Caucasian people today. Jeremiah's Scribe Baruch sent these lost sheep an Epistle called "The Epistle of Baruch" which he wrote to the nine and half Tribes in, "The Apocalypse of Baruch" LXXVIII thru LXXXVII starting on page 124. It is written in Hebrew and English, excellent read.

The name *children of Israel* were given to all seven Churches not only to Pergamos in Rev 2:14 but to all Churches in Acts 10:36. The Churches listed below were to go worldwide and spread Christ's Gospel "roll" and "little book" called the Gospel to all nations and tongues just as Ezekiel 3:1-5 and Rev 10:9-10 states. Proof is in how Ephraim as the Unicorn of England evangelized and translated the Holy Bible into English as the King James Version in 1611AD. This is historical fact evangelizing the whole world. This evangelization of the world included their brother Manasseh as the United States of America and at one time identified as the most Christian nation in the world that has sent Missionaries worldwide.

Timeline and definitions of the Seven Churches of Jesus Christ

1<u>st</u> **Ephesus**- 30-314AD Greek meaning, *a city in Asia Minor*
2<u>nd</u> **Smyrna**- 315-597AD Greek meaning, *a city in Asia Minor*
3<u>rd</u> **Pergamos**- 598-880AD during the Dark Ages and in Greek as the children of Israel (Rev 2:14) in Greek means, *fortified* and *a tower or castle*. This is the period of time that the European nations such a France, Germany, England and other countries became fortified castles with Christian armies.
4<u>th</u> **Thyatira**- 881-1163AD Greek meaning, *a city in Lydia in Asia Minor* during the Dark Ages of punishment.
5<u>th</u> **Sardis**- 1163-1446AD Greek meaning, *a city in Lydia in Asia Minor* during the Dark Ages of punishment.

Note: The last two Churches slowly began falling away from Christ's first love where he gives a dire **WARNING** to all seven Churches in Rev 2:5, **"Remember therefore from whence thou art fallen, and repent, and do the first works; or else I will come unto thee quickly, and will remove thy candlestick out of his place, except thou repent"**. This warning was to all seven Churches to be in a constant or "often" state of repentance as Heb 9:25-26 tells his Christians. This warning was not only to the Churches but to each individual Christian.

6<u>th</u> **Philadelphia**- 1447-1729AD Greek meaning, *a city in Lydia in Asia Minor* at the beginning of the industrial revolution and the founding of America. According to the Strong's Concordance, this Church is a king of Pergamos with great fortifications and castles with armies. Philadelphia was the beginning of great wealth and leisure and in Greek means, *fond of brother or brotherly love, friend, associate, neighbor, triumph, victory, conquer* etc. This time period was the evangelization of the world through the French, British, Italian and American empires by the King James 1611 English Bible as the Children of Israel, the eleven lost tribes to include the remnant of Judah.

7<u>th</u> **Laodiceans**- 1730AD to Present time, there is no good report on this Church for it is a liberal socialist Church that is spiritually *wretched, miserable, poor, blind and naked*. At the beginning of this Church, it was good but fell away not heeding the warnings given in Rev 2:5 and 3:2-5. The Greek meaning, *a people or one's populace with justice as its decision and execution, judgment, punish, vengeance, public bond together socially, bind or be in bonds* and *to sing as acting* [Holly Wood movies and Broad Way Shows]. This Church and the world have become liberal, socialist and communistic to be spewed out of God's mouth in Rev 3:16, **"I will spue thee out of my mouth"**. They failed to hear Christ's warnings so they were spewed and blotted out of Christ's mouth just as the verses above warned. The word "will" in future tense is a warning that it will happen if the situations is not corrected thru an often repentance.

This is the spiritual condition of the modern Church for naked means to be without a white garment to overcome our shame due to the lack of repentance that wash our robs clean. By not repenting "often", God spued them all out of his mouth and took their candlestick as warned in Rev 2:5 and blotted them out of the book of life in Rev 3:5. His servants, that at one time were true born-again Servants, are cast into outer darkness in Matt 22:13 due to failure of continued repentance. Study Matthew chapter 22 and all the parables as warnings. White robs or garments are found throughout the Old and New Testaments as a symbol of our vest of Salvation. To keep our garments undefiled and spotless before God and Jesus, we must wash it through the act of repentance of prayer "often" in Heb 9:25-26 with Jesus as our High Priest. If we fail to repent of our daily sins "often", spots will build up and spoil our garment. We will be blotted out of the book of life as clearly stated in Rev 3:5 and confirmed in Christ's parables in Matt 25:30 with shame of nakedness just as the Church is found in Rev 3:16-17. This is biblical fact as these verses state.

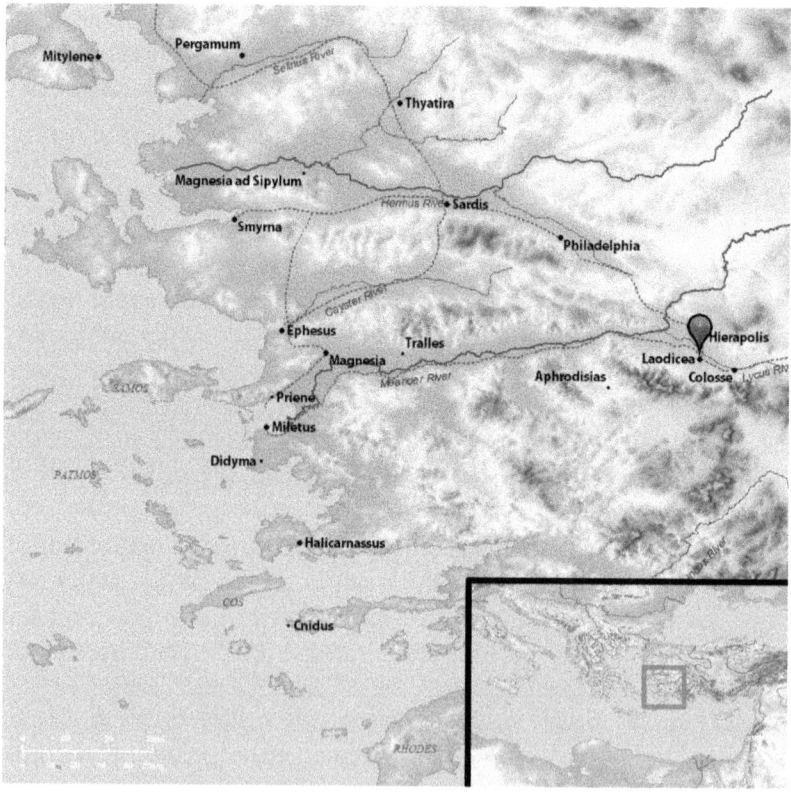

Location of the seven Churches of Asia Minor

Time of Trouble called the Tribulation

The seven-year Tribulation Period goes by several names that takes place in the last days or latter days as by the following definitions:

Jacob's Trouble: It is important to understand the definition of <u>Jacob</u> and <u>Trouble</u>.

Jacob: (Jerm 30:7) 3290, *heel-catcher as a supplanter*, 6117, prime root, *to swell out or up, to seize by the heel, circumvent as if tripping up the heels, to restrain as if holding by the heel, take by the heel, stay, supplant, utterly*, 6119, *a heel as protuberant, a track, the rear of an army, heel as horse hoof, last, lier in wait by mistake for, foot, steep*, 6120, *a lier in wait*. Jacob's name was changed to Israel in Gen 32:28 and 34:10 and in Hebrew ref. 3478 Israel means *he will rule as God, Jisrael, a symbolic name of Jacob given to his posterity*, 8280, *to prevail, have power as a prince*, 410, *strength, mighty especially the **almighty of any deity, God**, goodly, great, idol mighty, power, strong, Comp. **names is "el"***. In Hebrew "el" means **the name of God**, 352, *a chief, a mighty man, an oak*. These are the definitions given to Jacob as the father of the twelve tribes of Israel as a name to be an inheritance of his progenitors called the house of Israel as the Church to be named after God himself, Israel. This means that all born-again Christians/Believers under both Covenants are to be called Israel for we inherited God's name Israel at spiritual birth just as all children are given their fathers name at physical birth. This is why God changed Jacob's name to Israel for all Godly men that accepts his command under the Temple/Church Gospel to be named after his own Spirit, Israel. This is why Christians of the Church of Pergamos is called "the children of Israel (God)" in Rev 2:14 and also in Acts 10:36. The tween birth of Esau and Jacob is found in Gen 25:24-26 where Jacob grabbed Esau's heal as a form of a breach at birth for Jacob was given the inheritance instead of Esau as the firstborn. An example of a breach is also found in Gen 38:29-30 with the twin birth of Pharez and Zarah where Zarah's hand came out first but Pharez was born first creating a breach within Israel's line of Kings. The Throne of King David came from the birth of these two children where the Pharez or Parises line of Kings were later to be overturned to the Zarah or Ephraim line of Kings given to Joseph passed directly to Ephraim and Manasseh as the family name birthright inheritance in Gen 48:16, I Kings 11:25 and 12:19-20. These Ephrathite line of Kings of Zarah as a breach became the Kings of England and the European Hebrew family Monarchs as they migrated into Europe in II Esdras 13:40-46 and Joshua 14:2-3. Queen Elizabeth claimed that she was of the linage of King David and a chart on my wall lists every king form David to King Charles. The house of Israel is called the children of Israel as the Church in Matt 10:6, 15:24, Act 10:36, Rev 2:14 and Eze 3:1-5 given to the Church to be called the lost sheep of the children of Israel as Kings. All Christians that

41

are not of the twelve Hebrew tribes inherit the name Israel which is the name of God by our spiritual birth into his family as a grafting into the olive tree [Church] in Romans 11:23-24. Clearly by definition, all Christians of Christ's Church as his Bride is called Israel and Jerusalem as in Rev 21:9-21 and Jerm 3:14-20.

Trouble: (Jerm 30:7) Hebrew meaning, 6869, *tightness, a female rival, adversary* [name of Satan], *adversity, affliction, anguish, distress, tribulation, trouble*, 6862, *narrow, a tight place i.e. trouble, a pebble, an opponent as crowding, adversary, affliction, anguish, close, distress, enemy, flint, foe, narrow, small, sorrow, strait, tribulation, trouble*, 6864, *a stone, a knife, flint, sharp stone*, 6696, *to cramp, formative or hostile, adversary, assault, beset, besiege, bind up, cast, distress, fashion, fortify, in-close, lay siege, put up in bags*. This definition is speaking of Daniel's 70th week prophecy of seven years called the Tribulation Period which is a time for Satan in Hebrew ref #7854 as *the adversary or an opponent of God as an arch enemy*. In Greek, Satan in #4567, means *the accuser as the Devil*.

<u>Note</u>: II Esdras 16:74 clearly tells us, **"Hear, O ye my beloved, saith the Lord: behold, the days of trouble are at hand, but I will deliver you from the same"**. The word trouble means wrath upon man as *affliction, anguish, distress as tribulation* just as the definition explains. Clearly by this verse and many more, the Church will be taken prior to Gods WRATH upon man.

Time of Trouble: Dan 12:1. Daniel describes this event as a single period of time covering all seven years of the Tribulation or Daniel's 70th week with seven years in total. He divides this time period in Dan 12:7 as **"be for a time, times, and an half"** **"to scatter the power of the holy people, all these things shall be finished"** or 3½ years in reference to Rev 10:7 **"the mystery [Gospel] of God shall be finished"**. The Gospel is finished, according to this verse, at the blowing of the 7th Trumpet marking the middle of the Trib. Dan 12 6-7 is broken into two parts! Verse six and the first part of verse seven is speaking of the worders that take place in the first half of the Trib that last for *"a time, times and an half"* or 3½ years. The last part or verse seven speak of another 3½ years involving the scattering of the Holy People which is the sealed 144,000 spoken of in Rev 12:14 to escape the wrath of the Anti-Christ. The Gospel is finished in Rev 10:7, 11:7 and Dan 12:7 at the blowing of the 7th Trumpet in the middle of the seven years of Tribulation. When we study the definitions of trouble as listed above, we clearly see that the seven-year period for Satan the Devil's is broken into two 3½ year time periods of 1260 days or 42 months. The first half is to bring vengeance upon the nations of Mystery Babylon to be destroyed and the last half is to bring distress, anguish, wrath and sorrow to all ungodly man that takes the Mark of the Beast for 42 months or 3½ years in Rev 13:5.

Day of Trouble: in Nah 1:7, Isa 22:5, Hab 3:16 and Jerm 51:2, has the same definition as listed above. The word day in Greek means, 2250, *the time space between dawn and dark or the shole 24 hours*. It also means, *judgment and day time*. This definition implies that Day of Trouble means, judgment of Satan (adversary) during the Tribulation when we combine all definitions above.

Day of Wrath, Rev 6:17, wrath in Greek means, 3709, *punishment, anger, indignation* and *vengeance*. Romans 5:9 tells us, **"Much more then, being now justified by his blood, we shall be saved from wrath through him"** and this verse justifies I Thess 1:10, 2:16 and 5:9 where it clearly states that the Church is not of WRATH. Luke 21:36 and Dan 12:1-2 verifies those that maintains an "often" repentance will be worthy to escape and be delivered from wrath. If you were Christ, would you bring anger, indignation and vengeance on your Bride, no you would not, for those that are found worthy would escape or be delivered just as these verses state.

Wrath to Come: I Thess 1:10, 2:16 "Wrath is come", Rev 11:18. Same definitions as above.

Wrath of the Lamb: Rev 6:16. This is the wrath that the Lamb or Christ as the Lion brings upon the nations and ungodly man during the seven-years of Tribulation.

Great day of his Wrath is come: Rev 6:17 same definition as above.

Having Great Wrath: Rev 12:12, same definition as above.

Wrath of God: Rev 14:10, 14:19, 15:1, 15:7 and 16:1, the same definition as above.

Note: When we compile all the definitions of wrath from the verses above, we clearly find that both the first and last halves of the seven-year Tribulation Period is considered to be VENGEANCE which is WRATH.

Synopsis of Jacob's Trouble: When we analyze the Hebrew meaning of the word *Jacob* and Trouble, we come up with a very interesting conclusion. *Jacob* was to be the symbol of a heel, foot or horse hoof representing all twelve tribes traveling worldwide by foot or horse and wagon. Their world travel was to be scattered to lay in waiting to be supplanted into the world's wilderness as an army. Jacob's name was changed to Israel so this definition is speaking to the house of Israel as twelve tribes or nations called the four Beast as **"four living creatures"** in Eze 1:5 as a <u>Lion</u>, <u>Man</u>, <u>Ox/Calf/Cherub</u> and <u>Eagle</u> in Eze 1:10, 10:14 and Rev 4:7. Ezekiel 1:15-20 describes the four living creatures which are the four brigades of Israel as a wheel traveling worldwide to be Christ's

Church in Matt 10:6 and 15:24 and to fulfill the Great Commission in Matt 28:18-20. This account is covered in detail in the third chapter paragraph two of this book. Now let's define the meaning of <u>trouble</u> and in Hebrew means; *adversity, affliction, distress and anguish as tribulation.* It also means being used as a weapon of a stone, knife, flint or sharp stone and to lay siege as in fortifications during war. When we combine these two definitions, the term **Jacob's Trouble** means that Jacob of the house of Israel as many nations (Gen 48:19) were to travel by foot and horse being supplanted into the world after their time of lying-in wait after 2520 years of punishment for idolatry. They were to be a fortified weapon of war as a sharp stone, flint or knife as an army. This was to take place during the Church Age to spread the Gospel fulfilling the Great Commission given to the Church as the house of Israel to be finished at the middle of the seven-year Tribulation Period. Keep in mind that the Christian portion of the house of Israel produced the seven Churches in the wilderness as listed in Rev chapters one thru three. The Church is raptured or taken in I Cor 15:51, I Thess 4:14-18 and Dan 12:1-2 to start the seven-year period of the trouble of wrath, "Jacob's Trouble." According to these verses all seven years consist of trouble or wrath, therefore, the Church has to be taken first for the Church is not to see wrath, I Thess 1:10, 5:9 but to be delivered in Dan 12:1-2 and escape in Luke 21:36. Also note that WRATH begins at the opening of the 6th Seal in Rev 6:12 where it clearly states that Wrath has come in Rev 6:16-17. Through calculation, we can place the 6th Seal at the 1 year and one month mark of the first half of the Tribulation as explained in the blowing and length of the 5th Trumpet lasting five months and the 6th Trumpet lasting 1 year, 1 month, one day and one hour. That would place the blowing of the 5th Trumpet at the two-year mark of the 1st half of the Trib. making each of the seven Seals and the first four trumps lasting approx. 2.2 months each. This means that the 6th Seal would be 6X2.2= 13.2 months or approx. at the 13th month mark of the 1st half of the Trib.

The house of Jacob is called Israel in Gen 32:28 that became the lost sheep of the house of Israel in the wilderness as a fruitful nation called the children of Israel in Eze 3:1-5 confirmed in Matt 21:43-44 and the Church in Matt 10:6, 15:24, Acts 10:36 and Rev 2:14. By these Scriptures, the Church is called the house of Israel as the children of Israel.

<u>Note</u>: These definitions were taken from the New Strong's Exhaustive Concordance of the Bible copyright 1995.

Division of the Seven-year Tribulation Period into two halves'

Before we get into the timeline of Revelation and Prophetic Books, let's review the length of the Tribulation Period by days, months and years as recorded in the Scriptures. Properly dividing the seven-year Tribulation into two parts is very important and what separates the pre, mid and post Tribulation believers. The only time in Scripture the Tribulation is spoken of as seven years are found in Dan 9:24-27 and Apocalypse of Baruch 28:1-2 where it is called one week completing Daniel's 70th week Prophecy of 69 weeks already completed. One week represents seven years where one day is one year. All the other Scriptures divide the seven years into two parts either as 42 months or 1260 days (Rev 11:3) as times, times and a half (Dan 12:7). Now let's break the seven years of Tribulation into two halves for we must understand why it is broken into two parts as 1260 days for the first half and 42 months for the second half. Apocalypse of Baruch 27:1-13 and 28:1-2 clearly explains the dividing of the seven years of Tribulation into twelve parts broken into two halves for verses 1-2 clearly state, **"Nevertheless, whosoever shall understand will then be wise. For the measure and reckoning of that time are two parts weeks of seven weeks"**. We know that each week represents one year for a total of seven years where each year is 360 Hebrew days. If we multiply 7 years by 360, we get the Tribulation lasting 2520 days. The number 2520 is very important to understand for it represents a period of punishment upon the nation of Israel as a people in Leviticus 26:3-24 in either days or years. Lev 26:18 states **"And if ye will not yet for all this hearken unto me, then I will punish you seven times more for your sins"**. A normal punishment is seven times 360 or 2520 days equaling seven years. A maximum punishment for idolatry would be *seven times more* or 360-days times 2520 days which is 907,200 days. When we break it down and divide 360 years into 907,200 days it becomes a total of 2520 years of punishment.

Examples of national punishment of 2520 days or years upon Israel:
Gen 41:26: Daniel's interpretation of Pharaoh's dream of a seven-year famine in Egypt lasting 2520 days or seven years.
Eze 4:4-6: gives us the exact number of days given to both houses of Israel and Judah, a max punishment for idolatry which is a total of 390 years in verse 5 for the house of Israel and 40 in verse 6 for Judah totaling 430 years punishment each. We know that each house served 70 years as time served in captivity to Assyria and Babylon so if we subtract 70 from 430 years, we get 360 years which is a normal punishment on a Hebrew Callender of 360 days. Normal punishment would be 7 times 360 or 2520 days. Maximum would be 360 days times 2520 days or 907,200 total days divided by 360 is 2520 years. Why is 2520 years so important to understand?
Lev 26:18: tells us that their punishment was to be **"seven times more for your sins [idolatry]"** or 7 X 7. Again, seven times 360 is 2520 days but seven times more would be 2520 years of punishment as listed above.
The house of Israel under Ephraim went into captivity to Assyria in approx. 721BC when their 2520-year max punishment began. Their punishment ended in approx. 1799AD when England, the birthright tribe of Joseph in Gen 48:19 and in Duet 33:17 as the unicorn became a world sea power. They became the

47 Common Wealth nations of Great Britain the greatest sea power in history flying the flag of a lion and unicorn.

The house of Judah went into captivity to Babylon in approx. 586BC ending their 2520-year punishment in approx. 1934AD during the Jewish Holocaust that propelled Israel into becoming a modern nation in 1948AD fulfilling Matt 24:32-36, **"Now learn a parable of the fig tree"**. Ladies and Gentlemen, this is Biblical prophecy being fulfilled in front of our eyes if we are willing to see!

The Tribulation Period: last for seven years or 2520 days by Biblical fact in Dan 9:27 and Apocalypse of Baruch 27:1-13 and 28:1-2. These verses are clear that the Tribulation Period last for seven years divided into two parts of 1260 days and 42 months divided at its half-way point. Rev 11:2-3 divides the first half of the Trib for the outer court of the new temple to be trod under foot by the Gentiles for 42 months or 1260 days. This same period of 1260 says are allotted to the two Witnesses to preach and teach lasting 3½ years. These two events occur in the first half of the Trib for in Rev 11:7 the two witnesses are killed by the Anti-Christ immediately after he gains full power marking the middle of the first half at the blowing of the 7th Trumpet in Rev 11:15. The first act of the Anti-Christ is to kill the two Witnesses! The Anti-Christ takes full power and given 42 months to reign in Rev 13:7 at the middle of the seven-year Tribulation. This fact is clear if you are willing to understand the timeline as laid out within this book. When we add 1260 days for the two Witnesses and 42 months allotted the Anti-Christ, we get 2520 days of punishment that God serves upon humanity.

We must note that Baruch was the Prophet Jeremiah's Scribe and a Prophet within his own right. He wrote the book Baruch in the Apocrypha and it was considered a part of the Holy Scriptures of the King James Bible up till approx. the 1800's when it was removed. The Apocrypha was placed between the Old and New Testaments prior to its removal where man eliminated it from the KJV Bible not God. When he wrote this book he states *"that the word of the Lord came to Baruch the son of Neriah"*. This Author accepts these writing as Gospel and God inspired his writings according to verse 1:1. The following verses clearly divides the Tribulation into two halves confirming Dan 9:27.

Twelve Parts of the Tribulation according to the Syriac Apocalypse of Baruch 27:1-13:

1st Half of Tribulation 1260 days punishment by Vengeance
During the 7 Trumpets

1st Part: There will be the beginning of commotions
2nd Part: There will be slayings of the great one's
3rd Part: There will be the fall of many by death
4th Part: The sending of desolation

5th Part: Famine and the withholding of rain
6th Part: Earthquakes and terrors

<u>2nd Half of Tribulation 42 months ungodly WRATH by the 7 Vials</u>

7th Part: [Wanting]
8th Part: A multitude of portents and incursions of the Shedim
9th Part The fall of fire
10th Part: Rapine and much oppression
11th Part: Wickedness and unchastity
12th Part: Confusion from the mingling together of all those things
Aforesaid

Unknown Secret of 1st Half of the Seven-year Tribulation of Vengeance Punishment WRATH with mercy

Note: The coming of Jesus to take his Church in I Thess 4:13-18 at the beginning of the 1st half of the Tribulation is confirmed in I Thess 5:4-6 **"that day should overtake you as a thief"**. His coming is a SECRET for the timing of the appearance of a "thief" in the dark of the night is always secret as an unknown time and date.

<u>Tribulation timeline</u>: in reference to **"forty and two months"**, **"time, times an half"** and **"a thousand two hundred and threescore days"** as 1260 days, all equate to 3½ years. This divides Daniel's 70th week prophecy of Seven years into two periods. The first 3½ years is vengeance of 1260 days and the 2nd wrath of 42 months totaling 2520 days or seven years. Many Christians believe that the Tribulation Period only last for 42 months but the book Apocalypse of Baruch proves differently. We must understand that the Holy Bible, especially Daniel, is the bases for all Prophecy but many writings such as the books of Jasher, I and II Enoch, the Apocrypha and Apocalypse of Baruch are history books written by great God inspired Patriarchs that supports the Holy Scriptures. God expects Christians to dig and study to find his truths. This Author has studied them all and incorporated them into this book as inspiration supporting history to the Holy Bible of the KJV. Baruch was Jeremiah's Scribe and a Prophetic writer himself as proven in the book of Baruch. The Scribe Baruch wrote in his book The Apocalypse of Baruch 26:1 (XXVI) **"And I answered and said: will that tribulation which is to be continue a long time, and will that necessity embrace many years?"**. This question is answered in 28:1-2 where it is listed as seven years. Chapter 27:1-13 (XXVII) breaks the seven-year tribulation into twelve parts as listed above. Chapter 28:1-2 (XXVIII) clarifies the length of the tribulation where Baruch states that Jacobs Trouble last for **"two parts weeks of seven weeks"** which is seven years. This verse is clear that seven weeks or seven years are divided into two

parts just as Dan 9:27 states, **"And he shall confirm the covenant with many for one week: and in the midst of the week he shall cause the sacrifice and the oblation to cease"**. This seven-year period called the 70th week is seven years and Daniel also divided this period into two parts at the middle or 3½ year mark. This verse confirms Baruch 28:1-2. The timeframe for this verse is set in Baruch chapter 30:1 (XXX) where it states, **"And it will come to pass after these things, when the time of the advent of the Messiah is fulfilled, and He will return in glory, then all who have fallen asleep in hope of Him shall rise again"**. This verse is speaking of Christ coming in the clouds to be delivered as written in Dan 12:1 and to be **"accounted worthy to escape"** in Luke 21:36. Christ coming to take his Church is in Glory, not when Christ comes in power and glory with fire, but where he takes his Church fulfilling I Cor 15:51-52 and I Thess 4:13-18 **"which sleep in Jesus"**. The word "sleep" couples Baruch 30:1 and I Thess 4:14 as the same event when Christ comes in the clouds to take his Church which will be glory-full. This coming allows Christians to be *delivered* for Dan 12:1 state, **"shall be a time of trouble [seven years as the Trib]"** and **"at that time thy people shall be delivered"** for in Greek means in ref# 4421, *to fly away*. Research these Scriptures and definitions for yourselves.

Christ's Church is to be delivered from the Time of Trouble as stated in Dan 12:1 and escape by being found **"worthy to escape all these things that shall come to pass"** in Luke 21:36. The word "escape" in Greek means in Ref# 1628 *to flee out*, 1537, *from out of place or time, abundantly above, up*, 5343, *to run away, to vanish, flee away* where both words represent an upward movement. Some Christians believe that the Church is not going to be Raptured and want this verse to mean that God is going to protect his Church during the Tribulation by moving them somewhere on earth for protection. According to this Greek definition, the Church will vanish or be taken out of placed or time as flying away in an upward movement which means off the earth into the clouds just as I Thess 4:13-18 states. Clearly in these two verses, Christ's Church is taken when the Church age is finished **"advent of the Messiah is fulfilled"** in Baruch 30:1 and when Christ's earthly Kingdom is moved to Heaven in Rev 4:1-2. The Old Covenant under blood sacrifice (Dan 9:27) and New Covenant of the Gospel cannot overlap, therefore, the Church has to be taken away during the seven- years of Trib. To better understand, study I and II Thessalonians where I Thess. describes clouds as an upward movement where the Church is taken as a *vanishing out of place or time* by this definition at the beginning of the Tribulation. II Thessalonians is where clouds are described as a downward movement at his coming in power and glory with fire. I and II Thessalonians clearly describe two different evens of Christ's comings as one upward and one downward indicating two distinct diverse movements. The Time of Trouble or Daniel's seventh week last seven years that is divided into two parts as Baruch states. The dividing factor is 1260 days allotted to the two

Witnesses for the first half for exactly 3½ years later they are killed in Rev 11:7. 42 months is allotted to the Anti-Christ in the last half just as Rev 13:5 states. These verses describe two separate periods of time, one assigned 1260 days and the other 42 months indicating a distinct difference between the two periods.

The 1st half of the seven-year Tribulation is *vengeance on Babylon* as the ungodly house of Israel and 2nd half is *wrath on ungodly man*. The following verses again divide the seven years of Tribulation into two individual periods of time given to the two Witnesses in the 1st half in Rev 11:3 called vengeance. Forty-two months allotted to the Anti-Christ in Rev 13:5 as wrath on ungodly man, each lasting 3½ years with a total of seven years or 2520 days. We must note that the 1st half is in days where the 2nd half referred to as months which indicate there is a distinct division between the two halves of 2520 days that represent a number of punishments. The max discipline for national idolatry was 2520 years for the house of Judah and Israel where the seven years of Tribulation represent 2520 days, so national or individual punishment can be in days or years.

1st Half: is to complete the Gospel where the Church is taken at the very beginning and replaced with the two Witnesses preaching for 1260 days in <u>Rev 11:3</u>. The Saints under the Alter in the 5th Seal in Rev 6:9 are Saints saved during this period of time. Note that when John and Daniel wrote these prophecies the Hebrew calendar year was only 360 days with 30-day months. The first half of the Trib. is vengeance where God allows Satan's and man's wrath upon the nations of the world as recorded in Jerm 25:1-38 noting verses 26-27. Jerm 25:11, 50:15, Eze 24:8, 25:12-17 clearly state that vengeance is upon Babylon and in Jerm 49:38 places this event in **"the latter days"**. These verses are speaking of the destruction of Mystery Babylon the whore in Rev 14:8. The 1st half of the Tribulation is vengeance wrath by these stated Scriptures. Dan 12:1 called this seven-year period **"a time of trouble"**, Jerm 30:7 calls it **"the time of Jacob's trouble"** which is WRATH for in Hebrew wrath means vengeance. I Thess 1:10 states that Christians are to escape **"delivered us from the wrath to come"**, Luke 21:36 **"Watch ye therefore, and pray always, that ye may be accounted worthy <u>to escape all these things</u> that shall come to pass, and to stand before the Son of man"**. I Thess 5:9 **"For God hath not appointed us to wrath"** speaks of the whole seven-year period. The word *"all"* and *"shall come to pass"* in these verses clearly states that true Christians **"that may be accounted worthy to escape"** as the Church are to escape the wrath of the whole Tribulation Period. In the book of Revelation, the word WRATH is first spoken of in 6:16 at the opening of the 6th Seal which is within the first two years of the <u>1st half</u> of the Trib after the wars of the four horsemen. This proves that the 1st Half of the Trib. is considered WRATH on the evil nations of Babylon's economy, not ungodly man. During this time, the 3rd Temple

49

is rebuilt and blood sacrifice established and the outer court trodden under foot by the Gentiles for 42 months or 3½ years as recorded in Rev 11:2 in conjunction with the two Witnesses during the 1st half of the Tribulation in Rev 11:3. This brings up a very important subject for it appears there is a biblical contradiction. Compare the following verse and let's figure out this somewhat inconsistency.

Important Note: Blood Sacrificing and the outer court is mentioned several times in the Scriptures all listing a different length of time, WHY? The following verses will explain:

Rev 11:2&Dan 9:27 **"But the court which is without the temple leave out, and measure it not; for it is given unto the Gentiles: and the holy city shall they tread under foot forty and two months"**, which is 1260 days or 3.5 years during the 1st half of the Trib.

Dan 8:11-14 Speak of the **"daily sacrifice was taken away"**, **"sanctuary was cast down"** and **"sanctuary and the host to be trodden under foot"** and in verse 14 the vision was to last for 2300 days, **"two thousand and three hundred days"** which is 2300 days, 6.38 years or 76.6 months. This means that the daily sacrifice only lasted for 220 days into the first half of the Trib before it was taken away. If we look at time chart #3, we can better understand for this event took place during the opening of the 3rd Seal at the 220th day of the 1st half, 2520 in seven-years subtract 2300=220 days or at the 7.3-month mark into the 1st half of the Trib.

Dan 12:11&11:31 **"And from the time that the daily sacrifice shall be taken away, and the abomination that maketh desolate set up, there shall be a thousand two hundred and ninety days"**, which is 1290 days or 3 years and 7 months that occur at the 3-year 7-month mark or after 30 days into the 2st half of the Trib.

Dan 9:27 **"And he shall confirm the covenant with many for one week: and in the midst of the week he shall cause the sacrifice and the oblation to cease"**. This verse is saying that God shall confirm the covenant with the Jews for one week or seven-years and in the middle of the seven years the blood sacrifice will cease. This is Daniel's 70th week prophecy or the Tribulation Period of John's book of Revelation consisting of 2520 days of punishment in total.

 II Thess 2:2-7 **"so that he as God** [Anti-Christ] **sitteth in the temple of God, shewing himself that he is God"**. Rev 13:4-8 is where the Dragon or Anti-Christ sat on the throne in the Temple for all the world to worship and is when he decrees that he is god, the Apotheosis ending all Jewish traditions to include blood sacrifice.

Note: In regard to the Daily Sacrifice being taken away and the temple trodden under foot, there seems to be a discrepancy in days of time between Dan 11:14 of 2300 days, Dan 12:11 of 1290 days and Rev 11:2 of 42 months or 1260 days. Study the #3-time chart and the reason will be in the explanation below.

Explanation

Why are there a difference in time between these verses? The reason is very simple if we apply all the other verses within the Bible that reference when Satan the Anti-Christ called Abaddon or Apollyon comes into full power in II Thess 2:2-7, Rev 9:1&11 and Rev 13:5. These three verses are the key for it clearly states that the Anti-Christ is released from the bottomless pit in the 5th Trump at the two-year mark of the 1st half of the Trib. It takes the Anti-Christ 1½ years to come to full power at the middle of the seven years of Tribulation for he has no power given to kill till his inauguration ceremony is complete at the 1290-day mark. We must understand that he becomes the Anti-Christ at the 42-month mark (Rev 13:5) in the exact middle of the seven years but does not receive absolute power till the 1290th day when his ceremonial inauguration is complete. Dan 12:11 explains where he received absolute power, **"and the abomination that maketh desolate set up"** when he sets in the temple claiming himself to be god (II Thess 2:1-7) in the middle of the seven years plus 30 days. There are three different dates that must be explained!

Dan 8:11-14 Daniel's vision states that the "daily sacrifice" and "sanctuary trodden under foot" would be taken away for 2300 days. This would place this event during the 7th month of the 1st half of the Tribulation when the 3rd Seal of the black horse is opened bringing world economic collapse. Why? *Synopsis*: We know that the New World Order hates all religions and destroys Christianity, Muslims and Jews during WWIII (Eze 38&39 war) at the beginning of the Trib. in preparation for the coming of the Anti-Christ. We can see how Christians are being persecuted in our current time period and its only going to get worse. So, when the new Temple in Jerusalem is built at the beginning of the seven-years of Tribulation and the daily sacrifice begins in Dan 8:11-14, 9:27, 11:31, Matt 24:15 and Dan 12:11, the new One World Order government shuts down the "daily sacrifice" within the first 220 days in the newly built temple for political hatred of religion. The Anti-Christ will not be released from the bottomless pit for another two years so these verses are speaking of a political move on religious abhorrence.

Dan 9:27 Clearly state that the **"daily sacrifice"** will be taken away **"in the midst of the week"** when the Anti-Christ sets in the temple and declares himself to be god. *Synopsis*: The taking away of the daily sacrifice in this verse is simply to confirm and to reiterate that the taking away has already been compete when he sets in the temple to be god showing his hatred for religion.

Dan 12:11 This synopsis is hard for it took allot of prayer and study and asking

Jesus to show me the meaning of this verse. Why the difference? **"And from the time that the daily sacrifice shall be taken away, and the abomination that maketh desolate set up** [30-days], **there shall be a thousand two hundred and nineth days"** or 1290 days. The wording *"set up"* and "power was given unto him" in Rev 13:5 is the key. These verses took place one month after the middle of the Tribulation that starts his rule for 42 months or 1260 days, so why a 30-day difference? It is a ceremonial inauguration event that last for 30 days "set up" for all to take the MARK of the Beast which is a governmental decree and when the Anti-Christ can set upon his throne within the new built 3rd temple. This power was given unto him one month after taking full control of the world to kill all that did not take the mark. He was to be god of the world in II Thess 2:3-7, Matt 24:15 and Rev 13:5. We must consider where his power came from, **"and power was given unto him to continue forty and two months"**. If Satan the Anti-Christ is the second most powerful being in the universe other than God, who has the authority to give him power? His power and authority were not given to him by God but from the people of the world *"and powers were given unto him"* which is ceremonial powers by the nations of the world. This ceremony lasted for thirty days. God did not give but only allowed the Anti-Christ this power. It is power given from the people just as Caesar, Hitler, Stalin and all the other great evil dictators of history. This is a ceremonial event where the people of the world freely accept mentally, physically and spiritually the Anti-Christ to be their human god through free-will. It is this Author's belief that the taking of the Mark of the Beast will be a part of this ceremony where it takes 30 days to mark all the people of the world to accept the Anti-Christ as their god. The Anti-Christ has full power at the 42-month mark, at the exact middle of the Tribulation, where he immediately kills the two Witnesses in Rev 11:7. At this point in time, the Gospel is **"finished"**, "finished their testimony" [Rev 10:7, 11:7 and Dan 12:7 seven is the number of completions] where the Holy Spirt is taken from earth fulfilling II Thess 2:7. The Anti-Christ gives the world 30-days to take the Mark for he cannot start killing people till the Mark is completely implemented. At this point in time, after 1290 days from the beginning of the seven-year Trib., any person refusing to take the MARK will be killed. He takes his power at the beginning of this 30-day period where he now has man given powers through the people to kill the two witnesses in Rev 11:7 when the Gospel is finished and God's restraints through the Holy Spirit is removed from earth just as II Thess 2:6-7 states. Satan cannot kill the two Witnesses till restraint of the Holy Spirit is removed which means the words **"withholdeth"** and **"letteth *will let*"** be taken away.

Rev 11:2 Outer court of the Temple is **"tread under foot forty and two months"** or 1260 days. *Synopsis:* This verse is speaking only of the outer court and the city of Jerusalem, not of the "daily sacrifice" where the people of the world were to tread under foot for 42 months during the period of the two Witnesses which is 3½ years.

What does the word Finished mean?

The word "finished" in Dan 12:7, Rev 10:7 and 11:7&15 at the blowing of the 7th Trumpet is the completion of Christ's Gospel at the end of the first 3½ years in the middle of the Trib. When the two witnesses are killed in Rev 11:7, **"finished their testimony"**, the Gospel is "finished" when the "holy people" are scattered in Dan 12:7 **"all these things shall be finished"** at the middle of the seven-year Tribulation as also stated in Rev 10:7 at the blowing of the 7th Trumpet in 11:15. The word "finished" in these verses means that Christ's Gospel and the working of the Holy Spirit on earth are complete. Gods plan of Salvation is finished where all Saints throughout time can be judged in Heaven. This event takes place in the middle of the Tribulation as found in Rev 14:7. We must note that the Gospel is finished but Daniel's 70th week concerning Jerusalem in Dan 9:24-27 will not be finished till the end of the Tribulation for all that can be saved are killed in the middle of the Tribulation.

Example of mercy wrath of death: Rev 14:12-16 was a mercy death by the Lamb sitting on a cloud having a sharp sickle taking by death all living Christians, **"here are they that keep the commandments of God, and the faith of Jesus"** stated in verse 12. Prior to God's wrath there are examples such as in Jasher 5:5&21 where God took all faithful through a mercy death prior to the flood. The Church as his Bride is taken without seeing death prior to the Tribulation, Noah's and Lot's family saved prior to God's destruction by wrath with other examples throughout the Scriptures. God's faithful people do not see wrath just as Rom 5:9, I Thess 1:10&5:9, Dan 12:1 "delivered" and Luke 21:36 "escape" where these verses clearly state.

The first half of the Tribulation is *Vengeance upon the nations as the daughter of Babylon.* The Western Christian culture is called the daughter of Babylon for it is an offspring as stated in Isa 47:1-5. It is called **"O virgin daughter of Babylon"** for it was once the virgin bride as Christ's Church of Laodiceans spued out of God's mouth as a now perverted Christian nation. Verse three, **"I will take "vengeance" upon her** and verse 4 calls them, **"As for our redeemer, the Lord of hosts is his name, the Holy One of Israel"**. Christ's Church is called the house of Israel in Matt 10:6 and 15:24. Babylon was once tender and delicate as the Church but in verse one they fell away, **"O daughter of the Chaldeans; for thou shalt no more be called tender and delicate [the Church]"**. The Church within Babylon did not heed the warning given in Rev 2:5 and 3:5 for they failed to repent and fell from grace just as the Roman/Babylonian Church of Laodiceans were spewed out of God's mouth in Rev 3:16. Their candlestick was removed and spewed out **"I will spue thee out of my mouth"**. Jeremiah 51:33&45 and Rev 18:4 give a better identity of who Babylon was for it states in Jerm 51:33, **"the God of Israel [the Church]; The daughter of Babylon is like a threshingfloor"**, and verse

45, **"My people [the Church], go ye out of the midst of her"** and Rev 18:4, **"Come out of her, my people [the Church]"**. A threshing floor is where wheat is separated from the chaff or Godly from the ungodly. Clearly the Church as the house of Israel is called the daughter of Babylon. We know that the lost sheep of the house of Israel were given the responsibility of being the Church for Christ himself sent his Gospel by the twelve Apostles to only them in Matt 10:6, 15:24, Acts 10:36 and Eze 3:1-5. The western Church and the world accepted and maintained the old Babylonian BAAL religion of old through the Jewish Masonic Cabala from ancient Egypt during their enslavement. The god of Baal worship (Chief god of the Canaanites) is the religion of the Masonic Order called the Illuminati, the angel of light and knowledge where almost every town in the world has a Masonic Lodge. It is the Satanic religion of the world financed and controlled by America and Great Britain as its leader through the York and Scottish Rite Masonic Lodges which is the house of Israel that was once righteous nations, "tender and delicate" in Isa 47:1. This is a historical documented fact so study this subject for yourself. The 1ˢᵗ half of the Tribulation is a vengeful wrath through love just as a parent would lovingly punish their child for saved Christians are present during this time period. The Church has been taken or raptured so it is not present but millions of people will be saved by the Gospel of the two Witnesses in the 1ˢᵗ half under the authority of their two olive trees and candlesticks given in Rev 11:4 as authority of the Church. The 2ⁿᵈ half of the Tribulation is WRATH through anger as you would punish a godless hard-core criminal without mercy for no Christians are left. They have all been killed according to Rev 13:8&15 and 11:7. Only the 144,000 sealed Christians protected by God and people that has taken the Mark of the Beast are left, all other people have been killed by the Anti-Christ including the two witnesses, *"as many as would not worship the image of the beast should be killed"* in Rev 13:15.

Luke 21:22-23 Vengeance in this verse indicate a different period of time other than wrath, **"For these be the days of vengeance, that all things which are written may be fulfilled"**. Verse 23 speak of wrath in a different context as a "WOE" meaning of great distress also indicating it occurs in a different time. Vengeance and Wrath is separated into two different periods as the 1ˢᵗ and 2ⁿᵈ half of the Tribulation.

Isa 63:4 Study verses 1-8, **"For the day of vengeance is in mine heart, and the year of my redeemed is come"** meaning Christian believers are present that do not receive wrath but punishment. The word vengeance in Hebrew means, 5359, *revenge, avenged, quarrel*, 5358, *to grudge, or punish, take vengeance* and in Greek, II Thess 1:8, 1557, *vindication, retribution, punishment*. The Hebrew meaning of wrath, 5678, *an outburst of passion, anger, rage* and in Greek, I Thess 5:9, 3709, *desire as a reaching forth or excitement, violent passion or justifiable abhorrence, punishment, indignation,*

54

vengeance. If we closely study the different meanings of vengeance and wrath between the Hebrew and Greek, they mean basically the same for punishment. There is one difference that I can see; VENGEANCE is a punishment of LOVE as punishment of a child and WRATH is a punishment of a HATE crime or justifiable abhorrence. This means that the 1ˢᵗ half of the Tribulation is punishment from God to the nations out of love, verse 7, **"I will mention the loving kindness of the Lord"** as you would punish your child, but the 2ⁿᵈ Half is punishment to hateful ungodly man as a hard-core criminal.

<u>Rev 11:3</u> power of the two witnesses to prophesy for **"a thousand two hundred and threescore days"** equals the first 3½ years of the Trib. that fall under vengeance not wrath.

<u>Rev 11:11</u> the two witnesses dead in the streets of Jerusalem for **"three days and an half"** or 3½ days finishing the Gospel of Christ at the end of the first half of the Trib after completing their assignment of 1260 days. The first act of the Anti-Christ is to kill them when he is given power in Rev 13:5 at the beginning of his 42-month reign.

<u>Rev 11:9</u> the world sees the two witnesses' dead bodies for **"three days and an half"** or 3½ days lying dead in the streets of Jerusalem on international TV. Three-and one-half days is symbolic to the 3½ years of the two Witnesses preaching and teaching to the world. Three and a half is one half of seven where seven is the number of Completion.

2ⁿᵈ Half or 3½ years of the Tribulation is not a Secret for it can be calculated to the day

WRATH by Justifiable Anger

<u>Note:</u> The Secret of the coming of Christ as a thief in the night occurs in I Thess 4:14-17, I Cor 15:51 and Rev 4:1-2 when Christ's Throne is set in Heaven, marks the beginning of the seven-year Tribulation. The beginning of the 2ⁿᵈ half of the Trib will occur in exactly 3½ years so it is a known set date and cannot be as a thief or a secret coming.

<u>2ⁿᵈ Half:</u> God brings WRATH and judgment upon ungodly man with the pouring of the seven **"vials of the wrath of God"** in Rev 16:1-17 and this wrath began at the sounding of the 7ᵗʰ Trumpet in Rev 11:18. The 2ⁿᵈ Half of the Tribulation is *Wrath on ungodly men having the MARK* as hard-core criminals in Rev 13:16-17 and Rev 14:9-10, **"If any man worship the beast and his image, and receive his mark in his forehead, or in his hand, The same shall drink of the wine of the wrath of God"**. The following verses

clearly indicate 3½ years allotted for this period of wrath.

Rev 12:6&14 confirmed in Dan 12:12 The woman fled into the wilderness for **"a thousand two hundred and threescore days"** equating to 3½ years at the beginning of the 2nd half of the seven-year Tribulation. In verse 14 the woman flies into the wilderness for a **"time, times and half"** or 3½ years to escape the Anti-Christ during his 42 months reign in Rev 13:5 also indicating that this event occurs at the 7th Trump in the middle of the Trib. We must note Dan 12:12, **"blessed is he that waiteth, and cometh to the thousand three hundred and five and thirty days"** or 1335 days. The number 1335 divided by a 30-day month equals 44.5 months, that occurs at the 3 year and 3.5 months into the 1st half of the Trib. This would be two and a half months prior to the middle of the Tribulation. This time period has to be speaking of the specially selected sealed 144,000, 12 thousand from each tribe, that are scattered into the wilderness to escape the Anti-Christ in the last half of the Tribulation period. This blows the idea that the Tribulation period only last for 42 months or 3½ years. According to this verse, they departed on their trip into the wilderness two and ½ months before the middle of the Trib., therefore, lasting 1335 days in total which is 3.7 years. This would place them at the 3 year and 3½ month mark of the 1st half of the Trib. Daniel 12:12 gives them a special blessing. The 144,000 called "the woman" as the children of Israel, flee into the wilderness at the 1185-day mark of the 1st half of the Tribulation, 75 days prior to Satan the Anti-Christ taking full power at the 3½ year mark. God gave his people 75 days to escape or the Anti-Christ would have caught and killed them. Satan did not have the authority or power to kill till his 42 months of power was given as the apotheosis at the 42-month mark in the middle of the trib. If we fail to break down the seven years of Tribulation into two halves, we cannot understand the differences of time in these verses in how they overlap in time.

Dan 12:7 confirms Rev 12:6&14 to scatter the power of the Holy People **"for a time, times and an half"** equals 3½ years the same verse as Rev 12:6. Daniel blesses the 144,000 in Dan 12:12 where they flee into the wilderness for 1335 days or 75 days prior to the Anti-Christ taking full power. This occurs at approx. 3-year 2.5-month mark of the 1st half of the Trib. allowing them 1.5 months to flee into the wilderness to escape.

Dan 12:11 The taking away of the daily sacrifice occurs at the 3 yr. 5 mo. mark of the 1st half or 1290 days till the end of the Trib., **"there shall be a thousand two hundred and ninety days"** which is 3 years and 7 months in length starting at the 3-year 5-month mark of the first-half of the Trib. See time chart #3 on page twenty-nine.

Rev 13:5, the Antichrist is given **"forty and two months"** in the last half of the Trib. to complete his evil reign of 3½ years.

Note: Dan 11:31 and Dan 12:11 is where the Anti-Christ pollutes the sanctuary, **"a thousand two hundred and nineth days"** equals three years seven months which is also stated in Matt 24:14-15 at the end of the Gospel where the two witnesses are killed in the middle of the Trib.

What is "time, times and a half" spoken of in Dan 7:25, Dan 12:7 and Rev 12:14? Most interpreters take the term "time" to mean one year in reference to seven years of the Tribulation Period for that is the subject. Also, according to the subject of the Scripture, it can mean one day, one week or one year. Therefore, in these Scriptures the interpretation means "Time" is one year, Times equates to two years and a half time means one half year or 3½ years in total. The verses above cover all three as days, months and years. Rev 11:3, Dan 11:31 & 12:11-12 covers days; Rev 11:2, Rev 13:5 covers months and Rev 12:14 and Dan 7:25 covers years. Dan 7:25, the Anti-Christ time of reign is given his power for, **"shall be given into his hand until a time and times and the dividing of time"** or 3½ years as stated above. Rev 13:5 gives him power for "forty and two months". These two verses give the Anti-Christ power for 42 months or 1260 days which is 3½ years.

Important Notes:

1st Note: Crucial Scriptures of Rev 9:1 opening of the 5th Seal and Rev 9:13 blowing of the 6th Trumpet are key verses that establish the timeline for the whole book of Revelation. We need only to go backward from the blowing of the 7th Trumpet to understand the timeline. It is simple if we study this sequence! We know that the 7th Trumpet marks the middle of the 1st half of the seven years of Tribulation for the Gospel is "finished" when the two witnesses are killed, Rev 10:7 and 11:7 confirmed in Dan 9:24&12:7. We know that the two witnesses were given 1260 days or 42 months to preach and teach the Gospel in Rev 11:2-3 which clearly marks the end of the finishing of the Gospel at the middle mark of the Trib. Rev 9:15 clearly tells us that the 6th Trumpet lasted one hour, a day, a month and a year or for a total of 13 months a day and an hour. Rev 9:5 tells us that the 5th Trumpet lasted for five months. Simple, if we add 13 months allotted for the 6th Seal and 5 months of the 5th Seal, we get 18 months or a total of 1 and ½ years placing the blowing of the 5th Trumpet at the two-year mark of the 1st half of the seven-year Tribulation Period. Now we know that from the time John, representing the rapture of the Church, was taken into Heaven in Rev 4:1-2 up to the blowing of the 5th Trumpet was two years. We also know that during this two-year period the 7 Seals were opened and 4 Trumpets blown making 11 events that occurred in a 24-month period. If we divide 11 events into 24 months, we get approx. 2.2 months per event. It is simple math for each of the 7 Seals and first 4 Trumpets is estimated to last only 2.2 months each. When we add all this time up, we get 1260 days or 3 and ½ years to the middle of the Tribulations consisting of the

1st half of the Trib. In reality, this clearly breaks the seven-years of Tribulation into two 3½ year periods totaling seven years. The 1st half is vengeance on the nations and the 2nd half are wrath on ungodly men. We must also note that it is believed Jesus's ministry lasted for 3½ years representing the time allotted in the 1st half to the two witnesses for their Gospel to be finished at the 3½ years mark. Christ's Ministry is a symbol or representation of the two witnesses that lasted for only three and half years where the Church was taken at the beginning of the seven years leaving the two Witnesses 3 ½ years in place of Christ's Church. The Scriptures are clear that Christ's Bride as the Church is not of WRATH, I Thess 1:10&5:9, Dan 12:1 and Luke 21:36 for the key words are *delivered, saved* and *escape*. Christ's Ministry is complete when the two Witnesses are killed in Rev 11:7 for they were chosen to endure wrath in place of the Church during the 1st half of the seven-year period.

2nd note: We must note that John and Daniel had to be on the same calendar for the Scripture to be correct, therefore, they both used the old Hebrew calendar which means one year was 360 days with 30-day months.

3rd Note: The whole seven years of Daniel's 70th week in Dan 9:24 is to **"finish the transgression and to make an end of sins"** of God's people [only for the Jews of Jerusalem] and the sins of the world for God's Kingdom of his Church has been taken. The belief that the Tribulation is only 42 month is false for clearly Dan 8:14 lists 2300 days or 76.6 months, Dan 12:11 lists 1290 days or 43 months and Dan 12:12 lists 1335 days or 44.5 months which are far more than 42 months. By these verses, the Tribulation has to lasts for seven-years. Daniel's 70th week consisting of seven years is broken into two parts considered to be <u>vengeance</u> and <u>wrath</u> according to Luke 21:20-26. These verses are speaking only to Jerusalem for verse 20 states, **"And when ye shall see Jerusalem"** to fulfill sin and all Prophecy under the Old Covenant Law of Moses, blood sacrifice that is not fulfilled. Luke 21:22 **"For these be the days of vengeance, that all things which are written may be fulfilled"**. These verses cover all seven years of wrath where Dan 9:24-27 fulfills the prophecy of Jerusalem's 70th week. The 1st half of the Tribulation brings vengeance to the nations which is a form of wrath for many Christians are present. Luke 21:23 during the 2nd half states, **"for there shall be great distress in the land, and wrath upon this people** [ungodly people and Jews]**"**. Wrath is upon godless man called "this people", meaning, they are the ungodly people and Jews of the world that took the Mark.

4th Note: The Scriptures are clear, people can only be saved during the 1st Half of the seven-year Tribulation Period of <u>VENGEANCE</u> upon the nations of Babylon which is the current world economic system controlled by NY, London and all the other international Stock Exchanges. There is a distinct difference between the first half of Vengeance and last half under Wrath called the Beast System. This is where many Christians go wrong for the 1st half is under the Gospel of the two witnesses for 42 months or 1260 days in Rev 11:2-3 guided by the Holy Spirit after the Church is taken into the clouds in I Thess 4:14-18, I Cor 15:51-52 and Dan 12:1-2. We must note that the Holy Spirit is not taken when the Church is taken for it has to work during the 1st half giving authority to the two Witnesses. The Anti-Christ's power is not released till the Gospel is finished in Rev 11:7 when the two witnesses are Killed when the Anti-Christ is given full power. The Anti-Christ and the Holy Spirit cannot co-exist just as II Thess 2:7, **"only he who now letteth will let until he** [Holy Spirit] **be taken out of the way"**. This is why each of the two witnesses have their own individual olive trees and candlesticks which is equivalent to the seven candlesticks of the Church that has been taken away. The Holy Spirit has to be present as long as a candlestick representing the Gospel, the Church or the two Witnesses. If the Church was still present with their candlestick, the two Witnesses would not be necessary. The last half or 42 months of the Anti-Christ in Rev 13:5 is a period of time having total WRATH upon ungodly man without Gods Spirit, all have taken the Mark of the Beast except the Sealed 144,000 where all that refuse is killed. The Gospel is finished at the blowing of the 7th Trump that takes place in the middle of the Tribulation when the two Witnesses are killed after "a thousand two hundred and threescore days" or 3½ years just as in Rev 10:7, 11:7 and Dan 9:24&12:7 state. Note that the words to finish the Gospel is in the seventh verse of all three of these chapters, the number 7 is God's number of completion. This event divides the seven years into two parts of WRATH, three and half years of Vengeance of Wrath on the nations and three and half years of hard Wrath on evil men having the MARK. No one can be saved under the Gospel during the last half of the Trib. for the Gospel is finished at the mid-point of the Tribulation just as these verses indicate. Rev 13:7&15 clearly state, all that do not worship the image of the beast are killed leaving only the people that take the MARK and the Sealed 144,000 Hebrew Christians that God protects. There is no one left to be Saved during the last half of the Tribulation of 42 months of WRATH given to the Anti-Christ to finish his evil. You may say, how about babies, they are of God before they reach the age of accountability, yes, but these times will be different. All the mothers of these babies having the Mark of the Beast will willfully inject their children and themselves with COVID type DNA or AI altering nano-bot drugs making these babies along with mankind non-human but transhuman just as the Mark of the Beast. It makes them ineligible to enter Heaven due to the sin of the mother and father. All people to include babies at birth will receive the mark.

Chapter 4

Chronology of events in the book of Revelation Chapters 1 thru 22

To better understand prophecies of this book, we need to chronologically place each event in order by an actual timeline. This Author must note that the inspiration of this timeline came directly from the Holy Spirit and not from me! The book of Revelation can be confusing for time in some chapters appear to skip around. With study, we can place events of each chapter in the proper consistent commentary timeline in chronological order. If we fail in this process, the book of Revelation is almost impossible to comprehend by order of events. We know that Apostle John the Revelator was the author of the book of Revelation written on the Island of Patmos in approx 100AD. Christ himself commissioned John in Rev 1:11 to write down these prophecies in a book, verse 8, **"which is, and which was, and which is to come"** and Rev 11:17, **"which art, and wast, and art to come"**. These are prophecies of events in the past, present and future, therefore, the timeline commentary has to change back and forward making it very difficult to understand without guidance from the Holy Spirit. God made it this way for a reason, so that man would have to depend on his Spirit for understanding. If Christians of the Church are to understand prophetic events in conjunction with the Holy Bible, we must prove ourselves in Spirit by researching the proper timeline of each prophetic event guided by his hand. This means, each Christian has to be right with God physically, spiritually and mentally before he reveals these secrets through prayer and deep study.

Skeletal timeline of events in the book of Revelation by chapter

The Church timeline begins in Rev 1:1 and runs unbroken thru Rev 11:19 to mark the middle of the Tribulation of 3½ years. The timeline is still unbroken through Rev 16:17 saying, **"it is done"** at the pouring of the 7th Vial ending the seven-years of Tribulation. This verse states, **"And the seventh angel poured out his vial into the air; and there came a great voice out of the temple of heaven, from the throne saying, It is done"**. At this event, the seven-years of Tribulation is now done and complete but we still have six chapters 17-22 of commentary to go. The timeline of Rev 1:1 begins at Acts 2:1 when the Holy Spirit of God entered the Church at Pentecost in Rev 1:13&16&20 as the seven candlesticks and stars which is the seven Spirits of God. These seven spirits, which is the Church and its candlesticks, is taken to Heaven where it's located in Rev 4:1-5 ending approx. two thousand years of the Church age. The timeline of events including the Gospel continues. The beginning of the seven-years of Tribulation starts another era of time with the same unbroken timeline. The end of the seven-years of Tribulation is not the end of the timeline for it continues till the millennial is finished, the old earth and Heaven passes away and the new Earth and Heaven descends. We must understand that from Rev 1:1 to 16:17 the timeline is a continual constant time where John departs the script for brief commentary to explain certain events that take place in different time periods of the timeline. Chapters 12-14 and 17-22 are explanations of events that occurred at a certain moment of time during the ongoing timeline from Rev 1:1 to Rev 16:1-21. The seven-years of Tribulation is finished at the opening of the 7th Vial in Rev 16:17 when it clearly states **"it is done"**.

Let's break down John's commentary on a quick skeletal view chapter by chapter as we go: An in-depth view will be covered as we go later into each chapter.

There is an unbroken timeline from when John was chosen to write the book of Revelation to the blowing of the 7th Trumpet marking the middle at 3½ years and the 7th Vial ending the seven years of the Tribulation Period. Chapter 16 picks up from the blowing of the 7th Trumpet through the pouring of the 7th Vial in Rev 16:17-21. Chapter 13-14 does not break the timeline but commentary that skips through many different years of time and events. These events occur at a certain point of time within the timeline from the time Satan was kicked out of Heaven possibly thousands of years ago. It continues through the Church Age to the last Vial of wrath ending the seven years of Tribulation all the way through New Jerusalem descending out of Heaven after the old Earth and Heaven is passed away. The book of Revelation covers thousands or possibly millions of years.

Beginning of the Church Age in chapter 1 thru 3 Commentary

The timeline in Chapter 1 thru 3 occurs from Acts 2:1 at Pentecost approx. 30AD to Rev 4:1-2 when the Church is taken into Heaven. God personally gave John the Revelator the authority as his Church to record future Prophecy pertaining directly to Christ's Church called the lost sheep of the house of Israel in Matt 10:6, 15:24, Rev 2:14 and Acts 10:36. The unbroken timeline begins when the Holy Spirit entered the Church at Pentecost in Acts chapter two that began two thousand years of the Church Age. At our present time, we are at the end of the Church Age of Laodiceans. Revelation 1:1 through 3:13 has occurred in the past in reference to the Church of Ephesus to the later part of Laodiceans allotted time period which is our current time. We are now in the present timeline from Rev 3:14-19 till the Church of Laodicea is taken in Rev 4:1-2 in the future. This explains our past, present and future as the Church for we are at the very end of the age of the Church of Laodiceans. These three chapters explain the elements of the seven Churches and their allotted periods of time to include their identity up to the point when the Church is taken into Heaven in Rev 4:1-2. The taking of John into Heaven is clearly a symbol of the Church for Rev 4:5 places seven lamps or candlesticks and the seven Spirits of God listed in Rev 1:20 now in Heaven. Chapters 2-3 list each Church individually where they are given a candlestick and Spirit when John wrote his book placing each Church in the future tense listing each or their future deeds. In our current time, these Churches are now in the past tense except for the later part of the Church of Laodiceans that we are now in.

NOTE: It is important to understand who gave John the Prophecy to write in each chapter of the book of Revelation. It's clear that only Jesus and his Church as the Lamb of Judah in Rev 5:5 had the authority to open each of the seven Seals, Trumpets and Vials but some events Jesus delegated to Angels and the four Beasts which is his Church as the lost sheep. An important fact that most Christians completely overlook. God did not give Jesus his authority till he sat on his promised Throne given in Luke 1:31-33 where it is fulfilled in Rev 4:1-2 when the throne is "set" in Heaven and Jesus sets on King David's throne fulfilling Rev 5:5 as the Lion/Lamb of Judah. All three elements of Christ's earthly Kingdom had to be complete in Heaven before he received his authority which is King David's throne, the twelve tribes as the lost sheep and the Temple/Church. Christ's earthly Kingdom is complete when John representing the Church is taken into Heaven.

The first line in RED after the beginning of each chapter identifies who gave John the authority to write. Chapter 1-3 sets up the beginning of the Church Age that last for approx. two thousand years. Rev 4:1-2 begins the seven years of Tribulation of Wrath.

Rev chapter One: gives the Apostle John the authority to write future prophetic events that is going to occur for each Church in the future. This chapter list all the seven Churches and the elements of each Church having seven Stars (Spirits) and seven golden Candlesticks (the Church).

Rev chapter Two: list the first four Churches of Ephesus, Smyrna, Pergamos and Thyatira with their good and bad deeds. Verse 5 gives all seven Churches a dire **WARNING**, **"Remember therefore from whence thou art fallen and repent, and do the first works; or else I will come unto thee quickly, and will remove thy candlestick out of his place, except thou repent"**. This warning was invoked only to the Church of Laodiceans in Rev 3:15 where they are spewed out of God's mouth.

Rev chapter Three: list the last three Churches of Sardis, Philadelphia and

Laodiceans with their good and bad deeds. The Church of Laodiceans is the only Church that list no good deeds and considered to be wretched, miserable, poor, blind and naked where they are spued out of God's mouth in verses 15 thru 17. God gives the seven Churches another dire **WARNING** in verse five, **"He that overcometh, the same shall be clothed in white raiment; and I will not blot out his name out of the book of life, but I will confess his name before my Father, and before his angels"**. This is the Church of Babylon listed in Rev 14:8 and chapters 16 thru 18 where they refuse to repent of their sins so they did not overcome death for they are clearly blotted out of the Book of Life. Rev 3:20-22 is speaking of the Church age where if any man hears his voice and open the door, he will come into them. Jesus says that he, **"and am set down with my Father in his throne"** at this moment of time closing out this chapter and two thousand years of the Church Age.

Major Events: in the Past and Present
The completion of the Church Age approx. 2000 years takes place in the past and present.

We are in the present time and the Church doors are open, Rev 3:20, **"Behold, I stand at the door, and knock: if any man hear my voice, and open the door, I will come in to him, and will sup with him, and he with me"**. The Church door is currently open for only a short period of time so repent and accept Christ as your Savior while time is left!
The timeline from this point will be in the future.

New Covenant Church timeline (all approximate dates)

721BC The northern Kingdom of the ten tribes of the house of Israel went into captivity to Assyria, national punishment for idolatry would be completed in 2520 years or approx. 1799AD when England and America became an empire.
586BC The southern Kingdom of the house of Judah in Judea of Jerusalem went into captivity to Babylon, national punishment completed in approx. 1934AD, Israel became a nation in 1948AD
30AD Christ's Crucifixion and establishing the Church at Pentecost
38AD First above ground Church established in Ireland by Joseph of Arimathea
350AD Fall of Roman and Catholic Church founded began the dark Ages subverting light of truth
1215AD Magna Charta of England creating a Christian rule of law under the Church to this day
1455AD Invention of the printing press where the Holy Bible was the first book ever printed
1492AD Discovery of the Americas described in Isaiah chapter 18 and Jerm 23:3-8 **"I will raise unto David a righteous Branch and a King shall reign**

and prosper" the throne of England

<u>1611AD</u> King James Bible of England completed in mass print to evangelize the world

<u>1780AD</u> approx. Manasseh (United States) house of Israel completed 2520-year punishment

<u>1800AD</u> approx. Ephraim (Briton) house of Israel completed 2520-year punishment

<u>1934AD</u> approx. Judah (modern Israel) house of Judah complete 2520-year punishment

<u>1948AD</u> Modern Israel became a nation after 1878 years falling to Rome in 70AD fulfilling their national punishment of 7X360years=2520 years becoming a new nation in 1948AD.

Note: *These facts can be found if you research ancient British and English history.*

(See Time Chart #4)

Note: Times seven punishment of the Northern Kingdom of the house of Joseph given King David's Throne in I Kings 12:19-20 called the house of Israel (Ephraim and Manasseh) and the Southern Kingdom of the house of Judah is found in Lev 26:18 and Duet 28:22. The Dark Ages fell within the time period of punishment to the Hebrew kingdoms for God's people were under punishment. Their birthright blessing of greatness would not begin till completion of punishment and correspond to the dates above that appears to be extremely accurate. These dates prove the validity of the Scriptures. Because of idol worship, extreme punishment was required of both kingdoms. A normal punishment for a nations sin represented one-year of 360 days multiplied by one year for each day or 360 years of punishment. An extreme punishment would be X7 or 360 years times seven totaling 2520 years which is the ultimate punishment under Mosaic Law for national disobedience of idol worship. It is interesting to note that the number 2520 which is a number of punishments shows up as the length of the Tribulation Period. When we divide two into 2520 days, we get 1260 days or one half of the seven-year Tribulation which is the length of the ministry of the two Witnesses and of Christ's ministry, 3½ years.

Rev Chapter Four

<u>Taking/Rapture of the Church</u> in Rev 4:1-2 and starting of the Seven years of Tribulation Timeline: begins moments after the taking of the Church and this event triggers the seven-years of Tribulation) **A door in Heaven was opened by Jesus and took John and Christ's Church into Heaven for John was the symbol of the Church:** One of the most important chapters of the Bible. **Note**: Rev 3:21 where Jesus sets with God on his Throne but two verses latter in Rev 4:2 Christ's earthly Throne of King David is now set in Heaven where he sets upon it. Luke 1:31-33 is now fulfilled where Christ received his Throne and Kingdom given power to be the Lamb and Lion of Judah to open the

seven Seals, Trumpets and Vials during the seven years of Tribulation. He did not receive his power from God till he received his earthly Kingdom. Verses 1-2 translates God's earthly Kingdom of the throne of David, the 12 tribes as the four Beasts of Rev 5:7, Eze 1:10 and 10:14 as the lost sheep of the house of Israel (Matt 10:6 & 15:24) that represent God's spiritual Temple/Church into Heaven where Christ sets upon his newly set Throne. Verse 3-5 describes the 24 elders and the Church standing before the Throne as the seven lamps (candlesticks) of fire and the seven Spirits of God (the seven stars are the angels of the seven churches) as referenced in Rev 1:20. Verse 6-8 describe the four Beasts of the twelve Tribes of Israel as recorded in Eze 1:10&15 and 10:14 also standing before the Throne of Jesus. Chapter four places the Church, King David's Throne and four brigades of Israel as the twelve tribes of Israel in Heaven prior to opening the Seals, Trumpets and Vials of wrath.

Important Note: The Holy Spirit of the Church was not taken to Heaven when the Church was removed for its job was not finished. Millions of people during the 1st half of the seven-years of Tribulation still has to be saved under the Two Witnesses, Olive Tree, and Candlesticks for the Churches candlesticks has been taken away to Heaven. The Gospel is finished in Rev 10:7, 11:7 and Daniel 12:7 fulfilling II Thess 1:10 moments prior to the Anti-Christ taking full power in Rev 13:5. When Satan as Abaddon received his power to kill the two Witnesses in Rev 11:7, the Holy Spirit is taken and the Gospel is finished. This fact is in Scripture if we are willing to study and place events in proper sequence as Revelation states.

Major Events: in the Future
Verse 1- Apostle John representing God's Kingdom consisting of his Temple/Church, Throne and his people of the twelve tribes of Israel or four brigades as the Lion, Calf, Man, and Eagle are taken or Raptured into Heaven to fulfill Prophecy.
Verse 2- Christ's Throne is set in Heaven where Christ sets upon it promised in Luke 1:31-33. Christ's Kingdom consists of David's Throne, Temple/Church and the 12 Tribes of Israel all taken to Heaven in Rev 4:2. This event gives Christ as the Lamb power from God to set on his own throne and the authority to open the seven Seals, Trumpets and Vials.
The Seven-years of Tribulation begins.

Note: Christ received his power from God when he sets on David's throne in Rev 4:1-2 and Satan receives his power by the people of the world authorized by God in Rev 13:5 to set on his throne in the new rebuilt Temple in Jerusalem claiming himself to be god or the Apotheosis as man god.

Rev Chapter 5 (Timeline: occurs at the very beginning of the Tribulation just prior to the opening of the 1st Seal) **Given by the Lamb of the Tribe of Judah**

(Jesus) sitting on his throne having the written book (the Gospel): describes Christ setting on his newly set Throne having a "book written" sealed with seven seals (seven Spirits of God). He is the only one given authority by God to open the seven Seals, blow the seven Trumpets and pour the seven Vials of wrath. It describes in how the twenty-four elders, the seven lamps or the seven golden candlesticks as Christ's Church and the four beasts, which are the four brigades of the twelve tribes of Israel as the lost sheep, Matt 10:6&15:24, now stand before Christ's newly set Throne in Heaven. These are the three elements of God's Kingdom spoken of in Luke 1:33. This clearly confirms that the taking or Rapture of the Church as the Lamb of God is now in Heaven at the beginning of the seven-years of Tribulation. All three elements of Christ's Kingdom have to be complete where he is sitting on David's Throne before he has the authority (God given power) as the Lamb to open the 1st Seal. The timeline continues unbroken and explains events that takes place at the very beginning of the Tribulation moments before opening of the 1st Seal.

Important Note: Rev 5:5-6 describes the identity of Christ's Church that most Christians do not consider. When a person personally accepts Christ and born into his Spirit/Church, they become an Israelite of Christ's lost sheep and grafted into the tree of life as explained in Rom 11:24-26 where all Christians, either true Hebrew or grafted gentiles, are called an Israelite of Jerusalem. This is proven in Rev chapter 21 where New Jerusalem descends out of Heaven adorned as a bride for her husband [Jesus] as the Church. This chapter lists Jerusalem's four walls and foundations built upon the twelve Apostles and its gates representing the twelve tribes of Israel making God's earthly kingdom consisting of the twelve tribes of Israel and the twelve Apostles as the Church/Temple governed by David's Throne and it is called New Jerusalem. Therefore, the Church is called Israel for Jerusalem is the capital of Israel called the Church for all of its inhabitants are faithful Saints going back to Adam. All Saints that enter New Jerusalem has to be called Israelites of Israel where they inherit the name "el", the God of Israel. All Christian Saints that enter New Jerusalem will be called Israel which is the inherited name of God. The Church is called Israel through Jacob called Israel **"the Lion of the tribe of Juda, the Root of David"** [King David's Throne]. Jesus is the cornerstone setting upon his newly set throne in Rev 4:1-2 when the Church is taken into Heaven at the beginning of the seven-years of the Tribulation.

Major Events: in the Future
This chapter establish Christ's Kingdom being in Heaven after Rev 4:1-2 and list the three elements of his Kingdom:
1st element, verse 5-6, the Lion of the tribe of Juda along with the calf, man and eagle as the four Beast of the 12 tribes of the house of Israel given the Church in Matt 10:6, 15:24, Acts 10:36, Rev 2:14 and Eze 3:1-5 by Jesus himself. The Church as God's earthly Kingdom is now in Heaven as David's throne (throne

of England), the four Beasts as the 12 tribes and the Temple/Church as the Lamb Lion of Judah.

2<u>nd</u> element, verse 6, the Church as **"the Lamb as it had been slain, having seven horns and seven eyes, which are the seven Spirits of God sent forth into all the earth"**. This is the Church with the Lamb of Christ its cornerstone.

3<u>rd</u> element, verse 6, King David's Throne in Heaven, **"And I beheld, and, lo, in the midst of the throne and of the four beasts"**. This is the newly set throne of King David in Rev 4:2 given authority and power through inheritance of Throne, Church and the four beasts that are the twelve tribes of the house of Israel.

Note: With these Scriptural facts, how can anyone say that the Church is not going to be taken prior to the seven years of Tribulation?

Rev Chapter 6 (Timeline: begins within the first 2.2 months of the 1st half of the Tribulation) **Authority given by the Lamb of Jesus to open the seven Seals:** Unbroken timelines where the seven Seals in chapter six and 8:1 are opened by the Lamb of Judah. Jesus called "he" having the authority opened all seven Seals. We also must note that the Lamb is Christ's Church, Beasts as the house of Israel and Throne is clearly set in Heaven prior to the wrath of the Six Seals. These three elements under the Lamb have the authority to administer the Seals, Trumpets and Vials as listed below. Christ came out of the twelve tribes as the four brigades or the four Beasts of Israel through his Temple/Church as the Savior establishing his Gospel where he personally gave his Church to his lost sheep of the house of Israel. This is proven in Matt 10:6, 15:24, Acts 10:36, Rev 2:14 and Eze 3:1-5 (roll) for the mentioned "roll" is the Gospel of the Lion or Lamb of Judah as the "little book", the Gospel. This is confirmed in Rev 10:9-10 where the "roll" and "little book" as the Scriptures that were given to the four brigades of Israel by Christ himself. The Lion is the 1st Beast mentioned in Rev 4:7 and 5:5 as the only creature that can open the seven seals, trumpets and vials for this Lion is the Lamb of Judah as the Messiah. Clearly Christ and his new Throne as the Lamb of God and the Church which is his Kingdom is in Heaven at the very beginning of the seven-years of Tribulation.

Major Events: in the Future. **Note**: each of the Seals and first four Trumpets last approx. 2.2 months each. The 5th Trumpet last 5 mo. and 6th Trumpet 13 mo. These are the only time markers given for a total of 18 months or 1½ years. We know that the 7th Trumpet blew at the very middle of the Trib. at the 3½ year mark, so, if the 5th and 6th Trumpet lasted 18 months then each of the seven Seals and first four Trumpets last for 2.2 months each.

Important Note: God gave authority and power to Jesus as the Lamb called "he" in each Seal to open all seven Seals. Jesus called "he" in these verses delegated his power to the four Beasts, the <u>Lion</u> of Judah [Jesus himself, the <u>Calf</u> of Ephraim and Manasseh, the <u>Man</u> of Ruben and the <u>Eagle</u> of Dan to open the 1st four Seals of the four horsemen. Christ's Church with Jesus as its cornerstone opened the first four Seals. The four Beasts as the Lion, Calf, Man and Eagle is Christ which is the seven Churches.

1<u>st</u> Seal- *Begins the seven years of Tribulation and ends at the 2.2-month Mark of the 1st half.* Rev 6:1 the Lion of Judah or Lamb of Christ said look "the White Horse" was released with a bow and crown to "conquer" thru politics of the UN and NATO alliance of today that takes us into the Tribulation Period. **Note**: The Lion of the Lamb or Christ opened the 1st Seal meaning that the other three beast as the Calf, Man and Eagle opened the next three Seals through the power of the Lamb or Lion. Rev 6:1 mentions the four beasts to occur in succession, *"one of the four beasts saying, Come and see"*, therefore, the next three beasts opened a Seal each, Red, Black and Pale horses as the Seals of the horseman.

2<u>nd</u> Seal- *Begins at 2.2 months and ends at the 4.4-month Mark.* Rev 6:3 the Calf brigade of Ephraim and Manasseh said look "the Red Horse" of Red Russia was released bringing War with the sword. The Eze 38-39 war begins from events occurring at this very moment into the Trib.

3<u>rd</u> Seal- *Begins at 4.4 months and ends at the 6.6-month Mark.* Rev 6:5 the Man of the brigade of Ruben the 1st born said look "the Black Horse" was released bringing economic collapse due to the Ezekiel 38 war.

4<u>th</u> Seal- *Begins at 6.6 months and ends at the 8.8-month Mark.* Rev 6:7 the Eagle of the tribe of Dan said look "the Pale Horse" was released to kill with sword, hunger and death with the beasts of the field (disease) after the Eze 38 war.

5<u>th</u> Seal- *Begins at 8.8 months and ends at the 11-month Mark.* Rev 6:9 Souls under the Alter wearing white robes held for **"a little season"**. The Saints cried with a loud voice saying **"How long, O Lord, holy and true, dost thou not judge and avenge our blood on them that dwell on the earth?"** This verse proved that in the timeline at the opening of the 5th Seal God had not started his wrath or judgment upon the nations which is Babylon for this Seal marks the 8th thru 11th month of the first half of the Trib. Clearly WRATH begins in the 6th Seal in Rev 6:16-17 with a nuclear war, **"And the heavens departed as a scroll"**.

6<u>th</u> Seal- *Begins at 11 months and ends at the 13.2-month Mark of the 1st half.* Rev 6:12 Kings and great men hid themselves in the rocks and caves from the wrath of the Lamb for "wrath is come". This Seal is the fall of Babylon the Great but do not identify it by Scripture, we must study to see that fact for the wrath mentioned in Rev 6:16-17 and 14:10 is speaking to the wrath on Babylon. Rev 14:8 **"Babylon is fallen, is fallen"**, Isaiah 21:9 **"Babylon, is fallen is fallen"** having identical wording. Isaiah 47:1-5 speak of this destruction and calls it the **"O virgin daughter of Babylon"**, meaning it was at one time a Virgin as the Church and an offspring as a daughter as the house of Israel in Matt 10:6, 15:24 and Acts 10:36. Clearly Babylon is America and Great Britain as the western Church for it was once **"tender and delicate"**, **"for thou shalt no more be called, The lady of kingdoms"** New York City and London in Isa 47:1&5. The sealing of the Saints in Rev 7:4-7 immediately after the opening of the 6th Seal set the timeline for the fall of Babylon is the next event in succession in Rev 14:8. Babylon the Great as the old system has to be destroyed prior to Satan the Anti-Christ being released from the bottomless pit in Rev 9:1 where he brings in the NWO (New World Order) at the two-year mark of the 1st half of the Trib. but does not take his throne till the middle.

Important Note: list of events that occur at the opening of the 6th Seal in Rev 6:12. Each one of these events are commentary out of sequence and can be placed within either the opening of a Seal or the blowing of one of the Trumpets by Scripture.

Note the 1st time chart in chapter two.

Souls under the Alter released in Rev 7:14-17 and Rev 14:7 "hour of judgment"

144,000 Saints Sealed in Rev 7:4-8, Rev 14:3

Fall of Babylon in Rev 6:12-17 (wrath), 14:3-8, 14:8 and chapters 17, 18 and 19:1-6.

Marriage Supper of the Lamb in Rev 19:9.

WRATH begins in Rev 6:17 at the 13th month mark of the 1st half, Rev 14:7 "judgement" 2nd Nuclear War where the Heavens scroll in Rev 6:14.

Rev Chapter 7 (Timeline: occurs during the opening of the 6th Seal at the 1 yr. 1 mo. mark of the 1st half of the Trib.) **Opened by the four Angels that holds the four winds of the earth:** Events in chapter 7 are in sequence that occur immediately after the opening of the 6th Seal in chapter 6. Four Angels standing on the four corners of the earth holding the four winds of wrath till the sealing of the 144,000 Saints, 12,000 from each of the twelve tribes of Israel as listed in verses 5-8. Verse 9-17 describes a great multitude of all nations, kindreds and people to include the four Beasts stood worshipping before the Lamb of Jesus setting on King David's Throne all wearing white with palms in their hands. Verses 13-17 describes one of the Elders asking **"What are these which are arrayed in white robes?"** Verse 14 answers the Elders question, **"These are they which came out of great, tribulation, and have washed their robes, and made them white in the blood of the Lamb"**. These are the Saints under the Alter at the 5th Seal in Rev 6:9-12 that could not be released till God's wrath upon man has come. The 6th Seal released these Saints from being under the Alter to stand before Christ's newly set Throne of David to stand before Christ himself for wrath has now come in Rev 6:17 at the opening of the 6th Seal. This indicates that wrath from the 1st thru the 5th Seal is wrath that man brought upon himself, not from God.

<u>Major Events</u>: that occurred in chapter 7 immediately after the opening of the 6th Seal in the Future:

Rev 7:3-8 the Sealing of the 144,000 Servants or Saints of God (by Christ himself) 12,000 from each of the twelve tribes of the house of Israel. Note that this event occurred at the 13th month mark of the 1st half of the Trib., look at the 1st time chart in chapter two.
Rev 7:9 a great multitude that could not be numbered stood worshiping Christ as he sat on his Throne in Heaven. Rev 1:4-17 describes the Saints under the Alter in Rev 6:9 at the 5th Seal now being before Christ's Throne. These Saints or Servants are now released so they can partake in the Marriage Supper of the Lamb that occurs at the opening of the 6th Seal as listed above.

Rev Chapter 8 (<u>Timeline</u>: occurs at the 1 yr. and 3.5 mo. mark at the opening of the 7th Seal thru the end of the 4th Trump of the 1st half of the Trib.) **Started by the 1st thru 4th Angels having the seven Trumpets:** When "he" the Lamb (Jesus) opened the 7th Seal there were silence in Heaven for ½ hour. The ½ hour is allotted for a silent incense of prayer as explained in verse four for all killed in the name of Jesus from the beginning of time. The opening of the 7 Seals is by seven Angels given seven trumpets to blow. These seven Angels are the seven Stars which is stated in Rev 1:20, **"The seven stars are the angels of the seven churches"**, meaning, these seven Angels are the seven Churches with Christ as their cornerstone being already in Heaven at the 11th month mark of the 1st half of the Trib.

<u>Major Events</u>: in the future
<u>7th Seal</u>- *Begins at 13.2 months and ends at the 15.4-month Mark.* Rev 8:1 prepares the seven Angels of the Church to blow the seven Trumpets.
<u>1st Trumpet</u>- *Begins at 15.4 months and ends at the 17.6-month Mark.* Rev 8:7 fire mingled with blood falls from Heaven killing 1/3 of trees.
<u>2nd Trumpet</u>- *Begins at 17.6 months and ends at the 19.8-month Mark.* Rev 8:8 great mountain cast into the sea turning 1/3 of the seas to blood.
<u>3rd Trumpet</u>- *Begins at 19.8 months and ends at the 22-month Mark.* Rev 8:10 a great star fell from Heaven called "Wormwood" making 1/3 of rivers and lakes bitter killing many. This indicates nuclear war for wormwood in Greek means "bitter" nuke radiation.
<u>4th Trumpet</u>- *Begins at 22 months and ends at the 24.2-month Mark.* Rev 8:12, 1/3 part of the sun, mood, and stars were darkened and 1/3 of day and night.

An Angel flying through Heaven saying Woe, Woe, Woe starting the 1st WOE, most likely caused by nuclear war.

Major Time Key

Rev Chapter 9 Major time Key occurs at the blowing of the 5th Trump at the 2 yr. Mark of the 1st half of the Trib. Started by the 5th and 6th Angel blowing the seven Trumpets: These two trumpets are the key in setting the timeline for the book of Revelation. Unbroken timeline where Rev 9:1 begins with the blowing of the 5th Trumpet that lasted 5 months. Rev 9:13 is the blowing of the 6th Trumpet that last one year, one month, one day and one hour or approx. 13 months where we know that the blowing of the 7th Trumpet in Rev 10:7&11:15 marks the middle of the seven-year Tribulation period. This would place Rev 9:1 at the two-year mark of the Tribulation when we add 5 months and 13 months subtracted from 3½ years in the middle of the Trib.

Note: The 5th Seal occurs at the 24 month or two-year Mark of the 1st Half of the Tribulation.

5th Trumpet- Major Events: the 5th Trumpet begins at the 24th month and last for 5 months ending at the 29.2-month Mark (Rev 9:5). Note: this is the 1st time marker given in Rev 9:5&10. -Beginning of the 1st WOE Rev 8:13. -Opening of the bottomless pit releasing Satan called Abaddon in Hebrew or Apollyon in Greek. -Beginning of the 2nd WOE in Rev 9:12.
6th Trumpet- Begins at 29 months and last for 13 months marking the middle of the seven years of Tribulation at 42 months or 3 ½ years.
Note: Rev 9:15 is the second time marker given and allows us to calculate when each of the seven Seals, Trumpets and Vials are opened. -The Angel blowing this Trumpet released the four angels bound in the river Euphrates **"which were prepared for an hour and a day and a month and a year for to slay the third part of men"**.

Rev Chapter 10 (Timeline: sounding of the 7th Trump marking the middle of the Trib.) **A mighty Angle come down from heaven**: giving John commentary as a continuation of the 6th Trumpet that occur just prior to the blowing of the 7th Trumpet that marks the middle of the Tribulation in Rev 10:6 and 11:15. In verses 1-5, Christ himself descended from Heaven with feet of flaming fire placing his right foot upon the sea and left foot upon the earth allowing the sounding thunders of the seven angels that John was told to seal up and not write. Rev 10:6 states **"that there should be time no longer"**, meaning, the Gospel is finished at the blowing of the 7th Trumpet. This event marks the middle of the Tribulation and completion of the Gospel confirmed in Rev 10:7, **"the mystery of God should be finished, as he hath declared to his servants the prophets"**. Rev 11:7 also confirms when the two witnesses finish their

Gospel, **"And when they shall have finished their testimony"** and again in Dan 12:7, **"that it shall be for a time, times and an half; and when he shall have accomplish to scatter the power of the holy people all these things shall be finish"**. This verse says that this event occurs at the end of 3 ½ years or time, times and a half.

This event marks the Middle of the Tribulation at the 3½ year Mark

Major Events: in the future:

Rev 10:2 John was given a **"little book"** to eat where it was bitter in the belly but sweet as honey in his mouth representing the Gospel of Christ. This same account was given to Ezekiel in Eze 3:1-3 where it was sweet in the mouth and bitter in the belly but called a **"roll"**. The *little book* and the *roll* are the Gospel of Jesus where Ezekiel was told to take it to the house of Israel in Eze 3:1. John was to take the little book to the Church before many peoples, nations, tongues and kings in Rev 10:11. Christ calls his Church the lost sheep of the house of Israel in Matt 10:6, 15:24, Acts 10:36 and again in Eze 3:1-5. In these verses, Jesus personally sent the twelve Apostles only to the twelve tribes of the lost sheep of Israel and to no one else.

7th Trumpet- Rev 10:7&11:15 sounded by the seventh Angel of the Church finishing the Gospel. This Trumpet is mentioned in Rev 10:7 and again in 11:15 to emphasize that it marks the middle of the seven-years of Tribulation. This also tells us that all events listed from Rev 10:7 through 11:19 occurs at the blowing of the 7th Trumpet.

Note: These verses clearly state that Christ sets his feet on earth which means this is an actual coming of Christ in the middle of the Tribulation. Again, this identifies the middle of the Trib. as a very important time. The 7th Trumpet is sounded twice, once in Rev 10:7 and again in Rev 11:15 as an indicator as being the middle of the Trib. This also means that all events that occur from Rev 10:7 through 11:19 occurred immediately after the sounding of the 7th Trumpet.

Rev Chapter 11 (Timeline: Commentary of events that occur during the 1st half of the Trib.) An Angel giving John commentary. A continuation of the 7th Trumpet. John's commentary of the unbroken timeline, the preaching and teaching of power given to the two witnesses in Rev 11:3 on earth in place of the raptured Church. Their power was for a period of 1260 days or 42 months during the 1st half of the Trib. We must note that Acts 1:8, **"and ye shall be witnesses unto me"** gave the Church power as Witnesses on the day of Pentecost and each Church a candlestick in Rev 1:20. This brings up a serious question that must be answered! If the Church is present during any part of the seven-year Tribulation given power as witnesses each having a candlestick, then why would Christ send two witnesses with power and a candlestick to preach and teach when it is the Churches responsibility? The answer is simple, the Church is taken into Heaven in Rev 4:1-2 prior to the seven years of Tribulation and establishing the two witnesses in Rev 11:3 for 1260 days at the beginning of the 1st 3½ years of the Trib. God gave that authority to the two Witnesses with power and olive tree and candlestick each. At the end of the 3½ years the Anti-Christ that just received power for 42 months of the last half of the Trib kills the two witnesses in Rev 11:7. They lay in the streets of Jerusalem for 3½ days. If the Church as Christ's Bride was present instead of the two Witnesses, Satan would have killed the Church instead. Do you think God would have allowed his Bride to be killed, NO! The killing of the two Witnesses represents the end of the Gospel and 1st half of the seven-year Tribulation so the Church cannot be present.

Major Events: Occur in the future:
The two Witness are given 42 months to preach and teach to the world in the absences of the Church given two olive trees and two candlesticks.
Rev 11:3 the two Witnesses given power for 42 months or 1260 days during the 1st half of the Trib.
Rev 11:7 the two Witnesses finish their testimony and killed after 3½ years at the end of the 1260 days by the Anti-Christ. They lay in the streets of Jerusalem dead for 3½ days when they ascend into heaven in a cloud just as the Church was taken into the clouds in I Thess 4:17. Being taken into the clouds is a symbol of the taking of the Church and Christ when he ascended into the clouds in Acts 1:9.
Rev 11:7 the Gospel is finished confirmed in Dan 9:7 and Rev 10:7&11:7.
Rev 11:14 the 2nd WOE is past and the 3rd WOE comes quickly.
Rev 11:15 Sounding of the **7ᵗʰ Trump**. The kingdoms of this world now belong to God where he can begin supernatural WRATH upon men for the Gospel is finished. Wrath has come in verse 11:18 where the Servants, Saints and Prophets (Rev 10:7) receive their judgment and rewards for man's kingdoms are now finished. According to chapter 10 and 11, the last three and half years of the Trib. belong to God so he can bring wrath upon those that take the Mark and worship the Beast. The beginning of WRATH upon ungodly man.
This event marks the middle of the seven years of Tribulation or 2520 days divided by two equals 1260 days for each of the two halves. Also note that 2520 years mark the max punishment for national idolatry given against the house of Israel and Judah.
"WRATH is come" for the pouring of the seven Vials are next.
Time to judge the dead and reward the Servants, Prophets, Saints, and evil ones that destroy the earth. **Note**: If God judges the Servants, Prophets, Saints, and the evil ones in the middle of the Trib. at the 7th Trumpet, then, the Gospel has to be finished!

Beginning of the 2nd Half of the Tribulation of 42 months
Reign of the Anti-Christ Rev 13:5

Rev Chapter 12 (Timeline: John's Commentary that span thousands of years from Satan being cast out of Heaven to the establishment of Israel and the birth of Christ to the 144,000 taken from the 12 tribes of Israel fleeing into the wilderness to escape the Anti-Christ during the last half of the Trib.) **A great wonder appeared in Heaven: a woman (ancient house of Israel that become the Church) clothed with the sun, and the moon having a crown of twelve stars:** showing John commentary on the nation of Israel in ancient and modern times where it produced our Lord and Savior as the Christ from the tribe of the Lion of Judah. This chapter describes in how Satan and his angels were cast out of Heaven possibly thousands of years ago and persecuted the woman which is ancient Israel as the twelve tribes. Satan has persecuted the child from birth throughout ancient and the modern Church age. Verse 14 describes the Tribulation period in how the woman (12,000 Sealed from each tribe of Israel) fled into the wilderness to escape the Anti-Christ for God will not allow the dragon to destroy his people. This chapter covers a period of time from when Satan the dragon was cast out of heaven up to the Tribulation covering thousands of years.

Major Events: in the Past, Present and into the Future
The birth of Jesus through a woman called Israel 2000 years ago and **"upon her head a crown of twelve stars"** (twelve Tribes of Israel). This Woman fled into the wilderness for 1260 days or time, times, and half a time during the last half of the Tribulation in the future.
A great Red Dragon (Satan) appeared in Heaven having seven heads and ten horns and seven crowns upon his heads. A war in Heaven between Michael the Arch Angel and the great Dragon, Serpent, Devil called Satan was cast out deceiving the whole world bringing great wrath upon man. The Dragon persecuted the woman which brought forth the man child but God protected the woman.

Rev Chapter 13 (Timeline: John's Commentary of the rise of the Beast System thousands of years ago till the Anti-Christ takes his power from it in the middle of the Tribulation for 42 months during the last half of the Trib. This is amplified commentary that took place at the sounding of the 5th Trumpet in Rev 9:1 when the Anti-Christ called Abaddon or Apollyon as the 1st Beast is released out of the bottomless pit along with his angels. At this time, he received his power by taking over the current world political system created by his own children that was already in place for thousands of years. By Scripture, the 5th Trumpet took place at approx. the two-year mark in the 1st half of the Tribulation. It took 1.5 years for the Anti-Christ to take full power, from the blowing of the

5th Trumpet to the 7th trumpet at the middle of the Tribulation. Rev 13:5 tells us that he had 42 months of power starting in the middle of the Trib through the last half or 3 and 1/2 years. Rev 13:11 creates the 2nd Beast (the false Prophet) that also reigns for 42 months.

Major Events: in the Past, Present and Future commentary of reoccurring events out of sequence.

The rise of the Anti-Christ Beast System that comes out of our current political dealings of the nations of the world (sea) during the past, present and future. We must note that during the war of the White and Red Horse of Rev 6:3-4 which is the Ezekiel 38 war, the Anti-Christ has not been released. When he is released at the 5th Trumpet at the 2-year mark of the 1st half, he becomes the Great Beast spoken of in Dan 7:3-7 that develops during the 1st half of the Trib. He claims full power in the middle of the Trib. and last for 42 months in Rev 13:5.

Another as the 2nd Beast called the False Prophet comes to power in Rev 13:11-18 for **"he had two horns like a lamb, and he spake as a dragon"**. The term *horns like a lamb* indicates that he is an imitation of Christ the Lamb of God for he had all the power of the 1st Beast as the world religious system.

All Saints, patriots, red necks, religious people that refuse to take the Mark of the Beast will be killed in Rev 13:15 when he has the power to kill the two Witnesses in Rev 11:7. No one can be saved during the last half of the Trib. for all are killed except the ones that took the Mark and the 144000 sealed protected by Jesus that flee into the wilderness. By Scripture, there is no one else left to be saved and if so, the Gospel has been finished and the Holy Spirit has been taken away in II Thess 1:7 when the two Witnesses are killed in Rev 11:7.

Rev Chapter 14 (Timeline: John's Commentary of events that occur during the 1st half of the Trib.) **A Lamb (Jesus) standing on Mt. Sion** giving John commentary in Rev 14:1-5. Verses 1-5 occurs at the beginning of the 2nd half of the Tribulation at the 3 ½ year mark after the blowing of the 7th Trumpet in Rev 10:7 and 11:15. John in chapter 14 identifies the Sealed 144,000 Hebrews from the twelve tribes of Israel, that took place at the opening of the 6th Seal at the two-year mark in Rev 6:12 thru 7:1-17 where he is reiterating this event. The Lamb of Jesus stood on Mt. Sion which is the earth with the prior sealed 144000 Saints. The next three events occurred in a chain of succession simultaneously by three angels conducting three separate events in Rev 14:6-11.

Major Events: occurs in the Future in different order
The Sealed 144,000 Rev 14:1, Saints standing on Mt. Sion with the Lamb of Jesus after the opening of the 7th Seal that starts the 2nd half of the Trib.
1st Angel Rev 14:6, having the ever-lasting Gospel preaching to the world to praise God **"for the hour of his judgement is come"**, the judgment of

Tribulation upon ungodly men.

Important Note: Why does an Angel preach the Gospel? Simple, the Church or two Witnesses are not present for they were taken or killed. The Church was taken prior to the beginning of the Trib. in Rev 4:1-2 and the two Witnesses were killed in Rev 11:7 when the Gospel is "finished" at the middle of the Trib. With the absence of the Holy Spirit, only an Angel would have the power to preach the Gospel during the last half of the Tribulation for the Holy Spirit was removed from earth. Note that his Angel had no candlestick such as the Church and the two Witnesses for in reality, the preaching of this Angel is a WARNING to evil men for God knows that there is no one left on earth that can be saved for the Gospel is finished. This is a tormenting reminder to the ungodly of Christ's Gospel even to the end. Satan the Dragon cannot kill an Angel as he did the two Witnesses! The Gospel was finished when the two Witnesses were killed in Rev 11:7 fulfilling II Thess 2:3-4 for the Holy Spirit and the spirit of Satan cannot co-exist on earth. An Angel that could not be killed was needed to preach the Gospel during the last half of the Tribulation as a warning to torment the ungodly. God always gives man a chance to the very end. Accord to these two verses, the "son of perdition", the Anti-Christ, cannot come till the Holy Spirit is taken away.

2st Angel, Rev 14:8, Babylon is fallen, the destruction of Babylon as the Great American western Christian Culture is spoken of in the past for this event occurs at the opening of the 6th Seal at the 13th month mark of the 1st half.

The **3nd Angel**, Rev 14:9, warns the world to not take the Mark of the Beast or they **"shall drink of the wine of the wrath of God"** for this occurs at the beginning of the 2nd half of the Tribulation.

Note: The events in Revelation chapter 14 are directed by Jesus himself sitting on a white cloud with a crown that is mind blowing. Rev 14:14-20 mentions two sharp sickles that take place killing millions of people. It is this Author's belief that these two sickles take place in the middle of the Tribulation where Christ takes his Saints through a mercy death a moment prior to the 2nd sickle. This takes place in Rev 11:7 and 13:15-16 where the Anti-Christ kills all people that refuse his Mark which is the 2nd sickle to include the two Witnesses.

Verse 12-16 explains the *1st Sickle of mercy*, verse 12, **"Here is the patience of the saints: here are they that keep the commandments of God, and the faith of Jesus"**, Verse 13, **"Blessed are the dead which die in the Lord from henceforth"**, these two verses is speaking of a sickle that kills thru a sweet death all righteous people so they will escape **"the wrath of God"** that occurs in the last half of the Tribulation verse 19. This 1st sickle is trusted in by Christ himself taking his righteous people. God always takes his righteous prior to bringing wrath on man just as prior to the flood in Jasher V:5&21, I Thessalonians 4:14-18 and 1 Cor 15:51-52. This fact is also found in Rev 13:15 that states, **"and cause that as many as would not worship the image** of the beast should be killed". This means that all people are killed except the ones that worship the Beast and the Sealed 144000 Saints, there are no one else left to be saved even if the Gospel was not finished at this time.

Rev 14:17-20 explains the **_2nd Sickle of WRATH_** where Christ himself takes all wicked people that refuse to worship or take the Mark of the Beast which is **"the great winepress of the wrath of God"**. There will be millions of ungodly people that will refuse to worship the Beast due to political, patriot or religious reasons. All Christians or anyone that refuse the Mark are killed leaving no one going forward into the last half of the Tribulation except the people that take the Mark and the protected sealed 144000 Saints. No one is saved during the last half.

WRATH upon ungodly man Begins

Rev Chapter 15 (Timeline: Events that occur at the beginning of the last half of the Tribulation just prior to the pouring of the 7 Vials of Great Wrath) **The seven Angels having the seven last plagues:** A preparation and commentary given to John in Rev 15:1 where he sees in Heaven a great and marvelous sign, **"seven angels having the seven last plagues: for in them is filled up the wrath of God"**. This verse clearly indicates that if the last seven plagues of the Vials are wrath, then, the first seven Seals and Trumpets also has to be "the wrath of God". Therefore, the full seven-year period of Tribulation is considered to be WRATH upon the nations and godless people. Verses 2 thru 5 describes the Saints that overcome the image of the Beast and his Mark standing in Heaven before a sea of glass singing the song of Moses and the Lamb magnifying the name of God. All that is going to be saved is now in Heaven to be judged. Verse 4 says, **"for thy judgments are made manifest"** for manifest in Greek means ref #5319, *to render apparent, shew publicly to appear* meaning that Gods judgment of his Saints has come and confirmed in Rev 14:7&20:4. If the Saints are judged at this point, the Gospel has to be finished for all is complete.

Major Events: occur in the future
Rev 15:1, the wrath of God comes on earth with the pouring of the seven Vials.
Rev 15:5, the Temple of the Tabernacle of the testimony in Heaven was opened indicating that the Gospel is finished, Rev 10:7, 11:7, 14:7 and Dan 5:26&12:7 and judgement of the Saints can begin.
Rev 15:7, one of the four Beasts, most likely the Lamb of the Church, gave the seven angels seven golden Vials full of the wrath of God to pour upon ungodly man.

Rev Chapter 16 (Timeline: The pouring of the 7 Vials during the last 42 months of the Tribulation) **A great voice (the Lamb) out of the temple saying**

to the seven angels: Chapter fifteen and sixteen continues the commentary of what the three angels in chapter 14 brings: 1. Preaching the Gospel to the world, 2. Babylon is fallen and 3. to not take the Mark of the Beast. Rev 6:17, 14:7 and 15:1 takes place at the same moment of time that begins the wrath of God at the opening of the 6th Seal. All three chapters occur in an instant at the opening of the 6th Seal in Rev 6:12 thru 7:1-8. These three chapters maintain the continual timeline that introduce the **"wrath of God"** upon ungodly man through the pouring of the seven vials of WRATH for all have been killed as listed above in chapter fourteen except the Sealed 144,000 and those that take the MARK. Chapter sixteen is the pouring of the seven vials of wrath. These two chapters maintain the unbroken timeline of the last half of the 42 months of the Tribulation Period where the pouring of the seven Vials occur.

Major Events: occur in the future
1st Vial Rev 16:2, poured upon earth by an Angel bringing a noisome and grievous sore upon the men that took the Mark of the Beast.
2nd Vial Rev 16:3, upon the sea turning it into blood of a dead man killing all in the sea.
3rd Vial Rev 16: 4, upon the rivers and fountains of waters and became blood.
4th Vial Rev 16:8, upon the sun to scorch men with fire and they repented not.
5th Vial Rev 16:10, upon the set of the Beast and his kingdom was full of darkness gnawing their tongues for pain and they repented not.
6th Vial Rev 16:12, upon the great river Euphrates drying it up for the way of the kings of the east (China) to cross over for the battle of Armageddon. We must note that this gathering to do battle is not with each other but to battle God at Armageddon. The three spirit frogs that come out of the Dragon, Beast and False Prophet is a calling as an invitation to all nations to come and do battle with God, **"which go forth unto the kings of the earth and of the whole world, to gather them to the battle of that great day of God Almighty"**. Kings of nation and the whole world come together in unity to fight God.
7th Vial Rev 16:17, upon the air bringing a great voice from the Temple of Heaven and the Throne which is Jesus saying **"It is done"**. The greatest earthquake in history occurred dividing Jerusalem "the Great City" into three parts and all cities of the nations fell. This earthquake caused every island to flee away and the mountains were not found, a great hail fell upon men at the weight of a talent causing man to blasphemed God for the plague was exceedingly great.   The **Seven-Year Tribulation is DONE!!!**

NOTE: The seven years of Tribulation is completed and John gives his commentaries of events in chapters 17-22 that encompass the Past, Present and Future.

John's Commentaries begin Chapter 17-22

Rev Chapter 17 The seven-years of Tribulation is over but John's Commentary continues by reverting back to prior events. (Timeline: John's Commentary that describes the Beast System as Babylon being destroyed at the 6th Seal of the 1 yr. 1 mo. mark of the first half of the Trib.) **One of the seven Angels having the seven Vials** told John this commentary in a more detailed account of Rev 14:8. This Angel explains the destruction of Mystery Babylon the Great. Again, this chapter takes place at the opening of the 6th Seal in Rev 6:12 at the one year and one month mark of the 1st half of the Tribulation. Rev 6:12-17 describes the destruction and wrath upon Babylon but the mystery within these six verses does not mention its name directly. This subject is so important it takes four chapters to explain, Rev 14:8, chapter 17, 18 and 19:1-6 for clarification. These chapters explain the old economic, political and religious systems over six thousand years that came out of the old Babylon, Assyrian, Greek and Roman systems that has plagued and killed world societies to this day for it is called Mystery Babylon in Rev 17:1-5. **"MYSTERY BABYLON THE GREAT THE MOTHER OF HARLOTS AND ABOMINATIONS OF THE EARTH"** is nothing more than Satan's world system from the beginning of the earths foundation and God's creation of man polluted by Satan when he rebelled against God. This system is a combination of all of man's religious secret societies where the Roman Catholic Church dominates during the last days. Satan the Devil is using this system of old to establish his end time New World Order to be man god of the earth for he knows his time is short.

Rev 17:6-18 describes the Anti-Christ Beast system as a Woman having seven heads and ten horns. This is Satan taking over the established Anti-Christ system when he came out of the bottomless pit in Rev 9:1 at the blowing of the 5th Trumpet and the son of perdition in II Thess 2:3 and Rev 17:8&11. Satan is now released from the pit so he can personally take control of his already established New World Order after the destruction of Mystery Babylon. The old political and religious systems of Babylon have to be destroyed before his new system can come into power making its destruction the most important and discussed event in the book of Revelation.

Rev Chapter 18 (Timeline: a continuation Commentary of the fall of Babylon in the 1st half of the Trib.) **A very powerful Angel coming down from Heaven** with a mighty cry saying, **"Babylon the great is fallen, is fallen"** as a continuation of chapter 17.

Rev Chapter 19 (Timeline: Also, a continuation Commentary of the fall of Babylon in the 1st half of the Trib.) **A great voice of much people in Heaven saying Alleluia giving** commentary in Rev 19:1-10 takes place immediately after chapter 14:8 and chapters 17 and 18 for it states **"And after these things I heard a great voice of much people in heaven"**. These chapters explain the destruction of Babylon and this timeframe is confirmed in Rev 19:1-4 referring to the destruction of "the great whore" meaning that it occurred immediately before the Marriage Supper at the opening of the 6th Seal in Rev 6:12 also at the one year one month mark of the Tribulation. Rev 19:1-4 and 19:7-10 gives a timeline when the Marriage Supper of the Lamb (the Church to marry her Bride Groom Jesus) took place. According to these verses, immediately after the destruction of "the Great Whore" of Babylon at the opening of the 6th Seal the Marriage Supper of the Lamb occurred. That means, the Church has to be in Heaven at the opening of the 6th Seal estimated to be at the one year and one month mark of the 1st half of the Trib.

Rev 19:11-21 is commentary on Jesus coming back to earth in power and glory with his angels at the very end of the seven-years of the Great Tribulation of the battle of Armageddon.

Rev 19:20-21 the Beast and False Prophet along with the remnant that took the Mark of the Beast were cast into the Lake of Fire.

Rev Chapter 20 (Timeline: Commentary in the future after the seven years of Tribulation is complete where Satan is cast into the Pit for a thousand years and the Great White Throne of Judgment after the millennial reign where all godless sinners are judged) Rev 20:1-3 **An Angel from Heaven having the key of the bottomless pit**. is commentary on future events at the very end of the Tribulation Period when an Angel chains the Dragon as the Serpent which is Satan the Devil and cast him into the bottomless pit for a thousand years.

Rev 20:4-6 Commentary of a special group of Christians that were beheaded for not taking the Mark of the Beast. The only place in the timeline that this Author can place them is in Rev 13:15 when the Anti-Christ kills all Saints that do not take his Mark or worship his image. This could be when Christ scoops in his Sickle of mercy in Rev 14:14-16 and takes this group of people prior to his wrath upon ungodly man. They were beheaded by the Anti-Christ thru Christ's 1st Sickle of mercy not feeling the sting of death or suffering the 2nd Sickle of Death. They served with Christ for a thousand years during the millennial of Christ's rule on earth.

Rev 20:7-10 is commentary on when Satan the Devil is loosed for a very short time to deceive the nation at the end of the thousand-year reign of Christ. This Author believes that God used this incident to judge his people on earth at the end of the millennial to see who was loyal to him as true Christians and the unloyalty or unfaithful is cast into the Lake of Fire along with Satan, their tempter, to burn for ever and ever.

Rev 20:11-15 these verses are commentary that take place at the end of Christ's millennial reign when the books of life is opened to judge all unrighteous people that have ever lived called the Great White Throne of judgment. All that were judged at this final event were cast into the lake of fire and it is called the 2nd Death for rejecting Christ and his Gospel.

Rev Chapter 21 (Timeline: John's Commentary that describes New Jerusalem descending from Heaven after the old Earth and Heaven has passed away) **Apostle John's commentary** of the new Heaven and new Earth descending down out of Heaven consisting of New Jerusalem containing the Temple of

Jesus Christ as the Husband receiving his Bride. Chapter 21 describes in detail the structure of New Jerusalem from its twelve gates representing the twelve tribes of Israel to its four foundations as the twelve Apostles making New Jerusalem the Church.

Rev Chapter 22 (Timeline: A continuation Commentary of chapter 21 after the old Earth and Heaven has passed away) **An Angel showed John** a quick beautiful description of New Jerusalem in Heaven where there is no night or day but brightened by Jesus himself where Christians worship him continually. The timeline of these two chapters is indicated to be after the thousand-year reign of Jesus on earth which could be a thousand years or a million years into the future. Each chapter will be explained in more detail as we proceed through this book.

Chapter 5

The Biblical number of Punishment 7 or X7 and can be in days or years

Throughout the Scriptures, God attaches a number to punishment wither it be individual or national discipline of his people. Punishment is based on 7 as 7 years or maximum of X7 and can be either 2520 days or for maximin of years which is based on the Hebrew calendar where one-year equals to 360 days. We know that both the house of Judah and Israel fell to the worship of the old BAAL religion calling for the maximin punishment for idolatry. Maximin punishment would be 7X360 years that equates to 2520 years total. The punishment for each of the two houses, house of Israel and house of Judah, lasted for 2520 years after each of their captivities. The book of Revelation and Tribulation period is based on the minimum of seven years punishment or wrath and equates to 2520 days broken into two halves of 1260 days and 42 months each. This equates to Daniel's prophecy of the Tribulation Period that represents his 70th week prophecy. Rev 11:2 tells us that the two witnesses in the 1st half was allotted 1260 days to preach and teach the Gospel. Rev 13:5 allotted the Anti-Christ in the 2nd half to continue for 42 month which is also 1260 days. If we add 1260 days for the 1st half of the Trib. and 1260 days for the last half, we get 2520 total days of punishment, Lev 26:18&24. The Tribulation of wrath last seven years or 2520 total days which is God's punishment upon ungodly man and fulfills Daniel's 70th week or seven years which is 2520 days in Dan 9:24-27.

Important Note: God's number of completion 2520 keeps popping up and finally allowed me to discover the meaning of Dan 9:26 for it states, **"And after threescore and two weeks shall Messiah be cut off"**. Most Christian bible students understand verse 25 where it says that only 69 weeks of Daniel's 70 weeks has been fulfilled but how does 62 weeks play into the Prophecy. Really, it is pretty simple if we think about it. If we subtract 62 from the completed 69-weeks, we get 7 weeks that we know pertains only to the Temple Mount in Jerusalem for Dan 9:24-27 is speaking only to the Jews and the Temple in Jerusalem. Verse 26 speaks of 7 weeks of Daniel's Prophecy that deals in years not days, so, if we multiply 7 weeks times 360 Hebrew calendar days, we get 2520 years pertaining to this Prophecy. Very, very interesting! How does this play into the 69 completed weeks of Daniels Prophecy? We know that the 1st and 2nd Temples was destroyed by first Babylon in 586BC and the second by Rome in 70 AD. The 62 weeks in verse 26 has to account for the building of the 3rd Temple at the very beginning of the Tribulation for Dan 9:27, 8:11 and 12:11 is speaking directly to restarting of the blood sacrifice within the new Temple. This proves that Dan 9:26 pertains to the Temple Mount. The answer to the question, there will be 7-weeks or approx. 2520 years from the building of the 2nd Temple to the building of the 3rd Temple for the answer is in the numbers. The 2nd Temple was completed in 515BC so if we add 2024AD of our current date, we get 2539 years. Daniel's prophecy pertains to 2520 so the rebuilding of the 3rd Temple is 18 years overdue. This could be due to lost calendar days between the Hebrew and Roman calendars or the fact that the Lord is tarrying. The seven year or one week of Daniel's prophecy is overdue and imminent.

The last part of this verse, **"shall Messiah be cut off"** should also be explained. The 1st Temple was the only Temple that maintained the Holy of Holies where God reside with his Hebrew people. The purpose of the 1st Temple was simply to pave the way for the coming of the Messiah and the Jewish High Priest had fallen so far from God's Commandments, God abandoned the Temple. When Jerusalem fell to Babylon in 586BC, the Prophet Jeremiah took all the artifacts within the Holy of Holies and buried them somewhere outside of the walls of Jerusalem, Jerm 3:16 and II Maccabees 2:3-8 where it is not to be found till the last days. When the Holy Spirit left the Holy of Holies in the 1st Temple, Jesus was cut off for God knew that the High Priest of Judaism would reject the coming Messiah and have him killed. Jesus was cutoff when the 1st Temple was destroyed and the Ark of the Covenant removed. The 2nd Temple had no Holy of Holies or Ark where God resided with his people, the Messiah was cutoff opening the path for Jesus our Messiah. The Ark of the Covenant to fulfill Jewish Prophecy has to be found to rebuild the 3rd Temple, but we must be aware that the 3rd Temple is not to be of God but of the Anti-Christ where he claims himself to be god, therefore, the Anti-Christ has to be a Jew for the Jewish faith to accept him.

We must note that some Christians believe that the Tribulation last for only 42 months which is not true by Scripture and proven in the follow verses. The different names of time. Paragraph *6, *7 and *8 below, overlap into the 1st half of the seven years of Tribulation and destroys the idea that the trib. last only 42 months. It is clear by these Scriptures; the seven years of Tribulation is broken up into two halves of 1260 days or 42 months each totaling 2520 days or seven years. Daniel's prophecy considers the Tribulation to be one week where one day equals to one year tallying to seven years called the 70th week prophecy.

Names of Dividing of Time into three- and one-Half years

<u>**"time and times and dividing of time"**</u> Dan 7:25, **"time, times, and an half"** Dan 12:7 equals 1260 days or 3½ years in reference to "scatter the power of the holy people" which is the fleeing woman into the wilderness during the last

half of the Tribulation.

"a thousand two hundred and threescore days" in Rev 12:6&14 referencing the woman fleeing into the wilderness where she is nourished for **"a time, and times, and half a time"** in Dan 7:25 and Rev 12:14 equals 3½ years in the last half of the Trib.

"forty and two months" in Rev 13:5 in reference to the power given to the Anti-Christ during the last half of the Trib. for 42 months as 1260 days or 3½ years.

"forty and two months" in Rev 11:2 in reference to the outer court of the new Temple and holy city of Jerusalem being trod under foot by the Gentiles for 42 months during the 1ˢᵗ half of the Tribulation. This verse has to be in the 1ˢᵗ half for it states in verse 1, **"and them that worship therein"** for there is no worship in the last half for the Anti-Christ declares himself to be god setting in the temple.

"Prophesy a thousand two hundred and threescore days" in Rev 11:3 referencing the two witnesses given power for 1260 days or 3½ years during the 1ˢᵗ half of the Tribulation.

The next three paragraphs prove that the Tribulation last for more that 42 months or 3 ½ years.

*__"a thousand two hundred and ninety days"__ in Dan 12:11 refers to the daily sacrifice being taken away from the newly rebuilt Temple in Jerusalem that occur at the 1230 day or 3 years 5-month mark of the 1ˢᵗ half of the Tribulation.

*__"thousand three hundred and five and thirty days"__ or 1335 days in Dan 12:12 referencing the blessing given to the 144,000 that flee into the wilderness to escape the Anti-Christ which are the 12000 from each of the 12 tribes of Israel called the "woman". This woman is also found in Rev 12:6 where they flee for 1260 days. Note that there are 75 days difference between these two Scriptures, WHY? Seventy-five days gives the "woman" a head start to secure themselves in the wilderness for the Anti-Christ is not given the power to kill them till he received his authority for 42 months or 1260 days in Rev 13:5 which occurs in the middle of the Trib. God protects them.

*__"two thousand and three hundred days"__ or 2300 days in Dan 8:14 in reference to the new Temple in Jerusalem *"then shall the sanctuary be cleansed"*. This event occurs during the last half of the Tribulation. It is implemented at the 7.3-month mark of the 1ˢᵗ half during the 3ʳᵈ Seal of the black horse for it lasts for 2300 days of the 2520-day period of seven years. By this Scripture, the Tribulation has to last for more than 42 months.

Note: The three verses of Daniel referring to 1290 days, 1335 days and 2300 days apply to Daniel's 70th week Prophecy implies a full seven years or 2520 days, all more than 42 mo.

Now let's apply 2520-year punishment to the house of Judah as the southern kingdom and the house of Israel the northern kingdom as God's lost sheep to take place in the last days confirmed blessing given in Gen 49:1. They were to be his Church where it is given to the house of Israel by Christ himself in Matt 10:6, 15:24, Acts 10:36 (the Gospel) and Eze 3:1-5 (the Gospel).

The house of Israel as the northern kingdom went into captivity in approx. 740 to 721BC. Manasseh in 740BC and Ephraim in 721BC to Assyria. If we apply 7X360years we get 2520 years punishment against the house of Israel for idolatry. They are known to be called the unicorn of Ephraim the leader of Israel. Ephraim the Unicorn and Manasseh the Bull (Duet 33:17) as firstborn birthright brothers were given the birthright blessing to be called Israel in Gen 48:16 known as the lost sheep of the house of Israel in Matt 10:6, 15:24, Act 10:36 and Ezk 3:1-5 as Christ's Church. If we subtract 721BC from 2520 years, we get approx. 1799AD when punish upon the house of Israel of Ephraim was complete. This is approx. when England as the unicorn of Ephraim became the British Empire and America the Bull his brother Manasseh became a nation of America in 1776AD. We must note that Manasseh as America went into captivity approx. 20-years prior in 740BC which would place Manasseh's punishment being over in 1780 with the blessings of becoming a nation in 1776AD. We are speaking of historical facts in these numbers and verses.

The house of Judah as the Jews of Jerusalem of the southern kingdom went into captivity to Babylon in approx. 586BC. If we subtract 586BC from 2520 years when their punishment was complete, we get 1934AD. It took WW II with the Jewish death camps to establish Israel as a nation in 1948AD. These dates of the house of Israel as Ephraim the Unicorn and America as the Bull and Judah as modern Israel are right on the money in fulfilling Bible Prophecy.

To better understand, we need to review the history of God's people called Jacob as Israel. We know that God's people are called Israel, as Hebrew people of his divided earthly Kingdom into two houses, the house of Judah and the house of Israel in I Kings chapters 11 and 12. The northern kingdom of the ten tribes of Ephraim and Manasseh as the lost sheep of Israel dispersed into the world after the Assyrian captivity called the lost sheep of the house of Israel. Gen 48:16 clearly state that the name Israel was given to Ephraim and Manasseh only as a firstborn birthright not the Jews, so, when they departed into the wilderness the name Israel went with them. Jerusalem lay waste with no king for almost two thousand years before coming a nation again. In I Kings 12:19-24 the breached Throne of David (Gen 38:27-30, Amos 9:11 became the Throne of England to fill the breach) was taken from the Jews and given to the ten northern tribes called the house of Israel where they departed into the wilderness to never return to the land of Israel. This is why there is no throne in Israel today for it is in England as God's promise that there would always be a man sitting upon the throne of Israel through all generations, I Kings 9:5, II Chron 7:18, Ps 89:4 and Jerm 33:14-17. These Scriptures state a true fact so study them. The southern two tribes of Benjamin and Judah are called the house of Judah or the Jews that maintained King David's throne till the fall to Babylon in 586BC where David's throne was taken away and the destruction of the Temple in Jerusalem to the Romans in 70AD. It appears that David's throne has not existed for 2609 years but God promised that a man would always set on his throne through all generations promised in scripture above. David's throne has to exist in this world today by the promise of God. David's throne was breached in Gen 38:29-30 **"Pharez and Zarah"**, Judges 21:15, Isa 30:26, Jerm 14:17, PS 60:2 and Amos 9:11. I Kings 12:19-24 tells us how David's throne was taken from the Pharez line of Kings and given to Jeroboam of Ephraim an Ephrathite which is a Zarah line of Kings in I Kings 11:26 confirmed in Matt 21:43-44. The throne of David was taken from Jerusalem in these verses and given to the northern kingdom of the lost sheep of the house of Israel that departed into the wilderness eventually becoming the throne of England. This is confirmed as Christ's Church in Matt 10:6 and 15:24 by Christ himself.

In John's vision of the book of Revelation, both the house of Judah and Israel plays a large role. We know that the house of Judah as the Jews was responsible in maintaining Gods commandments of the Law of Moses through the Tabernacle and Temple in ancient times. In modern times this responsibility was taken from the Jews as a breach of King David's throne for God knew that the Jew would reject the Messiah at his coming. In Matt 21:42-44 God takes his earthly kingdom as the **"husbandmen"** of the Temple Priest of King David's throne controlled by the Jews and gave it to **"the stone which the builders rejected"** and **"and given to a nation bringing forth the fruits thereof"**. The "husbandmen" of Christ's parable in Matt 21:33-46 was taken from the Chief Priests within the Temple in Jerusalem and given to his lost sheep of Israel as Christ's Church called America and Great Britain scattered abroad as stated in James 1:1 and I Peter 1:1. The twelve Apostles were sent by Jesus himself only to the lost sheep scattered abroad just as James and Peter states. Gen 49:24 gives blessings to Joseph which is his two sons Ephraim and Manasseh as the Unicorn and Bull in Duet 33:17, symbols of the Christian nations of England and America. This is Christ's end time Church. The nation spoken of in this verse is the lost sheep of the house of Israel proven in Matt 10:6, 15:25, Act 10:36 and Eze 3:1-5, **"But go rather to the lost sheep of the house of Israel"** as a commandment to his twelve Apostles. We also know that these lost sheep became the Bull and Unicorn of Ephraim and Manasseh as **"shepherd, the stone of Israel"** as guardian to Christ's Church in Gen 49:24 and Duet 33:17, as the stone of Israel will **"with them he shall push the people together to the ends of the earth"** as Christ's Church, the British Empire controlled by the Throne of King David. Ladies and Gentlemen, these are historical facts if we properly research true English history.

Chapter 6

(Chapters One thru Twenty-Two commentary by the Author)

Revelation Chapter One The symbology of Apostle John representing the Church is extremely important to understand. If we fail to see this fact, we lose the true meaning of the book of Revelation. John was chosen as an ambassador to reveal future prophecies to the Church as a Servant, he represents the Church. Christians think that John's commentary is random but they maintain a specific and constant timeline that we must closely study if we are to understand the book of Revelation. The Apostle John is symbolic to the Church so when John was translated into Heaven in Rev 4:1, he represents the Church. Many Christian refuse to see this fact but it is logically and physically true by Scripture. This fact helps the puzzle fall into place. It will be proven by Scripture as we go through chapter four. Chapter one lays out the basic information of why this book was written and very important to understand in how the Church plays its part in John's revelations. To better understand the elements, time periods and purpose of the seven Churches, closely study the following.

Revelation chapter one gives the elements of each of the seven Churches which is very important: Rev 1:1 tells us that God has one Angel by his side called **"his angel"**. This is one single Angel assigned to God meaning that it can only be a part of the God Head which is the Father, Son and the Holy Spirit/Ghost. The Greek meaning of spirit and angel are basically the same, ref. #4151 (spirit), *an Angel, Christ Spirit, Holy Spirit breeze and blow* and #32 (angel), *a messenger, pastor, drive and angel.* God's single Angel has to be the Holy Ghost/Spirit sent to the Church in Acts chapters one and two different from all the other Angels as being singular. This would make "his Angel" distinctive from the seven Stars, seven candlesticks or the seven Spirits of the Church as being only one for the Churches are plural. Rev 1:4 speak of Christ's Throne being in Heaven where the seven Spirits or Angels stand before his Throne, meaning, Christ's throne is in Heaven prior to verse 8 when Jesus comes in power and glory at the end of the Tribulation. Rev 1:13 list **Seven individual golden candlesticks** (the seven Churches), Rev 1:16, **Seven individual stars** (Angel of each Church) and a **Two-edged Sword** (the Gospel of Christ). Rev 1:20 explains what the stars and candlesticks represent: This verse clearly state that the Stars are the angels of the seven Churches and the candlesticks are the seven Churches in different time periods with the Gospel at their core which is the two-edged Sword. Rev 1:4 mentions a **"throne"**

Important Note: With a deep evaluation of chapter one, we find that God's

Angel called **"his Angel"** is singular and separate from all the other angels of the Church. This would explain why "his Angel" the Holy Spirit is left behind when the Church is taken or raptured into Heaven in Rev 4:1-2. God's Spirit is needed by the two witnesses that is given each a candlestick and an Olive Tree so that millions of people will be saved during the 1st half of the Tribulation. Both a candlestick in Rev 1:20 and olive tree in Rev 2:7 are symbols of the Church as the tree of life, the Gospel of Jesus Christ.

The first three chapters of the book of Revelation is the beginning of a new area; a time dispensation called the age of the Church or the Church Age of time lasting approx. two thousand years. Chapter four through twenty-two is a special dispensation of time giving seven years of wrath upon the nations and ungodly man. This time period is broken into two parts which are Daniel's 70th week prophecy as the Tribulation Period. At the end of these two dispensations of time complete approx. six thousand years of man's self-rule on this earth where God's laws were given first to Adam, to Moses, to Christ and lastly to the Church to complete spiritual business of sin between God and his salvation to man through the nation of Israel as explained in Daniel 9:24-27. God is not in control of this earth for he gave that responsibility directly to his Church in Matt 28:18-20 where he gave all his power to the Church. Some Christians say, *"don't worry for God is in control"* is a false statement for clearly the Church was given control by Christ himself as the Great Commission. This authority was clearly given to the lost sheep of the house of Israel in Matt 10:6, 15:24, Acts 10:36 and Ezekiel 3:1-5 as the Church of the western Christian Culture evangelizing the world through the God given King James English Bible. The family of Ephraim and Manasseh which are Joseph's two sons are the Unicorn and Bull of England and the United State as brothers. They were given this authority in Duet 33:17, **"His glory is like the firstling of his bullock [bull of Wall Street]; and his horns are like the horns of unicorns [England]: with them he shall push the people together to the ends of the earth: and they are the ten thousands of Ephraim and they are the thousands of Manasseh"**. This verse is confirmed in Gen 49:1&22-24 where the two brothers were to be the end time Church, **"from thence is the shepherd, the stone of Israel"**. This is confirmed in Matt 10:6 and 15:24 as the lost sheep of the house of Israel where Jesus personally gave them the Gospel to preach and teach the world as his Church.

Rev 1:1-3 **"The Revelation of Jesus Christ which God gave unto him" "and he sent and signified it by his angel unto his servant John"**. God's Angel called "his angel" has to be the Holy Spirit as being one, singular, separate from all other Angels. Verse 3, **"Blessed is he that readeth and they that hear the words of this prophecy"** and **"things which must shortly come to pass"**. Apostle John wrote this book given by Christ himself to be given to the seven Churches for the last days. It is very important to understand by

Scripture exactly where John is physically located during each chapter for, he represents the taking of the Church. God introduces the Church through the Angels to his Prophet John as a Blessing to all Christians that read and study this book of his prophecies.

Rev 1:4-6 God commanded John to write the future prophecies that pertains to the Seven Churches in the context of the *past, present* and *future*. He states that the prophecy of this book was written to the seven Churches of Asia for the salvation of man to be Priests and Kings of the Earth washing our sins in his own blood. This period of time being Priests and Kings as the seven Churches represent the past two thousand years of the Church age fulfilling Matt 28:18-20. The Great Commission was given to the lost sheep of the house of Israel in Matt 10:6, 15:24 and Acts 10:36 with the authority of his transplanted Throne from Jewish Pharaz in Jerusalem to the Zarah bloodline of Ephraim as the house of Joseph in I Kings 11:26,28 and 12:19-24. The book of Esdras in II Esdras 13:40-46, I Maccabees 12:7-9&20-23 explain how the house of Israel migrated into the wilderness to a far land of Europe where they became Kings through King David's Throne of England. This is historical fact if you are willing to study and research as I have.

Rev 1:7-9 reveals Christ coming back to earth, in a downward motion, where **"he cometh with clouds"** bringing fire and smoke at the end of the seven-year Tribulation where the whole earth sees him.

Rev 1:9-10 John was imprisoned by the Romans on the Island of Patmos where he was visited by an angel in Rev 1:10 **"on the Lord's day"** which was the Sabbath where John was most likely in deep prayer by being in the sprit when he heard a great voice as a trumpet (Christ speaking).

Rev 1:11 He claims himself **"I am Alpha and Omega, the beginning and the ending saith the Lord, which is, and which was, and which is to come, the Almighty"**. This verse is speaking of the *past, present* and *future* of all seven Churches where John wrote his book on the Island of Patmos. John list the seven Churches of Asia as Ephesus, Smyrna, Pergamos, Thyatira, Sardis, Philadelphia and Laodicea. Each Church represent a certain period of time from the 1st Church of Ephesus till now the last Church of Laodicea covering one thousand nine hundred and eighty-nine years to present. We know there are to be seven Churches from the day of Pentecost in approx. 33AD till the end of the age (approx. 2024AD if the taking takes place this year) equivalent to 284 years per each Church period. The following represent approx. calendar dates for each Church period and definition by name. **Ephesus** (33-317AD) capital of the Roman province of Asia Minor. **Smyrna** (318-602AD) a city of Ionia Asia Minor. **Pergamos** (603-887AD) a city in Mysia Asia Minor and in Greek means, *fortified* and *a tower or castle*. This definition indicates the building of Europe's fortification during the dark ages. **Thyatira** (888-1172AD) city in Lydia Asia Minor. **Sardis** (1173-1457AD) a city in Lydia Asia Minor. **Philadelphia** (1458-1742AD) a city in Lydia Asia Minor and in Greek means, *a King of Pergamos, fond of Brethren, fraternal, a dear friend, fond or friendly, associate or neighbor*. Indicated the creation of America and the establishment of our Constitution in Philadelphia, the city of brotherly love. **Laodicea** (1743-to current date) chief city of Phrygia and in Greek means, *a place in Asia Minor, a people or one's own populace, the public bound together Socially, Justice or execution of judgment and punish*. The definition of the Church of Laodicea describes our current world of liberalism, communism, social justice and Holy Wood perfectly.

The dates listed for each Church period takes the seven Churches from Rev 1:1 through Rev 3:22 where the Church is taken from earth in Rev 4:1-2 when John is translated into Heaven. Rev 1:12-20 give the Church seven golden candlesticks and seven stars as their spiritual power given by the Holy Spirit or God's Angel called **"his Angel"** in Rev 1:1 and Acts 2:4,17&38.

Important note: We need to ask ourselves a serious question? We know that there are only one God, one Christ and one Holy Spirit, so, why are there seven Churches? Most Christians do not stop and think so I will explain. There is only one Church and one Gospel. Christ list seven Churches by a specific name with distinctive Greek meanings for each Church as listed above. There is only one Christ cornerstone, one Church and one Gospel that is broken down into seven different time periods. When each Church fulfills its time period of approx. 284 years each Church is renamed to the next one listed. Each Church name is given to one period of time or seven time periods in total. The definition of each Church describes their assigned time period and how each evolve through time. This can be the only reason there are seven distinct Churches, otherwise it makes no since.

Rev 1:12-15 John saw seven golden candlesticks and in the mist of the seven candlesticks was one like unto the son of man, clothed with a garment down to the foot and girt about the "paps" with a golden griddle, it had to be Jesus.

Rev 1:16-19 **"And he had in his right hand seven stars** plural); **and out of his mouth went a sharp two-edged sword** (singular)". This verse is speaking of the seven stars as seven different Churches and the sharp two-edged sword is Christ's Gospel. Verse 17-19 speak of Jesus being with his Church in the past present and future.

Rev 1:20 This verse is very important to understand for it is the last verse of chapter one. It describes the seven stars in Christ's hand as being different angels of the seven Churches which are the Spirits and seven candlesticks as the seven Churches described above. This chapter defines in how each Church has a distinguished individual candlestick and angel but the sword of the Gospel and Holy Spirit called "his Angel" is singular and never changes. At this point in time, John is still physically located on the Island of Patmos.

After reviewing chapter one, we find the follow elements of Christ's Church which is God's earthly Kingdom as stated in Rev 1:9.

The elements of God's Earthly Kingdom

Rev 1:1 the **Holy Spirit called "his Angel"** God's Angel singular that serve all seven Churches different from all other Angels in Heaven as the Holy Spirit of the God Head.

Rev 1:4 the **Apostle John** chosen by Christ himself to prophecy to the seven Churches, meaning, John was a symbol of the Church when translated into Heaven in Rev 4:1.

Rev 1:4 also mentions a **"throne"** which is King David's throne that Christ claim when it is set in Heaven in Rev 4:1-2 promised in Luke 1:30-33.

Rev 1:6 **"kings and priests"** are faithful followers worthy as Church members for ever.

Rev 1:9 **"the kingdom"** that never changes form ancient to modern times and consist of King David's Throne, twelve tribes of Israel and God's Temple/ Church for ever.

Rev 1:11 lists the **names of the Seven Churches** that span the last two thousand years.

Rev 1:13 list **Seven individual golden candlesticks** the seven Churches.

Rev 1:16, **Seven individual stars** one Angel Spirit for each Church not the holy Spirit.

Rev 1:16, a **Two-edged Sword** (the Gospel of Christ's WORD).

Rev 1:20 explains what the stars and candlesticks represent: This verse clearly state that the Stars are the angels of the seven Churches and the candlesticks are the seven Churches in different time periods with the two-edged sword as the (the Word) Gospel at their core. John 1:14, the Word is Christ. Chapter one describes the parable of Matt 21:33-46 as being the Temple of the old Covenant and the Church as the new Covenant both being placed under a "husbandman" in the absence of the Master for maintenance and leadership. This parable was for man to be under self-rule under a "husbandman", the Temple/Church. Matt 21:43-44, due to the Jews rejecting the Messiah, took the kingdom from the house of Judah (the Jews) and gave it to the house of Israel (Ephraim the house of Joseph I Kings 11:26&28) fulfilling the breach and the Throne transferred in I Kings 12:19-29 and from this Scripture has never changed.

Revelation Chapter two (The first four early faithful Churches)

Rev 2:1-7 **Ephesus**: (33 to 314AD) gives a grave WARNING to all seven Churches, list their good works but warns them of their bad works, **"Remember therefore from whence thou art fallen, and repent, and do the first works; or else I will come unto thee quickly and will remove thy candlestick out of his place, except thou repent"**.

Rev 1:8-11 **Smyrna**: (315 to 597AD) gives good works of their Church.

Rev 2:8-12-17 **Pergamos**: (598 to 880AD) is the city that Satan dwells and they still hold fast Christ's name.

Rev 2:18-29 **Thyatira**: (881 to 1162AD) list good and bad works dealing with the prophetess Jezebel. (Church began to fall away with warning)

Rev 3:1-6 **Sardis**: (1163 to 1446AD) Sardis is warned to be watchful for Christ has found them to not be perfect before God. Christ gave all seven Churches a dire warning, "He that overcometh, the same shall be clothed in white raiment; and I will not blot out his name out of the book of life, but I will confess his name before my Father, and before his angels".

Rev 3:7-13 **Philadelphia**: (1447 to 1729AD) has a little strength and kept God's Word. They slowly began to fall away from the Gospel.

Rev 3:14-22 **Laodiceans**: (1730AD to our current time period) The Church of Laodiceans fell away from God's word and became Babylon. This would explain the warning of Rev 2:5 where if the Church did not repent God would move their candlestick and in Rev 3:16 spewed this Church out of his mouth. Christ moved his candlestick from the Church body to each individual having a worthy heart that has overcome explaining Matt 18:19-20 where two or three that gather together in his name is his Church.

Rev 2:1-29 list the Church of Ephesus through Thyatira by name and gives their good and bad works. Note the timeframe of each Church above. After each Church is listed, the last verse pertaining to each Church is a WARNING to that individual Church. This warning is the same for each Church except for the first three Churches which is Ephesus, Smyrna and Pergamos where they are given an individual blessing after the initial warning. This indicates that each Church represents a certain timeframe for this identical verse is a warning given to all seven Churches, **"He that hath an ear, let him hear what the Spirit saith unto the Churches:"**. Each individual Church were commanded to listen to the Holy Spirit as a "warning" in Rev 2:5 and 3:2-5 or these warnings would take place if the Church failed to repent. The Church of Laodicea failed somewhere within their time period and these two warning were implemented by Jesus. They were spewed out of his mouth and their candlestick was removed from the Church body and placed into the hearts of the individual Christian. After this verse a special blessing is given only to Ephesus, Smyrna and Pergamos that obeyed and listened to the Spirit. Starting with the 4th Church of Thyatira, they began to fallaway and not listen to the Spirit by not repenting. Again, this indicates that each Church represents a different

94

blessing in their own timeframe or period of time. The special blessings given to the Church of Ephesus, *"To him that overcometh will I give to eat of the tree of life, which is in the midst of the paradise of God"*. The blessing to the Church of Smyrna is a little different, *"He that overcometh shall not be hurt of the second death"*. The special blessing to the Church of Pergamos, *"To him that overcometh will I give to eat of the hidden manna, and will give him a white stone, and in the stone a new name written, which no man knoweth saving he that receiveth it"*. Note that each blessing is different but starts with the word overcome. The last four Churches did not receive a special blessing but only the warning verse as quoted above, WHY? They were not listening to the Spirit! The first three Churches maintained Christ's Gospel called **"do the first works"** from Pentecost in Acts 2:1-11 up to approx. 885AD where the Roman Catholic Church (came into power approx. 610AD) became powerful throughout Europe and began to dilute the last four of Christ's Churches in their given time period. They failed in Christ's WARNINGS and began to not listen to the Spirit. We must note that in Rev 2:5 starting with the 1st Church of Ephesus to the last and current Church of Laodiceans, Christ gave all seven Churches a dire WARNING! This warning clearly states: **"Remember therefore from whence thou art fallen, and repent, and do the first works; or else I will come unto thee quickly, and will remove thy candlestick out of his place, except thou repent"**, Rev 2:5. Note that the word repent is mentioned twice in this verse as a failure to not listen to the Spirit. The 4rd Church of Thyatira had already begun to fall from Christ's "first works" so they were given a warning to repent in Rev 2:18-29 in which they did not repent. Verse 25-26 gave them another warning and it states, **"And he that overcometh, and keepeth my works unto the end, to him will I give power over the nations:"**. To overcome sin, a person has to maintain an "often" repentance (Heb 9:25-26) to enter Heaven just as the special blessing to the first three Churches indicate where they listened to the Spirit. Another note that we must understand is that each Church is called **"the children of Israel"** and verse 17 the **"white stone"** just as Pergamos is called by this name in Rev 2:14. Ephraim and Manasseh of Joseph is called **"the stone of Israel"** in Gen 49:24 to be Christ's Church in the last days. The Church called the children of Israel is confirmed in Matt 10:6, 15:24 and Acts 10:36 where Christ himself sent his Apostles. They were only to preach and teach to the lost sheep of the house of Israel as the children of Israel to be a white stone as Christians of the Church with Christ its cornerstone.

The most important word in this chapter is "overcome" or, **Overcometh** in Greek means, 3528, *to subdue, fig or literal to conquer, overcome, prevail, get the victory*. To overcome, subdue, conquer, prevail and victory to enter heaven is to repent of our sins continuously as in "often" as a direct reference to *listen to the Spirit*, **"let him hear what the Spirit saith unto the Churches"**. The following verses refer to "overcometh"; I John 5:4-5, Rev 2:7, 2:11, 2:26, 3:5,

3:12, 3:21, and 21:7. What does God expect that we must OVERCOME? Sins of this world through prayer asking for strength and repentance "often" found in Heb 9:25-26. If we fail to repent, then, we fail to listen to the Spirit just as Christ warned his Church. Therefore, if we as born-again servants fail to "overcome" which means we fail to repent of our sins in a timely or "often" manner, we will as Christians be blotted out and cast into outer darkness. We lose our salvation just as the warning in Rev 3:5 and Christ's parables state and will be spewed out of Gods mouth just as the Church of Laodiceans in Rev 3:15.

Revelation Chapter 3 Chapters one through three takes place from the time of Pentecost till the taking of the Church or Rapture estimated to be approx., 1,989 years based on the rapture being fulfilled in 2024AD. This period is called the Church Age. Chapters 1-3 pertaining to the Gospel is an unbroken timeline that continuously run from Rev 1:1 through the blowing of the 7th Trumpet at the middle of the Tribulation when the Gospel of Christ is finished in Rev 10:7, 11:7 and Dan 12:7. We must note that the Holy Spirit called "his Angel" will not leave earth when the Church is taken for it has to remain till the Anti-Christ is revealed and the Gospel is finished. Chapter three explains the spiritual condition of the last three Churches of Sardis, Philadelphia and Laodiceans that take place during the last days and the Churches final falling away. The Church of Sardis was the beginning of the falling for they refuse to listen to the Holy Spirit and for this reason, a dire warning is given to these last three Churches.

Rev 3:1-2 The warning to the Church of Sardis to be **"watchful"** for they had fallen **"for I have not found thy works perfect before God"**. They had fallen from their state of perfection by failing to repent given in Heb 6:1, they failed to listen to the Spirit for only a few true Christians remained.

Rev 3:2-5 These verses is a direct warning to not only the Church as a whole but to each individual Church member in how to maintain our spiritual state of perfection before Jesus. Closely read each of these verses for they list five things that the individual must do to enter Heaven and maintain our daily salvation to keep our perfect white Garments to be "worthy" to "overcome" and stand before Christ at his Marriage Supper given in Matt 22:2-15. Five things that an individual must do, according to these Scriptures, to be saved and to do "often" to maintain that salvation. Verse 3 explains, <u>receive</u> the Gospel, <u>hear</u> the Gospel, <u>hold fast</u> the Gospel, <u>repent</u> often of our sins and <u>watch or be watchful</u> for the coming of our Lord. Verse 4 tells us that if we maintain these five things, we will keep a white garment and be worthy to escape Hell and if we refuse or fail, then, verse five will take place in our lives, **Rev 3:5- "He that overcometh, the same shall be clothed in white raiment; and I will not blot out his name out of the book of life, but I will confess his name**

before my Father, and before his angels". Ladies and Gentlemen, this verse is perfectly clear, if we as born-again Christians and fail to repent in a timely or often manner of our daily sins, we will be blotted out of the Lambs Book of Life and not see Heaven just as five of the ten virgins in Matt 25:1-12 were cast out of the Marriage Supper where Christ himself stated, **"But he** [Christ] **answered and said, Verity I say unto you, I know you not"**. These five virgins were born-again Servants of God at one time but lost their salvation due to the lack of repentance. The term *"once saved always saved"* is not true for clearly if we fail to repent "often" we will lose our God given Salvation as chosen Servants. Again, the warning to the Church of Sardis, **"He that hath an ear, let him hear what the Spirit saith unto the churches"**.

Rev 3:7-8 To the Church of Philadelphia during the time frame of approx. 1447-1729AD when the house of Israel began to settle the western world spreading Christ's Gospel. Christ himself gave his Gospel as his Church "only" to the lost sheep of the house of Israel in Matt 10:6, 15:24, Act 10:36, Ezek 3:1-5 and David's throne of England as a symbol of the Lion in Rev 3:7 calling it the **"key of David"**. The last two thousand years of the Church Age is found in Jerm 23:3-6 as **"David a righteous Branch" "dwell safely"**. What is this Key? In Greek, the word key means in ref #2807 *a key as shutting a lock*, 2808, *to close or shut up* and goes on to say that no man can open or shut this "key" but **"he that is true"**, Jesus the Lamb of Judah. This key is the Gospel of Jesus given to King David's throne as its caretaker (husbandmen) called the Throne of England, the Unicorn of Ephraim. I Kings 12:19-20&24 where the throne of David is taken from Judah and given to the house of Israel and in Matt 21:43-44 calling them the children of Israel to be Christ's Church in the future. I Peter 1:1 and James 1:1 calls them scattered strangers abroad where they waited in the nations of Europe for the Gospel to come. They accepted Christ's Gospel when the twelve Apostles took the Great Commission in Matt 28:18-20 to the scattered strangers fulfilling history. The flag of England carries the three crouched lions of Judah as the birth tribe of Jesus. England is the only nation in the world that carries the "unicorn" as a national symbol in Duet 33:17 and the "bull" of America as their brother. The Scriptures are clear on this fact.

Rev 3:8-13 The Church of Philadelphia had a little strength and **"kept the word of my patience"** and due to this strength, God promised in verses 10-12 that his Church would not see **"the hour of temptation, which shall come upon all the world, to try them that dwell upon the earth"**. This verse is speaking of the seven-year tribulation period also promised in I Thess 1:10, Dan 12:1-2 and Luke 21:36 that the Church would escape wrath. Jasher 56:20 is very clear for it states, *"For I know that many and grievous troubles will befall you in the latter days, in the land, yea your children and children's children, only serve the Lord and he will save you from all trouble"*. By Scripture, the Church will not see the wrath of John's Tribulation. Again, verse 13 gives the identical warning to listen to the Spirit.

Rev 3:14-19 To the Church of Laodiceans no good deeds were listed for it was a wicked fallen away Church that Christ spewed out of his mouth and their candlestick was taken and moved as clearly stated in Christ's warnings to his Churches. Rev 3:16 clearly states, **"So then because thou art lukewarm, and neither cold nor hot, I will spue thee out of my mouth"**. No other Church was spewed out of God's mouth except for Laodicea! This verse is not given as a warning like Rev 2:5 and 3:5 but as a factual event that actually happened for this Church was wretched, miserable, poor, blind and naked. Naked is the key for it means shame for they lost their white garment of Salvation just as the Servant in Christ's parable at the Kings son's Marriage Supper in Matt 22:1-14. The "man" or guest which was a Servant having an invitation "bid to the marriage" meaning they were once born into Gods service as a chosen Servant had no wedding garment or white robe. He was cast into outer darkness with gnashing of teeth and blotted out of the book of Life just as Rev 3:5 warns. The word "naked" in Rev 3:17-18 means *shame* before God for not having the proper pure "white raiment" to stand before God at the Marriage Supper of the Lamb. We can lose our white robes and proven in Matt 22:11 [wedding garment], Rev 3:5 [white raiment] and 4:4 [white raiment]. If we lose our white garments, we cannot stand before the throne of God as in Rev 4:4 and Rev 6:11 [white robs] where all that enter Heaven is given a white robe in Rev 7:14 [washed their robs and made them white in the blood of the Lamb] through repentance. Rev 3:3 gives all the elements required to enter Heaven and they are, be watchful, perfect before God, receive and hear the Gospel, hold fast the Gospel, and repent to wash "often" and maintain our garments white. How do we sustain our white rob spotless before God? The following verses explains in how we wash and keep our garments pure white, Titus 3:5, **"by the washing of regeneration, and renewing of the Holy Ghost"**, I John 1:9, **"If we confess our sins, he is faithful and just to forgive us our sins, and to cleanse us from all unrighteousness"**, Jude 23, **"hating even the garment spotted by the flesh"**. Repentance is how we become worthy to overcome and escape God's wrath by not being blotted out of his book of life as explained in Rev 3:2-5. How often do we have to repent of our daily sins to maintain an acceptable white garment before Christ, Heb 9:25-26 tells us? Under the Old Covenant Law of Moses animal blood sacrificing was once a year but the New Covenant under the Church is "often" and in Greek means, *"as often as"*. The Greek dictionary relates "as often as" as to drinking or eating which means in reality, every day. In English, often means frequently which also can be related to eating and drinking as in every day. This means, repentance before Jesus should be included in our daily prayers or as often as a Christians commits to daily sins that render spots on our pure white garments of salvation. How many sins or spots do it take to pollute our garments, that depends on our personal relationship between each individual and Jesus Christ our Savior? Only Jesus knows our hearts.

Rev 3:20-22 Verse 20, **"Behold, I stand at the door, and knock: If any man hear my voice, and open the door, I will come in to him, and will sup with him, and he with me"**, this is the Gospel of Christ's Church being spread worldwide fulfilling the Great Commission of Matt 28:18-20 given directly by Christ himself to only the lost sheep of the house of Israel in Matt 10:6, 15:24, Act 10:36, Eze 3:1-5 and Rev 2:14 to be his Church. Verse 21, explain in how people that accept Christ overcome and set down with him in Christ's throne in the future for Christ is still setting with God on his Throne during this verse, **"and am set down with my Father in his throne"**. Christ's throne is not in Heaven at this moment of time as this verse clearly states but two verses later in Rev 4:2, Christ's Throne is **"set"** in Heaven. Verse 22, the last and final warning to the seven Churches, **"He that hath an ear, let him hear what the Spirit saith unto the churches"**. The last three verses span almost two thousand years of the Church Age on earth preparing the overcomers as his Church that accept Jesus and his Gospel maintaining an unbroken timeline. The next two verses change everything through a major event and transforms Christ's Church and King David's throne into Heaven creating a new area of time called the Tribulation Period. This major event is the Rapture or Taking of the Church!

Revelation Chapter 4 Chapter four marks the division between the Church age and the seven-year Tribulation Period with no break in time. John gives a short commentary in chapter four and five where several very important events take place at the same moment of time prior to the wrath of the Seals, Trumpets and Vials. This is not a break in the timeline but a beginning of a new Dispensation of time. There have been three dispensations of time pertained to Gods people such as from Adam to the Flood, the Flood to the coming of Christ and from Jesus establishing his seven Churches over a period of almost two thousand years till our current time period adding up to approx. six thousand years of the rule of man, 666, the number of man. During Rev 4:1-2, there are four major events that takes place simultaneously which are, **1st** A change of dispensation of time ending the Church age, **2nd**, the taking or Rapture of the Church of God's Kingdome into Heaven, **3rd**, King David's throne taken from earth to Heaven where Christ claims his Throne and sets upon it, Luke 1:31-33 and Rev 4:2 and **4th** the beginning of the Seven-year Tribulation Period of WRATH.

There are two important notes that should be closely studied where most Christians fail to see or understand. These facts are proven by Scripture if we are willing to study and pray for understanding. There are four different taking or raptures of Gods people prior to his judgment upon ungodly man and four specific comings of Christ onto Earth recorded in the Scriptures.

1st Note: God taking his people prior to WRATH on earth four different times

The **1ˢᵗ Taking** of God's people to avoid wrath is found in the story of Noah in Genesis chapter seven. There is also a story in Jasher 5:1-22 where God took all the faithful through death prior to the flood which could be thousands or possibly millions of faithful people of God that did not feel the sting of death. This was a mercy death. The book of Jasher is God's true Word found in Joshua 10:13 and II Sam 1:18 for the Hebrew meaning in # 3477 *the upright or correct record.* **2ⁿᵈ taking** of God's faithful is the story of Lot in Gen chapter 19 where his family was saved prior to the wrath upon Sodom and Gomorrah. The **3ʳᵈ taking** of the Church *in the clouds* prior to the wrath of the tribulation, I Thess 4:14-17, I Cor 15:51-52, Luke 21:36 and Dan 12:1-2. The Church or Bride do not see death. **The 4ᵗʰ taking** of Gods people prior to wrath is found in Rev 14:12-16 where Christ has the 1ˢᵗ sickle of mercy in his hand, **"Here is the patience of the saints: here are they that keep the commandments of God and the faith of Jesus".** God takes his saints through a mercy death prior to WRATH of the 2ⁿᵈ Sickle just as found in Jasher 5: 1-22 prior to the wrath of the flood. The 2ⁿᵈ Sickle is wrath of death or damnation in Rev 14:17-19, **"And the angel thrust in his sickle into the earth, and gathered the vine of the earth, and cast it into the great winepress of the wrath of God".** In Rev 14:12-20 there are two distinct different Sickles of death, the 1ˢᵗ is mercy of Gods taking his faithful people without the sting of death and the 2ⁿᵈ on ungodly man of pain, death and destruction into Hell.

2ⁿᵈ Note: Christ's coming onto the Earth or within the Atmosphere four different times

1ˢᵗ Coming on earth as a child to establish his Gospel as recorded in Matthew, Mark, Luke and John to die as our Savior and establish his Gospel. The **2ᵗʰ coming** is in the clouds to take his Church as recorded in I Thess 4:14-17, I Cor 15:51 and Dan 12:1-2. The **3ʳᵈ coming** as an angel which is Christ himself placing *his feet on earth* at the blowing of the 6ᵗʰ Trumpet in Rev 9:13 thru 10:1-2 to fulfill the events of the sixth trumpet lasting 13 months. This event is an actual coming of Christ where his feet physically touch earth. The **4ᵗʰ coming** of Christ is found in Rev 1:7 and 19:11-21 where he comes with his mighty angels *with clouds of fire* in power and glory at the very end of the Great Tribulation of WRATH.

The Rapture or Taking occurs and Vengeance/Wrath 1ˢᵗ half Tribulation begins

Rev 4:1-2 The taking of John symbolize the Rapture of the Church and the beginning of the Seven-year Tribulation Period. Christ's new Throne is now set in Heaven along with his earthly Kingdom that existed during ancient and modern times. Rev 3:21 clearly states that Christ sets with his Father on his Throne with a promise that his Church will set with him when he receives his

Throne in the future. Rev 4:2 fulfills Rev 3:21 for now King David's Throne is moved from earth to Heaven where Jesus receives it. Jesus is now given authority to claim his throne and he now sets upon his newly "set" Throne.

Important Note: The Holy Spirit is not taken into Heaven when the Church is taken for it to remain on earth till the Gospel is finished in Rev 10:7, 11:7 and Dan 12:1 that fulfills the prophecy of II Thess 2:7. The Holy Spirit has to be present to give power and protection over the two Witnesses where they receive each a candlestick in Rev 11:3-4. Rev 1:20 clearly tells us that the two candlesticks given to the two Witnesses represent the authority of the seven Churches that has been taken for it states, **"and the seven candlesticks which thou sawest are the seven churches"**. Why would the two Witnesses need a candlestick each if the Church was still present, they would not need them? The Church is not present during the 1st half of the Tribulation of 1260 days given to the two Witnesses in Rev 11:3-4, therefore, they need Candlesticks to represent the Church under Christ's Gospel till it is "finished" in the middle of the Tribulation.

These verses also initiate man's or Satan's Vengeance of Wrath on the Nations of Babylon till the opening of the 6th Seal where Babylon is destroyed and God's wrath upon ungodly man begins in Rev 6:17. The first thirteen months are wrath upon the nations of Babylon. The first five seals are Satan's wrath of depopulation and destruction of all Christianity on earth controlled by Satan and his earthly minions. Satan or man is in total control of all nations till Rev 11:15 at the blowing of the 7th Trumpet marking the exact middle of the 1st half of the Tribulation. God now takes control for all Kingdoms on earth, **"The kingdoms of this world are become the kingdoms of our Lord"**. God's wrath does not start till the 6th Seal as stated in Rev 6:17 at approx. the one year one month mark of the 1st half of the Tribulation. We must note that God's wrath during the first half of the Trib. is done through the hands of man, not supernatural for God has not taken control till the middle. The first six seals belong to Satan's rule as vengeance upon God's people to kill all Christians as a preparation for his rule on earth. For the Anti-Christ or Satan to declare himself to be the Apotheoses as god, he has to totally destroy Christianity during the first half of the trib. God allows Satan to do his wrath. After the Church is taken, a world revival begins where millions of people are saved, therefore, Satan is forced to kill all that do not worship him and the Beast in Rev 13:15 when he gains full power for 42 months in Rev 13:5 at the 7th Trumpet marking the middle of the Tribulation. This proves that the Tribulation last for seven years for Rev 11:3 gives the two Witnesses 1260 days or 3 ½ years in the 1st half for Satan the Anti-Christ is not released from the bottomless pit till the 5th Trumpet at the two-year mark. From the 5th trumpet to the 7th Trumpet is 1 ½ years for in Rev 13:5 the Anti-Christ is given full power for 42 months or 3 ½ years. God will not allow him to kill the two Witnesses and all others till the middle when he is given full power. The 1st half of the Trib. is for the two Witnesses and the 2nd half is for the Anti-Christ totaling seven-years.

Rev 4:3-11 verse 3 describe the beauty of Christ setting on King David's throne being set in Heaven. Verse 4 states who was in front of the throne which was the ancient **"Twenty-four Elders"** of Israel worshiping their King sitting on David's Throne. Verse 5 list lightings and thundering and voices coming from the Throne with seven lamps of fire burning and seven Spirits of God before the Throne. We know from chapter one that the seven lamps are the seven golden candlesticks or Spirits of God that are the elements of Christ's Church. This clearly places the Church in Heaven standing before Christ in front of his newly set throne of King David that Christ now claims promised in Luke 1:31-33. Clearly John represents the taking of the Church when he was translated into Heaven to write visions of prophecy.

Rev 4:6-11 is very important and a proving factor in identifying the lost sheep of the house of Israel as the Church in Matt 10:6, 15:24, Acts 10:36 and Rev 2:14. Who are the four beasts as the **Lion** (Jesus of Judah in Rev 5:5), **Calf**, **Man** and **Eagle** for the Scriptures clearly identify them to be the four brigades of the twelve tribes of Israel which are now in Heaven standing before Christ's Throne. Only the Lion of Judah had the power to open, blow or pour the Seals, Trumpets and Vials. They are the Church as a wheel traveling worldwide to spread Christ's Gospel fulfilling the Great Commission but now are in Heaven. These creatures are found in Ezekiel 1:10, 10:14, Rev 4:7 and II Esdras 11:39 as the four brigades of Israel which are living beasts with four faces and four wings with wheels for travel. These four beasts are the four brigades of Israel illustrating their encampment layout as they travailed by horse and wagon, ship and walking in the wilderness in ancient times and throughout the world in the last days. Numbers chapter two describes the bearing of their standards or flags as they traveled where the flag of the **Lion** represented Judah on the east side, the **Calf** of Ephraim on the west side, the **Eagle** of Dan on the north side and the **Man** of Ruben on the south side of their daily encampment. This is how the children of Israel was identified by tribe as they traveled during their forty years through the wilderness into the Promised Land and into the world during modern times as the scattered strangers abroad where James 1:1 and I Peter 1:1 sent their Epistles. The book of Numbers clearly identifies these four beasts as the twelve tribes of Israel broken down into four brigades listed in Rev 4:7. II Esdras 11:39 of the Apocrypha actually state that these four-beasts were to reign in this world, **"Art not thou it that remainest of the four beast, whom I made to reign in my world, that the end of their times might come through them"**. They were to reign *"through them* (the lost sheep of the house of Israel)*"* in the last days as the Church. II Estras 10:39 places this time period in the last days for it states, **"unto them that dwell upon earth in the last days"** where chapter eleven gives Esdras a vision of an eagle (believed to be the speckled bird in Jerm 12:9-15) as the lost sheep of the house of Israel given to Ephraim and Manasseh as the Bull and Unicorn that became the two eagles of Great Britain and America as brothers. If we study the listing of the twelve tribes in Rev 7:5-8 we find that Dan is not listed and Manasseh takes his place. Why? Dan sinned against his brothers of the other eleven tribes. The majority of Dan did not stay and fight for the Promised Land but departed by ship. God gave Ephraim and Manasseh the firstborn birthright in Gen 48:16-22 to be called Israel, not the Jews, so Manasseh received a double portion and was given Dan's inheritance of the Eagle in Rev 7:6 due to Dan's sin. The vision of the Eagle in II Esdras 11:1-39 is believed to be Ephraim and Manasseh due to their firstborn birthright blessing given by Jacob to Joseph to the two lads to be called Israel that became the lost sheep of the house of Israel. They received King David's throne in I King 12:19-20&24 by the authority of the Prophet Ahijah. The house of Israel was called the children of Israel in verse 24.

The twenty-four elders and the four beasts representing Christ's Church as the lost sheep first stood before Christ's throne worshiping Jesus our Lord when his newly set throne was placed into Heaven. This occurred at the very beginning of the Tribulation as explained in Revelation chapter four.

Wheel of Israel (The Church) in Eze 1:10-16, 10:2-19 in Heaven in Rev 4:7 as the four Brigades of Israel being Christ's Church, England the brothers of America

Evangelizing the World by Travel Isa 41:3 by Ship Wheel and then by horse and wagon.

represents their 40-year trek in the wilderness and Evangelization of the Church into the Wilderness of the World given by Christ himself to his lost sheep in Matt 10:6 and 15:24.

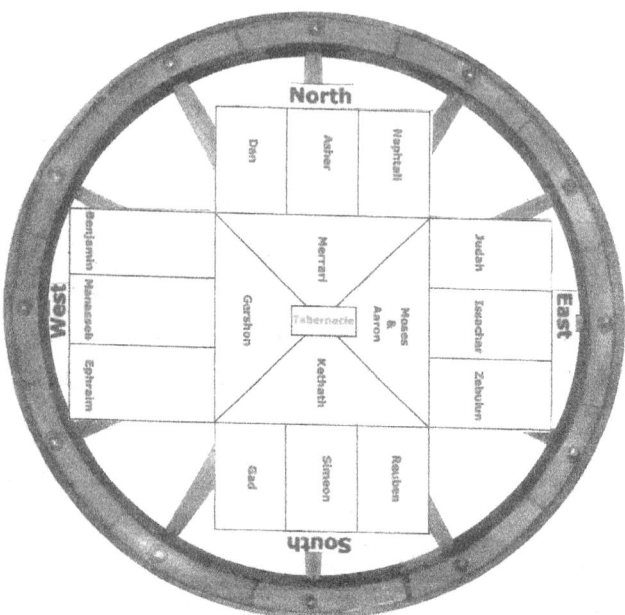

The House of Israel as the Lost Sheep of Israel Matt 10:6 & 15:24 the Wheel of the Church as the Lion, Man Ox and Eagle, Eze 1:10, 10:14 and Rev 4:7

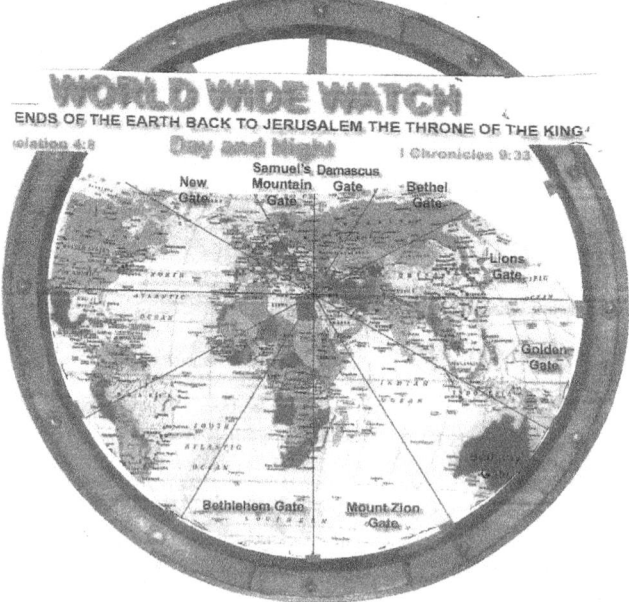

Described as a wheel "Now as I beheld the living creatures, behold one wheel upon the earth by the living creatures, with his four faces"

104

The Gates of Jerusalem represent the Encampment of the twelve Tribes in the Wilderness and the foundation of the Church of New Jerusalem in all of Rev chapter 21.

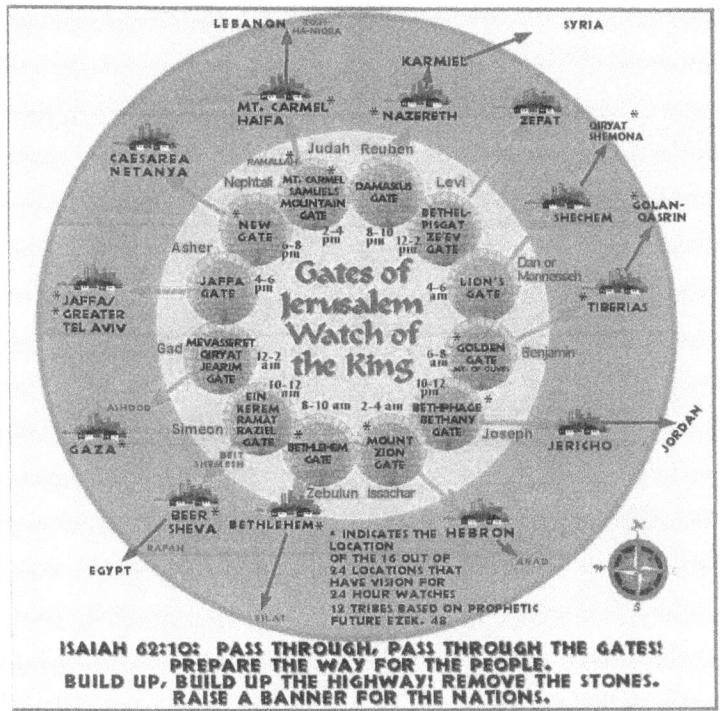

Revelation Chapter 5 This chapter is also John's commentary that takes place in a very short period of time at the very beginning of the Tribulation moments prior to the Seals being opened.

Rev 5:1-10 It had to be determined who has the authority to open the seven seals, trumpets and vials for no man on earth or in Heaven had that authority. Christ, the Lamb of Judah as the **Lion,** sat on the Throne having a written book (the Gospel) with seven seals in his right hand representing the Church as the lion, one of the four brigades of the house of Israel as the Lion, Calf, Man and Eagle. This proves that the Church is in Heaven at the very beginning of the Tribulation. Where did Christ get his authority? He received his authority from God when he sat on his Throne when it was set in Heaven the moment John was translated into Heaven in Rev 4:1-2. Christ's earthly Kingdom was moved into Heaven where Jesus received it as promised in Luke 1:30-33. The one that sat on the throne having the "little book", the Gospel in Rev 5:1 is explained in verse 6, **"And I beheld, and low, in the midst of the throne and of the four beast, and in the midst of the elders, stood a Lamb as it had been slain, having seven horns and seven eyes, which are the seven Spirits of God sent forth into all the earth"**, Jesus our Savior, as the slain Lamb, sat on the throne of King David representing his Church as its cornerstone of the Gospel, is the only one that had authority to open the seven seals. Therefore, Christ could not receive his power to open the Seals till he sat upon David's Throne as the Church given in Jerm 23:3-6 as a **"righteous branch"**. Christ's Church and Throne was taken into Heaven at the very beginning of the Trib. Christ had no authority or Throne till King David's earthly throne along with the Church was taken into Heaven in Rev 4:1-2 giving Jesus his Heavenly power to be King. Christ's earthly Kingdom of the twelve tribes, the Temple/Church and King David's throne is complete and now in Heaven at the very beginning of the Tribulation. The Throne of King David is the key and authority given to Jesus to open the Seals, Trumpets and Vials.

Rev 5:11-14 these verses explain how the Angels, the four Beasts as the Church called the lost sheep of the house of Israel, Matt 10:6, 15:24 and Acts 10:36, and the twenty-four Elders and ten thousand of thousands represent every faithful person from Adam stood before the throne worshiping the slain Lamb that sat on the Throne for ever and ever.

Revelation Chapter 6 The first Six Seals Maintains an unbroken timeline from the establishing of the Church in Acts chapter two through the seven Seals, Trumpets and Vials that ends in Rev 16:17-21 at the end of the seven-year Trib.

The four horsemen of the Apocalypse Rev 6:1-2 the 1ˢᵗ Seal opened only by the Lamb (Jesus) from the tribe of the Lion releasing the White Horse with the rider having a bow and crown "went forth conquering, and to conquer" through politics of world power. Note: the first four seals are opened by the Lamb but announced by the four Beast of the four Brigades of the house of Israel (the Church) as listen in Rev 4:7 with authority coming from Christ as the Lamb of Judah, the Lion setting upon his newly set Throne. This rider had a bow or great army with a crown meaning, he was a great political and military leader under a "white" flag of peace. This rider is believed to be the United States of America as head of the 30 member states of NATO countries under the power of the United Nations with the USA as its leader. This white horse is also believed to be the political and military power of the Great Whore of Babylon prior to its destruction in Rev 14:3-8, 17:1-18 and 18:1-24. It is also explained as Babylon in Isa 47:1-5 as "the lady of kingdoms" [represents the Statute of Liberty in the NY Harbor] where the Church as the bride is taken from her (Babylon or USA) in Rev 18:23. This means, the Church was once within Babylon called USA. White also represents *"peace"* through politics just prior to all-out WAR on earth, the white horse represents the last moments of peace. If we closely study, it appears that the white horse of the Apocalypse is the 1ˢᵗ of the four Beasts of Dan 7:4-7 and the four horsemen of Rev 6:1-8. They are all related for it places the pieces of the puzzle nicely together. The White Horse of Rev 6:1-2 is the same as the first beast in Dan 7:4 that was like a lion having eagles wings (USA having the symbol of the eagle) where his wings were plucked (war) and lifted up from the earth. This would explain the taking of the Church fulfilling Rev 18:23 where the bride was taken from Babylon as a man standing upon his feet given a man's heart, "and it was lifted up from the earth" where Babylon once was the Church but now broken for America's head and wings are removed. The Church was lifted and taken out of America Babylon.

Order of the Seals of the four Horsemen

We should note that the Four Horsemen of the Apocalypse are the preparations of political and military power of the Anti-Christ establishing his earthly kingdom in the first four Seals that appear during the first half of the Tribulation period. This is man's vengeance/wrath to the nations of the world to depopulate allowed by God, not God's wrath upon ungodly man in the second half. The 1ˢᵗ half is wrath upon the world by man through Satan where God allows it. These Horseman are the culmination of political power given to the son of perdition in 1 Thess 2:3. He is reveled in the first half of the Tribulation when released from the bottomless pit in Rev 9:1 at the 5ᵗʰ Trumpet which is at the two-year mark of the 1ˢᵗ half of the Trib. Being released from the pit has to occur before Gods wrath takes place upon ungodly man that accept the Mark of the

Beast at the beginning of the last half of the Trib. The Anti-Christ is given two years to prepare. It is important to understand the difference between the Satanic vengeance/wrath upon man of the first half verses Gods wrath of the second half of the seven-year Tribulation Period. These are two distinct or diverse types of wrath. The first thirteen months is Man's/Satan's wrath on the nations of the world that support the Babylon system to include Christians saved during that time period. Its Satanic wrath is to kill Christians, Patriots, all religions and depopulate man due to the Satanic hatred for humanity. The Church of Laodicea prior to the Church being taken fell into sin under the old BAAL religion of Babylon through the 501C3 tax exception controlled by the governments of the world. John warned the Church to come out of her (Babylon) in Rev 18:4. Millions of members of the Church of Laodiceans that is left behind will be saved during the 1st half. These are the so-called Christians that thought they were saved but left behind. The Anti-Christ as a man is working for Satan building his power base till Satan takes his body in Rev 13:3, not having full control of the earth till the middle of the Trib. when he kills the two witnesses and all that do not take the Mark of the Beast in Rev 11:7 and 13:15. Satan is released from the bottomless pit at the blowing of the 5th Trumpet where he is called Apollyon. The 5th Trump takes place at the two-year mark during the first half of the Trib. but Satan do not become the Beast till the middle of the Trib. when he takes the body in Rev 13:3, for 42 months, in the middle of the Trib. The last three and half years, 42 months, is wrath only for the wicked and ungodly that took the mark of the beast. We should note the importance of who has the power to open the 7 Seals, 7 Trumpets and 7 Vials for it explains the power structure in Heaven during the Tribulation of Wrath. The Four Beasts listed in Eze 1:10, 10:14 and Rev 4:7 represent the four Brigades of Israel as laid out in Numbers chapter two as the Lion (Judah), Calf (Birthright tribes of Ephraim and Manasseh), Man (Ruben first born son) and the Eagle (Dan/Manasseh). They are God's earthly kingdom and represent the Church during the last days just as Jesus gave the responsibility of the Church to the lost sheep of the house of Israel in Matt 10:6, 15:24, Acts 10:36 and Eze 3:1-5 as the Bull and Unicorn, USA and UK of England.

All the Seals and first four Trumpets lasted approx. 2.2 months each as explained within this book.

The four Horseman

1st Seal - Rev 6:1 - the **White Horse is the same as the 1st Beast of Dan 7:4** opened by **"he"** the Lamb or Lion which is Christ giving the rider of the White horse a bow (a gift) and crown to conquer with Political intrigue and military power. This Seal was opened by the Lamb (Christ) which is the Lion of the tribe of Judah, the 1st Beast of the four Brigades of the house of Israel as

Christ's Church with total authority. The four Beast of Rev 4:7, Eze 1:10 and 10:14 are completely different Beasts listed in Dan 7:4-8 as the Church where Christ himself gave them the authority to be his Church in Matt 10:6, 15:24 and Acts 10:36.

2ⁿᵈ Seal Rev 6:3-4 – The **Red Horse** 2ⁿᵈ Beast of Dan 7:5 opened by **"he"** the Lamb and announced by the 2ʳᵈ Beast of the Ox or Calf of Ephraim and Manasseh, the firstborn birthright tribe releasing the Red Horse with a great sword taking peace from the earth by killing one another. This Seal starts the WAR of Ezekiel 38 and 39 and begins WWIII, a limited nuclear war! This red horse is believed to be the 2ⁿᵈ Beasts in Dan 7:5 and Rev 6:4 where the Red Bear of Russa plucks the wings off the 1ˢᵗ Beast of Dan 7:4 called the White Horse which is a partial destruction of Babylon America that became the Beast (the Dragon or Anti-Christ) in Rev 13:3, **"And I saw one of his heads as it were wounded to death; and his deadly would was healed"**. This is a partial destruction of the NATO Beast where America is destroyed or plucked off the white horse of peace but survives with the deadly wound. NATO of Europe is revived as the Beast and False Prophet in Rev 13:1-8 after the battle between the White and Red Horses. The white horse survives to become extremely powerful where European NATO rebuilds and no nation can fight against him in Rev 13:12&14, **"which had the wound by a sword, and did live"**. The white horse of Rev 6:1-2 was almost destroyed by the red horse or red bear of Russia meaning that the head as its leader called Babylon America was removed but grew a new head through the leadership of the European NATO confederation. America is Babylon the Great as a military power and destroyed, but its economic system is not completely finished till the opening of the 6ᵗʰ Seal at the one year one month mark of the 1ˢᵗ half of the Tribulation. The 2ⁿᵈ Seal in Rev 6:3 called the **Red Horse/Beast of Dan 7:5** opened by **"he"** the Lamb where he is given a great sword to take peace from the earth (war). Seals one and two are the beginning of WW III called, the battle of Hamon-gog in Eze 39:11 and Joel 3:2&12 where the dead bodies are buried.

Note: It is this Author's belief that the war recorded in Ezekiel 38 and 39 is a war started by Russia the Red Horse along with China. God puts Hooks into the Jaws of Gog and Magog to go to war in Eze 38:4 where it takes seven years to burn their weapons in Eze 39:9. This verse means that the Ezekiel war at the 1ˢᵗ and 2ⁿᵈ Seals had to take place at the very beginning of the seven-year Tribulation for it takes seven years to burn their weapons. If we closely study current world events, it would appear that Russia and China are planning together to attack and destroy America. We also know through current events, the Deep State of Biden's Government is planning with China to take over America by invasion, physically, economically and militarily. China lures Russia into attacking America using a limited nuclear strike destroying America as the Crown (head of NATO) with a bow (military). China double crosses Russia by backing out at the last moment and allowing

NATO along with China to destroy Russia just as Ezekiel 38:22 and 39:1-6&9 states. China and the Democratic Communist Deep State government of the future Anti-Christ Beast System is working together to destroy America and Russia. This explains why Russia loses the war for all the American Christians and pundits believe that Russia wins this war where the Bible is clear that Russia is destroyed.

3rd Seal Rev 6:5-6 - **Black Horse** is opened by the 3rd Beast called "he" the Lamb which was the MAN the Brigade of Ruben. He is carrying a pair of balances in his hand representing worldwide hunger and famine created by WWIII between the White and Black Horses. The black horse represents the 3rd Beast of Dan 7:6 as the Leopard and on his back had four wings of a fowl. This Beast also had four heads and domination of the world was given unto him where the Anti-Christ rises to power. The red bear as the red horse goes to war with the white horse removing or killing its head as the rider taking its bow (military) and its crown (leadership) which is the United States, the head of NATO. In the process, the red Bear or red horse of Russa is destroyed but severally wounds the head of the white horse. As always, the destruction of war brings famine and then death! The Black Horse represent weight balances to shackle or enslave the earth through hunger opened by the Lamb announced by the 3rd Beast or Brigade of Israel as the red hand of a Man bearing the flag of Ruben. The sign of a red hand is found all over England to this day where bundles of newspapers are wrapped in a red string and ropes are made with one red string inside.

4th Seal Rev 6:7-8 - **The Pale Horse**- is opened by "he" the Lamb but announced by the 4th Beast or Brigade of Israel as the Eagle of Dan releasing the Pale Horse. The rider that sat on this horse was called Death and Hell that followed him. This rider was given power to kill the fourth part of the earth with sword and hunger and beasts of the field, disease. The pale horse is the 4th Beast of Dan 7:7 that was dreadful, terrible, strong exceedingly with great iron teeth to devour and break in pieces and to stamp the residue of the earth with his feet. We must note that the four horsemen and the four Beast of Daniel chapter seven is closely related to NATO as the military arm of the United Nations and the red bear of Russa representing different periods of time and power. The Pale Horse of death to kill 1/4th of the people of earth by hunger and disease. Opened by the Lamb announced by the 4th Beast (Eagle of Manasseh/Dan).

Synopses of the four horsemen of the first four Seals and four Beast of Daniel chapter seven is this. The White horse is our current NATO and UN military and political system that takes the world into the seven-year Tribulation Period. This white horse is already in power when it is let lose in Rev 6:1-2 where it controls the world but is challenged by Russia the Red Bear as the 2nd Beast of Dan 7:5. The moment the red horse is released in Rev 6:3-4, the white and red horse goes to war which this Author believes to be the war of Ezekiel chapter 38 & 39 which is the battle of Hamon-Gog in Eze 39:11 and also called Jehoshaphat in Joel 3:2&12. Hamon-Gog in Hebrew means in #1992, *multitude of Gog, an emblematic place in Palestine*, 1993, *to be in great commotion or tumult, to rage war, moan and clamor.* The term Hamon-Gog is the people of Russa of the north that came down to do battle in the location of the valley of Jehoshaphat. The results of this war take place in the valley of Jehoshaphat which is near Jerusalem in Israel and Joel 3:2&12 explains this war when the red horse is released. Jehoshaphat in Hebrew means, #3092, *a valley near Jerusalem.* The Red Horse and the 2nd Beast of Dan 7:5 called the Bear is one and the same. The Red Bear plucks the wings off the white horse of Rev 6:2 which is the Beast of Dan 7:4 in the battle of Eze 38&39 and Joel 3:2&12 where the Red Bear of Russa is destroyed found in Ezekiel 38:22-23 and 39:1-11. Before the red bear of Russa is destroyed, it plucks the rider or leader as its head off the white horse and its two wings. The bear wounds the white horse but don't destroy it for its head is miraculously healed in Rev 13:3 where it later becomes the Anti-Christ Beast System.

5th Seal Rev 6:9-11 - is opened by **"he"** the Lamb of Christ describing Christians under the Alter that were souls slain for the word and testimony of God. They cried with a loud voice saying how long O Lord do we stay under the Alter and they were all given white robes. Remember in Rev 3:5 as a warning for those that overcome will be given **"white raiment: and I will not blot out his name out of the book of life"** for those Christians that maintain a constant or "often" repentance in Heb 9:25-26. Yes, we can lose our white robs meaning our Salvation if we allow our white robs to become spotted without an "often" repentance. These crying Christians were told that they should remain under the Alter till their fellow servants as brethren should be killed as they were to be fulfilled. If they were members of the Church, they would not be under the alter but with Jesus by his throne for they were killed at the beginning of the Trib. after the taking of the Church. An important note is that the Saints under the Alter cried out to Jesus saying **"How long, O Lord, holy and true, dost thou not judge and avenge our blood"**. This verse indicates, as of the 5th Seal, God had not started wrath or judgment of the nations of the world.

Wrath and Judgment Begins

6th Seal Rev 6:12-17 - opened by **"he"** the Lamb of Christ of the 1st Beast called the Lion of Judah. Four major and very important events occurred at the opening of the 6th Seal. A great nuclear war turning the sun into black as sackcloth, the moon to blood, stars fell to earth which indicate nuclear missiles creating a shaking and the skies departed as a scroll moving mountains and islands. To escape nuclear war, all men great and poor hid themselves in the rocks of the earth from God **"For the great day of his wrath is come"**.

Four major events occurred in Chapters six and seven after the opening of the 6ᵗʰ Seal

1ˢᵗ Event: Rev 6:12-16 describes a great earthquake, the sun becomes black, the moon to blood, the stars fell to earth (missiles of war) and the heavens departed like a scroll indicating a nuclear war from the falling missiles causing the earth to become dark. Gods WRATH begins in Rev 6:17, **"for the great day of his wrath is come"** creating more war on the earth beginning God's WRATH upon man.

2ⁿᵈ Event: Rev 7:1-8 describes the **Sealing of the 144,000 Hebrews**, 12,000 from each of the twelve tribes of Israel as listed below. It is this Authors belief that the whole of chapter seven occurred a split second after the 6ᵗʰ Seal was opened prior to this nuclear war. God would have saved his sealed servants from this nuclear destruction. It is very important to determine which tribes are listed in order of birth written by Moses in Gen chapters 29 and 30, the blessings of Jacob given in Gen 49, by Moses in Duet 33 and the most important in Rev 7:4-8. All the listings of the twelve tribes are in Biblical order by spelling. The recording by John in Rev chapter 7 and by Moses in Numbers chapter two is very important to note. It is extremely significant to understand why Manasseh replaced Dan in Rev 6:6. He was the Grandson of Jacob where he received a double portion of blessing as a firstborn birthright through Joseph. Ephraim and Manasseh, Joseph's two sons, were the only tribes that received the right to be called Israel when Jacob gave the two lads the authority of the family birthright blessing to be above the other eleven tribes in Gen 48:13-22. In Rev 7:6 Manasseh replaced Dan as the eagle which is key in understanding.

3ʳᵈ Event: The nuclear war in Rev 6:12-17 is the **fall of Babylon the Great** expounded on in Rev 14:3-8, Rev 17:1-18 and Rev 18:1-24 as John's commentary placing this even at the opening of the 6ᵗʰ Seal.

4ᵗʰ Event: According to events in Rev 19:4-10 that occur in a quick immediate order, it places the **Marriage Supper of the Lamb** immediately after the fall of Babylon the Great. The results of the opening of the 6ᵗʰ Seal in Rev 6:12 completes the four major events of that very important seal.

Revelation Chapter 7 Unbroken timeline and the twelve tribes listed by birth and blessings given. This Chapter is a continuation of the events that occurred in the opening of the 6ᵗʰ Seal.

Rev 7:1 four Angels stood on the four corners of the earth holding the four winds that the wind should not blow. The word wind is key, winds in Greek means (417) *the quarter of the earth, meaning plural, wind* (109) *to breath unconsciously, respire, air as natural circumambient*, (5594) *to chill or wax cold* as in Matt 24:12. By this definition, one wind is ¼ so you need four winds to go around the earth. I believe the winds represent God holding back his spirit from the earth and the reason no one can be saved after the middle of the Tribulation for the Gospel is finished in Rev 10:7, Dan 12:7 and **"wrath is come"** in Rev 6:17. The Greek meaning for spirit explains in ref. 4151, *a current of air, breath, a breeze, a spirit, an angel* or *demon, Christ's spirit or the Holy Spirit*. These definitions indicate that Christ's Holy Spirit is being held back from the earth. Note in these verses that the four Angels did not release the four winds but began to hurt the earth and the sea but not till God's people were sealed. God's Spirit was held back from the earth and sea.

Rev 7:2-3 another Angel ascending from the east having the seal of the living God crying to the four Angels holding the winds back to not hurt the earth or sea **"till we have sealed the servants of our God in their foreheads"**. It still is not clear if the winds or God's Spirit was ever released again on earth.

Rev 7:4-8 describes the sealing of the 144,000 Servants of God. According to all the Scriptures listed within this book that describes how God preserves his Saints from wrath to come would indicate that the whole of chapter seven took place at the moment of the opening of the 6th Seal just prior to the described nuclear war in verses 12-17.

The Twelve Tribes of the house of Israel listed by Scripture:

Gen 29:32 thru 30:24 by Birth	Birthright Blessings given in Gen 49:3-22 – Duet 33:6-24		Numbers Ch 2		Rev 7:5-8
Conceived by Leah					
1.	Reuben	Reuben	Reuben	**East** Judah	Juda
2.	Simeon	Simeon	Judah	Issachar	Reuben
3.	Levi	Levi	Levi	Zebulun	Gad
4.	Judah	Judah	Benjamin	**South** Reuben	Asher
Conceived by Rachel					
5.	Dan	Zebulun	Joseph	Simeon	Nephthalim
6.	Naphtali	Issachar	Zebulun	Gad	Manasses
Leah's handmaid Zelpah					
7.	Gad	Dan	Issachar	**West** Ephraim	Simeon
8.	Asher	Gad	Gad	Manasseh	Levi
Conceived by Leah					
9.	Issachar	Asher	Dan	Benjamin	Issachar
10.	Zebulun	Naphtali	Naphtali	**North** Dan	Zebulon
Conceived by Rachel					
11.	Joseph	Joseph	Asher	Asher	Joseph
12.	Benjamin	Benjamin	*Simeon not*	Nephtali	Benjamin

Important Notes: In Rev 7:5-8 Manasses or Manasseh is mentioned in the place of Dan. This indicates that in the last days in Gen 49:1, Manasseh were to receive double portions of blessing and all the blessings that were given to Dan to include the symbol of the Eagle giving Manasseh the Bull and the Eagle (of America). He was one of the two leaders of the house of Israel. Also note that Ephraim his brother was not mentioned for Manasses was the firstborn of the two even though Ephraim received the Birthright. This is proven in Gen 48:20.

Ephraim and Manasseh were given the firstborn birthright blessing to only be called Israel in Gen 48:13-22 as leaders of the ten northern tribes called the children of Israel (house of Israel) in I Kings 11:26 (Jeroboam the Ephrathite), 30-37 (northern ten tribes called the house of Israel) and given the throne taken from Judah where Ephraim were to be **"over all Israel"** in I Kings 12:19-24. Ephraim and Manasseh were clearly called the house of Israel in verse 20 and the children of Israel in verse 24 confirmed as the Church in Acts 10:36 and the children of Israel again in Rev 2:14. Christ himself in Matt 10:6 and 15:24 calls his lost sheep the house of Israel and Act 10:36 Paul calls them the children of Israel to be Christ's Church in the last days.

There are two other listings of the Tribes of Israel that are most important to understand for the house of Israel were to be the Church in the last days. The following are the listings:

Rev 7:9-17 releases the Saints that are under the Alter described in Rev 6:9-11 at the opening of the 5th Seal. These are the Saints killed from the first five Seals estimated by this Author to be a approx. at the nine-month mark of the 1st half of the Tribulation as explained in Rev 7:14.

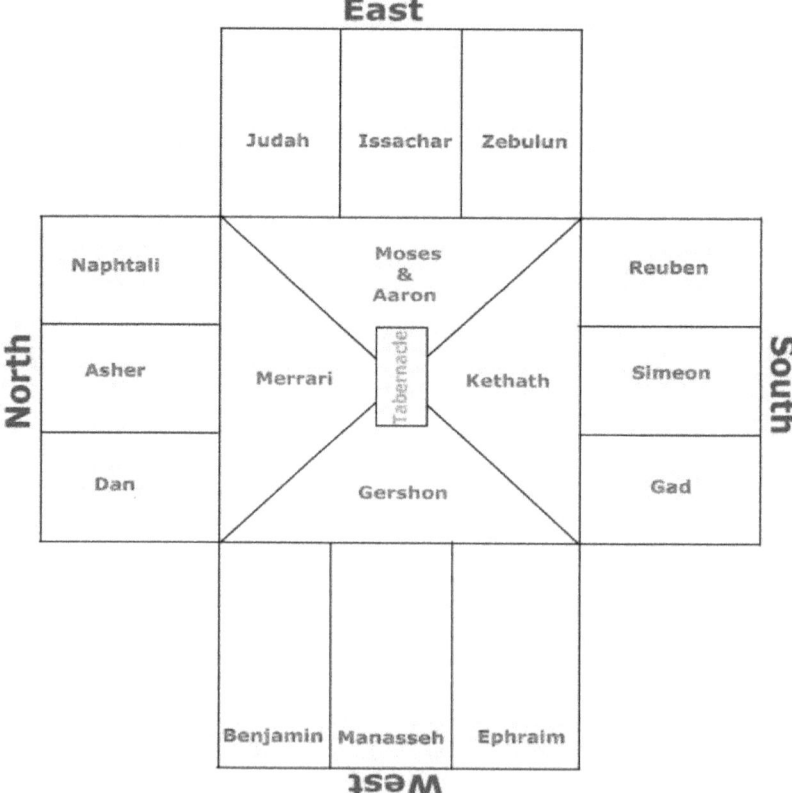

(This Illustration lays out the encampment of Israel during their forty-year

114

trek in the desert) Their encampment is shaped like a wheel where they are called a man, a lion, an ox and an eagle as a living-creatures in Eze 1:10&15 and Rev 4:7. The tribe of Levi the High Priests are in the center along with the Tabernacle.

Gen 46:8-24 listed by Moses Twelve Tribes that went into Egypt not by order of birth	Numbers 2:1-29 listed by Moses Twelve Tribes encampment during forty years trek in the wilderness and in the world, encampment every day shaped as a circle or wheel to the north, south, east and west Ezekiel 1:10&15&10:17-19 as the **four Brigades of Israel**	
1. Reuben	**East Side** 1st **Brigade**	1. Judah
2. Simeon	Ensign the Lion	2. Issachar
3. Levi		3. Zebulun
4. Judas	**South Side** 2nd **Brigade**	
5. Issachar	the Man red hand	4. Reuben
6. Zebulun		5. Simeon
7. Gad		6. Gad
8. Asher	**West Side** 3rd **Brigade**	
9. Joseph and two sons	the Ox or Calf	7. Ephraim
10. Manasseh first born		8. Manasseh
11. Ephraim		9. Benjamin
12. Benjamin	**North Side** 4th **Brigad**	
13. Naphtali	the Eagle	10. Dan
		11. Asher
		12. Naphtali
	Center Hub of the Wheel the Temple/Church	13. Levi

Rev 7:9-17 Identifies a great multitude of Saints that no one man could number. These Saints are the Saints that are under the Alter mentioned in the 5th Seal in Rev 6:9-11 that could not come out from under the Alter till certain events were complete. They could not be released from under the alter till God's WRATH upon man began with the opening of the 6th Seal in Rev 6:12&17 where they are now released in Rev 7:9-17. WRATH upon man begins.

If we closely study Ezekiel chapter one through 10, we find that the four beasts in Rev 4:7 as the Lion, Calf or Cherubim in Eze 10:15, Man and Eagle are the wheel as the same four beasts listen in Eze 1:10 and 10:14. Matt 10:6, 15:24, Acts 10:36 and Eze 3:1-5 is clear where Christ himself calls his lost sheep the children of Israel or the house of Israel as Israel's four brigades. This is listed in Numbers chapter two above. By Scripture there are thirteen tribes when we drop Joseph as King and add his two sons Ephraim (the Unicorn) and Manasseh (the Bull) to be Kings in his stead during the last days, I Kings 12:19-24, leaders of the other eleven tribes as the firstborn birthright blessing given in Gen 48:13-22 where only the two lads were called Israel. The other eleven tribes were called Israel only through the leadership authority of Ephraim and Manasseh that received the family birthright in Gen 48:16, **"The**

Angle which redeemed me from all evil, bless the lads; and let my name be named on them, and the name of my fathers Abraham and Isaac; and let them grow into a multitude in the midst of the earth". This scripture clearly states that the two lads, Ephraim and Manasseh, were to rule over all the earth to be called the house of Israel as the Church just as Matt 10:6, 15:24 and Acts 10:36 states. This is important Scripture that the modern Church refuse to teach. Ephraim and Manasseh were to be nations spread world wide just as James 1:1 and I Peter 1:1 calls them strangers scattered abroad.

Important Note: With all the Scriptures listing above of the tribes of Israel, we must consider the following verses to be true by God's Holy Word. The following verses clearly state that from the time God established his throne first with King Saul in the book of Samuel, there would be a man sitting on his throne through all Generations of time till his coming in the clouds to take his Throne, Kingdom and Church. This is the promise to Jesus in Luke 1:31-33. Christ claims and sits on David's promised throne in Rev 4:1-2. Psalms 89:4 and 145:13 clearly states that David's throne would be occupied through all generations and Jerm 33:17&24 and I Kings 9:5 state that there would always be a man sitting on his throne through all generations of time from the book of I Samuel 9:16 when he first established his throne through Rev 4:1-2 when Christ claims it. That means, King David's throne has to be in existence today with a blood linage of David sitting upon it by promise from God himself. The only royal throne in the world today that meets this criterion is the Throne of England where King Charles and his mother Elizabeth can trace their lineage back to King David. I have a chart on the wall of my office that trace by name every king from King David to King Charles of England. This information has been eliminated from your history books by Satan and his minions.

Rev 6:12&17 explained! Mystery Babylon represents Satan and evil man's BAAL religious systems such as the Roman Catholic Church, Masonry and the Illuminati that has persecuted Israel and Gods Holy people to include Christ's Church since Adam. The Saints under the Alter in the 5th Seal could not be released till Mystery Babylon was destroyed in the opening of the 6th Seal and the beginning of WRATH upon man in Rev 6:17. The multitude of Saints were not of the Church or Bride that was taken at the beginning of the Tribulation but killed during the first five Seals. When the old BAAL religious system was destroyed and the beginning of WRATH began, the Saints under the Alter could be released.

Note: The first six seals indicate a period of time it takes the minions of the Anti-Christ to build political power and physical armies bringing war to earth through the four horses of the apocalypse. This means, the vengeance and wrath that takes place on earth during this time period comes from the human followers of the Anti-Christ, not God. Gods Wrath does not begin till Rev 6:17

after the opening of the 6th Seal. From my studies, there appear to be three types of wrath that occur during the seven-year Tribulation. The **1st period of Wrath** (wrath of man on man planned world depopulation) takes place from Rev 6:1-16 with the opening of the 1st thru the 6th Seals creating death by war with the White, Red, Black and Pale Horses as vengeance upon the nations of this wicked world. The first six Seals bring death and destruction created by Satan and man through politics not God. This wrath is man's planned depopulation of the earth written about four hundred years ago. All Christians that are saved during this time period has to endure this period of mercy punishment vengeance and wrath as you would discipline your child. The **2nd period of Wrath** (wrath from man on man and Satan prior to his full power) begins in Rev 6:17**, "For the great day of his wrath is come:"** through Rev 11:15 with the sounding of the 7th Trumpet. The first six Trumpets are wrath from man and Satan upon the nations due to hatred for the Church. This is wrath on man through governmental politics. Rev 11:15 state, **"And the seventh angel sounded; and there were great voices in heaven, saying, The kingdoms of this world are become *the kingdoms* of our Lord"**. This verse indicates that the Wrath that occur through the Trumpets were aimed at the nations of the earth. This was God allowing man's wrath *to all the nations* of the earth to include Christians and marks the beginning of the sealing of the 144,000, 12,000 from each tribe of Israel. This period is from Rev 6:17 when God's wrath begins thru Rev 9:13 when Satan the Anti-Christ is released from the bottomless pit to the middle of the Tribulation at the 7th Trumpet when the Anti-Christ takes full power in Rev 13:5. **The 3rd period of Wrath** (supernatural wrath from God) occurs from Rev 15:7 through 16:21 consisting of the 1st through 6th Vials of great wrath to be applied to judgment of ungodly man that take the Mark of the Beast in the last half of the Trib. This wrath is of anger as you would punish a hard-core criminal. This is also proven in Rev 16:10 & 17:1-6 where the Angel that pours the vials explain who received the wrath, godless people that accept the Mark.

What is the ALTER of God in Rev 6:9
(Saints under the alter 5th Seal)

The God head represents the Father, the Son and the Holy Spirit and key in understanding what the Alter means to God. The Old and New Testaments connects his holiness and Spirit to his people and his plan to provide Salvation to any man that accepts him and his commandments through his Temple and Church. The Alter in the Temple/Church is a direct connection to the Alter in Heaven. It is the spiritual communication line between man and God. In the Temple the Alter is in the Holy of Holies under blood sacrifice and in the Church, it is in each Christian's heart as his Temple under Christ's blood of the Gospel, II Cor 6:16, **"for ye are the temple of the living"**, I Cor 6:19, **"know ye not that your body is the temple of the Holy Ghost"**. The Alter of God is in each Christian heart representing blood sacrifice, either by animal in the Old Covenant and by Christ's blood on the cross within the New Covenant.

Alter: the golden alter before the Throne in Heaven in Rev 8:3. Heb (4196) *an alter (2076) to slaughter an animal in sacrifice, kill, offer, do sacrifice and slay.* Greek (2379) *a place of sacrifice (2378) the act of sacrifice (2380) to rush, breathe hard or blow smoke by the act of sacrifice by fire.* It is very important to understand the definitions of Alter. In Hebrew, under the Law of Moses, the Alter represented a blood sacrifice to *slaughter*, *kill*, *offer* and *slay* an animal for our sins on the Alter of the Holy of Holies in the Temple by the High Priest once a year. In Greek under the New Covenant, it stands for a different meaning. The Alter in the ancient Temple is now in each Christians heart and represent a place of sacrifice, the act of sacrifice to breath hard by blowing smoke by fire as a sacrifice representing prayers of repentance. What does this mean? The Golden Alter in Rev 8:3 represents incense of prayers from all the Christian Saints, past, present and future as stated in Rev 11:17, **"which art, and wast, and art to come"**. The smoke and fire in Rev 8:4-5 says that the smoke mixed with fire is the prayers of repentance of the Saints gathered in a censer taken from the Golden Alter in the Temple in Heaven. The Golden Alter in Heaven is key in maintaining our salvation through repentance on earth to keep our robes pure and white so that we will not be blotted out of the Lamb's Book of life for our sins as stated in Rev 3:3-5, **"which have not defiled their garments"**. For a Christian to not defile their garment, they must maintain an "often" repentance before God as stated in Heb 9:25-26. The New Covenant under Christ requires an "OFTEN" repentance, not once a year.

 Note: Most of the Angels bringing wrath of the Seals, Trumpets and Vials either stood by or came out of the Alter (Alter of Prayer of Repentance) before fulfilling their assigned WRATH upon man.

Rev Chapter 8 Unbroken Timeline, 7th Seal & first four Trumpets and Beginning of Wrath

Rev 8:1-7 - 7th Seal Opened with silence in Heaven for one half hour. The space of one-half hour represents a moment of silent prayer respecting all the prayers of the fallen Saints killed by the wrath of war and martyred in the name of God during the opening of the first six Seals. In verse two, there were seven Angels that stood before God which are the seven Angels of the seven Churches in Rev 1:20 and each given a Trumpet to blow. The Angels of the Churches was given the authority to sound the seven Trumpets of wrath. In verse three thru five, another Angel came with a golden censer filled with the prayers of the persecuted fallen Saints before the Alter of God and cast them with smoke and fire onto the earth. In verse six the seven Angels prepare to blow their Trumpets. **Note**: The opening of the 7th Seal is a marker or dividing point in time where the first six Seals is vengeance wrath upon the nations or man on man ferocity such as world depopulation and secret society's hatred for Christianity representing goodness and purity. The Wrath displayed in the first 6 Trumpets come from Man and Satan to destroy the Church in preparation for the coming of the Anti-Christ incarnate. The opening of the first six Vials is God's hardcore supernatural WRATH upon ungodly man that worship the Beast. The vehemence of the seven Seals, Trumpets and Vials are all considered to be WRATH either by Man, Satan or God.

The beginning of WRATH in Rev 6:17
The 1st Half of the Tribulation is WRATH by Man not God

1st Trumpet Rev 8:7 - (Man's WAR) sounded by the Angel of the 1st Church of Ephesus bringing wrath of hail and fire mingled with blood cast upon earth burning 1/3 of trees and all green grass indicating a major nuclear WAR.

2nd Trumpet Rev 8:8-9 - (Man's WAR) sounded by the Angel of the Church of Smyrna casting a great mountain burning with fire into the sea turning 1/3 of the sea to blood, destroying 1/3 of sea life and 1/3 of ships indicating another nuclear WAR.

3rd Trumpet Rev 8:10-11 - (Man's WAR) sounded by the Angel of the Church of Pergamos casting a great star from heaven burning as a lamp falling upon 1/3 of rivers and fountains of waters making them bitter to drink. This star was called Wormwood killing many men due to its bitterness. In Greek "wormwood" means, #894, *a type of bitterness or calamity* and in Heb means, *to curse or a poison*. The word "wormwood" is mentioned as a bitter wrath in Jerm 9:15, Amos 5:7 and Rev 8:11. These verses indicate that this star was a nuclear missile of WAR started by a General as a punishment for forsaking Gods commandments in Jerm 9:12-15 **"the land perisheth and is burned up like a wilderness, that none passes through"**, it became a nuclear wasteland. This chapter was speaking to the lost sheep of the house of Israel where Christ left his Church in the wilderness as the USA and Great Britain, brothers where they became Babylon in the last days. Jeremiah 10:15-25 confirm this nuclear war by stating in verse 25, **"for they have eaten up Jacob, and devoured him, and consumed him, and have made his habitation desolate"** for this was to happen in the last days to the "pastors" in verse 21. Jerm 3:16&18 states a timeline **"in those days"** meaning in Gen 49:1 telling Jacob, **"that I may tell you that which shall befall you in the last days"**. The whole book of Jeremiah was written for the last day Church. The word "paster" in Jerm 10:21, Hebrew meaning ref 7462, *to tend a flock, graze, herdman, sheep, shepherd* indicate it was speaking to the last day Church. The tenants of the Temple under the Law of Moses in Israel were priests and in the New Testament are pastors or shepherds tending the flock of Christ's Church indicating that Jeremiah was speaking directly to the last day Church.

4th Trumpet Rev 8:12-13 - (Man's WAR) sounded by the Angel of the Church of Thyatira smiting 1/3 of light during night and day from the sun, moon and star. Verse thirteen identifies an Angel flying through Heaven saying **Woe, Woe, Woe** is coming to the next three Trumpets. "Woe" in Greek means, 3759, *grief* and woeful in Hebrew, #605, *to be frail, feeble or melancholy, desperate, incurable and sick.* This indicates that great wrath of grief and sorrow is next. With these facts, how can Christians say that the 1st half of the Trib is not considered WRATH when it clearly states in Rev 6:17 and Woe in Rev 8:13.

Revelation Chapter 9 Beginning of the 1st WOE Rev 8:13&9:12, unbroken timeline.

5th Trumpet Rev 9:1-10 – Two years mark of the 1st half of Trib: Sounded by the Angel of the Church of Sardis where a star or one of the seven Angels of Christ's Churches fell from Heaven opening the **"bottomless pit"**. Verse 3-10 describes the locust that came out of the pit to torment man for five months. The term five months are mentioned in verses 5&10 which is extremely meaningful for this Trumpet is the first key in establishing a timeline for the Seals, Trumpets and Vials.

Rev 9:11-12 Give the name of their King, in Hebrew he is called Abaddon and in Greek, Apollyon. In Hebrew Abaddon means, *Angle of the Abyss* and in Greek, #3, *a destroying angle.* In Hebrew Apollyon also means, *the Angel of the Abyss* and in Greek, 623, *a destroyer as Satan*, 575, *separation, departure, cessation, completion, reversal*, 3639, *ruin, death, punishment, destruction.* These two names separate man from God as Lucifer the Angel of light and Satan as the destroyer of man's souls. The names of Abaddon and Apollyon are names of Lucifer, Satan the Devil himself where he is released from the bottomless pit onto the earth bringing death to man, where he is given full power for 42 months in Rev 13:5 after the blowing of the 7th Trumpet that marks the middle of the seven-year Tribulation Period.

The 5th Trumpet in Rev 9:1-12 is sounded by an Angel called a "star" falling from Heaven having the key to open the bottomless pit. When the pit was opened the smoke darkened the sun bringing locusts with great power to sting men without the Seal of God but to not hurt the green grass. The men with the Seal are the 144000 in the 6th Seal at approx. the **10th month mark** of the first half of the Trib. As scorpions, they were to torment man for five months and man will seek death but not find it for death will flee from them. Verse 7-10 describes the shape of the locust and they hurt men five months. Verse 11, they had a King over them which is the Angel of the bottomless pit called in Hebrew Abaddon and in Greek Apollyon. This creature is Satan the Devil to soon be the Anti-Christ man god. Verse 12 ends the 1st WOE. These verses clearly show in how Satan comes onto the earth in the 5th trumpet but does not take his power for 42 months as the Anti-Christ till Rev 13:5 is fulfilled in the middle of the seven years.

6ᵗʰ Trumpet Rev 9:13-21 - Sounded by the Angel of the Church of Philadelphia where he releases the four Angels bound in the river Euphrates. They commanded an army of horseman of two hundred thousand, thousand or two million soldiers to kill 1/3 of man from the fire, smoke and brimstone (modern nuclear and conventional warfare) that came out of their mouth. This event lasted for **"an hour, and a day, and a month, and a year for to slay the third part of men"**. These verses are speaking of a great war with China where they cross over into Europe on a dry Euphrates Rever and China is destroyed by the upcoming Anti-Christ. China, to date, is the only nation in the world that boast they can produce a two-million-man army. These verses describe their power being in their mouth and tails indicating modern warfare of tanks, planes and missiles indicating that this wrath is from man not God. This nuclear war destroys 1/3 of man. The people of the world still refused to repent of their worship of gold and silver idols, devil worship that they cannot see, hear or walk.

Major Event: Satan is released from the Bottomless Pit at the two-year mark of the first half of the Tribulation as explained in the note below. He has 1 ½ years to gain full power in Rev 13:5.

Important Note: The 5ᵗʰ Trumpet lasted five months as stated in verses 5 and 10 which give us the first major key in determining the timeline of the book of Revelation. The 6ᵗʰ Trumpet gives the 2ⁿᵈ key in nailing down the timeline for it last one year one month one day and one hour or approx. 13 months up to the very middle of the Trib. We know that the 7ᵗʰ Trumpet marks the middle of the seven-years of the Tribulation Period, therefore, when we add five months and 13 months, it gives us a total of 18 months or 1½ years. When we subtract one and half years from three and a half years we get two years, therefore, the 5ᵗʰ Trumpet was blown at the two-year mark of the first half of the seven-year Tribulation. This is an accurate calculation that is completely overlooked and a fact that we as Christians cannot ignore. From this computation, we can determine the length of the seven Seals and first four Trumpets to be approx. 2.2 months each when we divide these eleven events into 24 months or two-year period. The last half of the Tribulation is simple for all we have to do is divide 7 Vials into 3½ years and we get 6 months per each Vial. We must understand that God has his own timeline and we as fallible man can only compute what is logical to us as humans.

Revelation Chapter 10 Continuation of the 6th Trumpet and unbroken timeline

Rev 10:1-7 Another mighty Angel came down from Heaven clothed with a cloud and rainbow upon his head with his face as the sun and feet as pillars of fire indicating this is Christ Jesus. He had a "little book opened" which is the

Gospel or Holy Bible where he set his right foot upon the sea and left foot on the earth roaring as a lion. This is Christ the Lion of Judah crying and seven thunders uttered their voices which I believe to be the Angels of the seven Churches. This "little book opened" is the Gospel of Jesus and the same as the "roll" in Eze 3:1-5 where both Apostle John and the Prophet Ezekiel were to go preach to the lost sheep of the house of Israel as Christ's Church to take place in the last days. The subject of the book of Ezekiel is in direct reference to the living creature listed as a Man, Lion, an Ox and an eagle in Exe 1:10 and 10:14. This living creature is the four brigades of the house of Israel, Christ's lost sheep scattered abroad in James 1:1 and I Peter 1:1 where Jesus himself sent his Gospel in Matt 10:6 and 15:24. After the voices shouted their message, John began to write but a loud voice from heaven told him to not write and seal it up just as Daniel was told to seal it up till the time of the end in Dan 12:4. At this moment of time, the mighty Angel with his feet on the earth that had the little book looked up to God in Heaven and shouted in verse 6, **"that there should be time no longer"**. The term **be time no longer** is very important for it differentiates the middle of the 1st half of the Tribulation as a separation point from the 2nd half. The phrase "time no longer" ends the time of man's self-rule. As long as the world is under man's self-rule, God could not show any type of supernatural wrath. Time stopping in this verse distinctly indicates a break or marker of time separating the first and second half of the seven-years. Chapter 11 explains the difference between the two halves of 1260 days given to the two witnesses in Rev 11:3 and 42 months given to the Anti-Christ as Satan in Rev 13:5-7. These as two different periods of time equaling 3 ½ years each. The difference in days in the 1st half and months in the 2nd half is a distinct factor in dividing the two halves.

The END of the 1st Half or Mid-Mark of the seven-year Tribulation

7th **Trumpet Rev 10:7-11&11:15** – Sounded by the 7th Angel of the Church of Laodiceans with the authority of Jesus as the Lamb or Lion of Judah.
Rev 10:7 This is one of the most important verses in the book of Revelation for at this moment, the sounding of the 7th Trumpet marks three major events:
Event 1: it marks exactly the middle of the 1st Half of the seven-year Tribulation Period.
Event 2: verse seven states, **"But in the days of the voice of the seventh angel, when he shall begin to sound, the mystery of God should be finished, as he hath declared to his servants the prophets"**. This verse match Rev 10:6 where there will "be time no longer" where man's self-rule ends and the Gospel is "finished". These verses mark the middle of the Tribulation where Gods Word, Christ's Gospel of the Church and all Prophecy given *to his servants the prophets* are "finished". This completion of time is confirmed in Daniel 12:7 and Rev 10:6&7 when it states **"that there should be time no longer"** and **"the mystery of God should be finished"**. The last sermon given

on earth will be when the two Witnesses are killed by the Beast in Rev 11:7 for it states, **"And when they shall have finished their testimony, the beast that ascendeth out of the bottomless pit shall make war against them, and shall overcome them, and kill them"**. No man can receive Christ or God after this point in time for God's Spirit of the Gospel is finished on earth and taken away fulfilling II Thess 2:7 at the middle point of the seven-year Tribulation. This event begins the 42-month reign of the Anti-Christ and the pouring of the seven Vials of WRATH on those that take the Mark of the Beast. This separate time period is to complete the 3 ½ years given to the Anti-Christ

Event 3: This event ends Gods Kingdom on earth where man rules himself in Rev 11:15, **"The kingdoms of this world are become the kingdoms of our Lord and of his Christ"**. An important note: the sounding of the 7th Trumpet is mentioned twice. The 1st time in Rev 10:7 and the 2nd time in Rev 11:15 indicating a time marker for certain events. The authority to rule the earth was given to Adam first, then to his Patriarchs, then to Jesus and through his Apostles to the Seven Churches. Research this fact for yourself for it is in the Scriptures. God is not in control of this earth today; the Church was left that responsibility and why the earth has become so evil. The Church has failed God and is why he spews the Church out of his mouth as stated in Rev 3:16. The salt of the earth is gone and Satan has taken over the Churches authority through infiltration.

Rev 10:8-11 A voice from Heaven told John to go to the mighty Angel with his feet on the earth and *"take the little book"* and eat it up making his belly bitter but sweet as honey in his mouth. John did as commanded and was told in Rev 10:11, **"And he said unto me, Thou must prophesy again before many peoples, and nations, and tongues, and kings"**. The little book spoken of in this chapter is the prophecies and Gospel given to John the Apostle to write the book of Revelation to preach and teach end time prophecy to the seven Churches.

Important Note: The story of the "little book" as the Scriptures of the Old Covenant and the Gospel of the New Covenant are also mentioned in Ezekiel 3:1-4 where the little book is called a "roll" and Ezekiel was told to eat just as John was told to eat. Both Ezekiel and John, the little book and roll was bitter in their belly but sweet in the mouth. Both were sent to the house of Israel to teach God's Word as the "roll" and "little book" is God's Holy Scriptures, Eze 3:1, **"eat this roll, and go speak unto the house of Israel"**. John was sent to the lost sheep of the house of Israel in Matt 10:6 and 15:24, **"but go rather to the lost sheep of the house of Israel"** which is the seven Churches. Clearly, the seven Churches were in Heaven at the blowing of the 7th Trumpet.

Revelation Chapter 11 A Continuation of Commentary from sounding of the 7th Trumpet. There are two accounts of the sounding of the 7th Trumpet. The first in Rev 10:7 and again in Rev 11:15. This means that all the commentary events spoken of from Rev 10:7 thru chapter eleven occurred immediately after the sounding of the 7th Trumpet in an unbroken timeline.

Rev 11:1-2 These verses are commentary by John in how he was given a rod and told to measure the newly rebuilt Temple and alter and the people that worship but to leave out the outer court. This is the new Temple in Jerusalem that the Gentiles shall tread under foot for forty-two months or 3 ½ years. The term in verse two, **"tread under foot forty and two months"** is key for it directly relates to Dan 11:31 and 12:11 that occur in the last half of the Tribulation after the blood sacrifice has been taken away.

Rev 11:3 **"And I will give power unto my two witnesses, and they shall prophesy a thousand two hundred and threescore days"** which is 3½ years or 1260 days exactly. These witnesses are the two olive trees and candlesticks standing before God on earth. We must note that this verse is speaking of the two witnesses that prophecy during the 1st Half of the Tribulation in place of the Church that has been taken. The term of "forty and two-months" verses "a thousand two hundred and threescore days" indicate two distinct different periods of time lasting 3½ years each. Forty-two months represent the last half of the Tribulation in reference to the New Temple and 1260 days represent the first half in subject to the two witnesses that the Anti-Christ kills in Rev 11:7.

Rev 11:4-6 speak of the two witnesses as the two olive trees having two candlesticks standing before God on earth. God sealed them from death during their 3½ years of preaching and teaching to the whole world for no man could harm them for fire would proceed out of their mouth and devour them. If anyone tried to hurt them, in the same manner they would be killed. Clearly, they could not be killed! These two witnesses had power over the earth and waters for it to not rain, turn water to blood and plague men as often as they willed.

Rev 11:7 The two witnesses are killed by the Beast or the Anti-Christ. We must remember that the angel Abaddon which is Satan the Anti-Christ was released from the bottomless pit in Rev 9:1&11 at the two-year mark of the 1st Half of the Trib. Satan has 1½ years to gain total power and the 7th Trumped marks the middle of the Tribulation where the Gospel is "finished".

Important Question: This brings up a very important question! If the Church was still present during the 1st half of the Tribulation, why would God have to send two witnesses also having two candlesticks that represent the Church? Rev 1:20 clearly state that a candlestick is the Church for it says, **"and the seven candlesticks which thou sawest are the seven churches"**. If the Church was present during the 1st half of the seven-year Tribulation, the two witnesses would not be needed. The Church has been taken just as I Thess 4:14-18, I Cor 15:51 and Dan 12:1-2 states to escape wrath confirmed in Luke 21:36 and I Thess 1:10. God has to send the two witnesses believed to be Enoch and Elijah for they never saw death. The Scriptures are clear that all men are to see a physical death as recorded in Heb 9:27. Their taking without seeing death is found in Gen 5:24 and II Kings 2:11. It is believed that Elijah is to return during the time of trouble in Malachi 4:5-6.

Rev 11:8-12 explain events after the death of the two witnesses in how they lay in the streets of Jerusalem for 3 and ½ days without burial and how the whole world rejoiced by giving gifts one to another due to their torment. After 3 and ½ days the two witnesses came alive and stood on their feet and the world feared, **"And they heard a great voice from heaven saying unto them, Come up hither. And they ascended up to heaven in a cloud; and their enemies beheld them"**. This event fulfilled prophecy for the two witnesses as Enoch and Elijah had never seen death. They died and was resurrected just as Jesus and all his Bride of the Church ascended into the clouds fulfilling the requirements of the death of a Saint as stated in I Thess 4:14-18. If a person is to see Jesus in Heaven, we must go through this process of dying and being resurrected just as Jesus to be like him, Christian. A lot of Christians fail to understand in why the Rapture or taking of the Church is necessary, this process has to be completed prior to wrath for the Church is not of WRATH as clearly stated in I Thess 1:10, 5:9, Luke 21:36, I Cor 15:51-52 and Dan 12:1-2. If you don't believe in the pre-tribulation rapture or taking of the Church into the clouds, then you don't believe in the Scriptures for they are very clear on this subject. My Heaven help you.

Rev 11:13 about an hour after the death of the two witnesses there was a great earthquake and a tenth part of Jerusalem was destroyed killing seven thousand people and a remnant of the people gave glory to the God of heaven.

Rev 11:14 the 2nd WOE is past and the 3rd WOE in coming.

End of the 2nd WOE and beginning of the 3rd Woe

7th Trumpet Rev 11:13 & Rev 10:7 - Sounded by the Angel of the Church of Laodiceans. This is the second time the blowing of the 7th Trumpet is mentioned for the first is in Rev 10:7. The blowing of the 7th Trumpet is significant for three major events occurred at this immediate time to be specified. It was to be highlighted in Scripture that the middle marker of the tribulation was to be clearly identified. The Gospel of Christ, all Prophecy and the end of man's self-rule are now completed and finished belonging to God. God could not begin his supernatural WRATH till man's self-rule is complete so he can bring justified judgment.

Rev 11:16-17 the twenty-four Elders and all Saints in Heaven fell down before God and worshiped him saying **"We give thee thanks, O Lord God Almighty, which art, and wast, and** in these verses **art to come; because thou hast taken to thee thy great power, and has reigned"**. This is also an indicator that God and Christ is now in full control with power and reigns the earth completing the Gospel and all is finished for the next verse confirms this fact.

Rev 11:18-19 there are several events that occur in these verses.

Event One: the nations or kingdoms of man are angry and Gods wrath is come.

Event Two: time for the dead in Christ to be judged and to reward the servants, prophets and saints that fear the name of God.

Event Three: God destroy them that destroy the earth.

Event four: The Temple of God was opened in Heaven and the ark of his testament was seen for the very first time ever and due to this great event, there were lightnings and voices and thundering and an earthquake and great hail.

Note: It is very important to understand that the three events that occurred in Rev 10:7 and Rev 11:18-19 all occurred immediately after the blowing of the 7th Trumpet marking the middle of the Tribulation.

Revelation Chapter 12 Commentary by John that can fit into the unbroken timeline of history in the Past, Present and Future skipping through time. Chapters 11 marks the middle of the Trib when the 7th Trumpet is blown in verse 15 and chapters 12-13 are John's clarification of events that occur prior to and during the first half of the Tribulation. Chapters 14-15 are events that occur in the middle of the Tribulation preparing to pour the seven Vials of WRATH. Chapter 16 begins the 2nd Half of the Trib. of Great WRATH with the pouring of the seven Vials.

The first verse is commentary describing past history back to Christ's Birth. We must remember throughout the book of Revelation it mentions God's Word and Church being in the *Past*, *Present* and *Future*, therefore, John's commentary also covers the past, present and future that do not break the timeline. The timeline runs from Genesis verse one through the last verse in Revelation and this "timeline" in God's Word has never been broken.

Rev 12:1 John was told to write of a great wonder appearing in Heaven, a woman clothed with the sun and moon under her feet with a crown of twelve stars. This woman being with child pained to be delivered in birth. Who is this woman? It is the twelve tribes of the house of Israel where Jesus our Lord was born out of the tribe of the lion of Judah, the Lamb of God. This Lion or Lamb was the only creature with the authority to open the Seals, Trumpets and Vials in Rev 5:5.

Verses 3&4 is commentary of past history where Satan called Lucifer was kicked out of Heaven.

Rev 12:2-4 There appeared another wonder in heaven called a red dragon having seven heads and ten horn with seven crowns upon his head where his tail drew 1/3 of the stars in Heaven where he was cast onto the earth. The

Dragon stood before the woman which was ready to deliver for, he was to devour her child as soon as it was born. This is Satan the Devil that has tried to kill Jesus, his Gospel and his Servants from the time that he was born two thousand years ago.

Rev 12:5 The woman birthed a man child who was to rule all nations with a rod of iron and his child was caught up unto God in Heaven where he sat on his throne. This verse has several important meanings. We know that the man child was Jesus Christ our Lord and Savior but he was caught up into Heaven where it is recorded in Acts 1:8-9. Jesus left his Apostles to spread his Gospel just as the Husbandmen in the parable of Matt 21:33-46. The question is, if Jesus was caught up into heaven, who was to rule all nations with a rod of iron as verse 5 states. According to Acts 1:8-9, and Matt 28:18-20, **"But ye shall receive power"**, Christ left his Church with full power and authority to rule with a rod of iron after his ascension into the clouds. Therefore, the term *"don't worry, God is in control"* is not a true statement for Jesus clearly left the Church in charge of the spiritual earth just a God first left it to Adam, the patriarchs and then to Jesus. The Christians that say God is in control is wrong for Christ clearly left the Church in total control and authority.

Commentary placing the woman at the middle of the seven-year Tribulation.

Rev 12:6 The woman as the twelve tribes of Israel or the sealed 144,000 fled into the wilderness to escape the Beast and Anti-Christ where God prepared for **"a thousand two hundred and threescore days"** (1260 days) or 3 and ½ years.

Commentary dating back possibly millions of years where Satan the Dragon and his angels made WAR with God and kicked out of Heaven.

Rev 12:7-9 Describes the war in Heaven between the Arch Angel Michael and Satan the Dragon with 1/3 of the Angels. Satan and his Angels lost the war and was kicked out of Heaven onto the earth to deceive the whole world.

Commentary of the 3rd WOE taking place at the 7th Trumpet in the Middle of the Trib.

Rev 12:10-17 A loud voice from Heaven crying, **"Now is come salvation, and strength, and the kingdom of our God"**. This verse is saying that salvation is come where man's kingdom is finished and God's Kingdom begins which the word "finished" occur in the middle of the Trib. The rest of this verse and verse 11 speak of how Satan the accuser was cast down accusing our brethren day and night but overcame by the blood of the Lamb and the word of their testimony. Verse 12 begins the 3rd WOE to the inhibiters of the earth

127

and sea for the devil is come down to you having great wrath because he knows that he has only a short time. Verse 13&14 says the Dragon that was cast out persecuted the woman [twelve tribe of Israel] which brough forth the man child, Jesus, were given two wings of an eagle to fly into the wilderness where she is nourished for **"a time, and times, and half a time"**, again 3 and ½ years or 1260 days. Verse 15-17 describes in how the woman escapes the Dragon from the flood that proceeded out of his mouth but the earth swallowed it up. The Dragon was wroth with the woman that kept the commandments of God and the testimony of Jesus Christ for they had God's Seal and could not be destroyed.

Revelation Chapter 13 John's Commentary occurs basically in the middle of the Tribulation and describes the rise of the great Beast maintaining the timeline.

Rev 13:1 Describes a **Beast that rises** out of the sand of the seas [the earth] having seven heads, ten horns with the name of blasphemy upon his head and horns which is Satan as the Anti-Christ. This is the political power of the nations establishing their Anti-Christ leader into power during political intrigue of the first half of the seven-year Tribulation. Time reverts in commentary back to the war taking peace from the earth in Rev 6:3-4, the war between the White and Red horses.

Rev 13:2 The Beast that John saw was like unto a leopard with feet as a bear and mouth of a lion where the dragon or Anti-Christ gave him power and the seat of great authority. This "leopard" is the military power of the Anti-Christ found in Daniel's vision in Dan 7:6. Note that the "leopard" is a symbol religious leader of military strength of German to this day. The Leopard Tank of power and strength. There are three great entities of authority during the seven years of tribulation which is the Anti-Christ as Satan the Apotheosis god, the Beast as the military leader and the False Prophet.

**Revelation 13:3
One of the heads of the beast
seemed to have had a fatal wound,
but the fatal wound had been healed.**
RevelationScriptures.com

Symbol of United Nations military power the 1st thru 4th
Beast of Daniel's Dream in Dan 7:6

This is an actual symbol of the NATO/UN statue of current Western power

Important Note: The war of Ezekiel chapters 38 and 39 at the very beginning of the seven-years of Tribulation created this beast. Closely study Daniel chapter seven and the four Beasts of Dan 7:3-7 as the **Lion, bear, leopard** and **beast with great iron teeth**. The Lion with eagles' wings that were plucked represent the first white horse in Rev 6:1 that had a bow of war and crown of great political leadership. This Lion is the western coalition of the United States, Great Britain and all the NATO powers of Europe that occurred during the Ezekiel war matching the current powers going into the tribulation Period. Our current western political system become this great Beast of Daniel. Note: white is the color of the UN with NATO as its military power. The Bear is the red horse of Russia in Rev 6:3 that takes peace from the earth creating world war where the white horse and red horse does battle called "Hamon-god" during the Ezekiel 38 war at the very beginning of the seven-year Trib. The bear of Russia is destroyed and buried in Ezekiel 39:6,9,11 & 15. Russia, during this great war, kills the head or crown of the white horse which is the United States as the NATO leader where "the wings thereof were plucked" fulfilling the head being killed in Rev 13:12&14. The first illustration in the pictures above. It kills the head but not the body. The head comes back alive in Rev 13:12 by being revived as the Leopard's military power under the Anti-Christ and given great authority. Note that after all these wars in Rev 13:2, the Leopard has the feet of a Bear (Russia), the mouth of a Lion (USA & UK) where the dragon (Satan or Anti-Christ) gave him great authority. All the worlds military powers that were not destroyed during the battle of the white

130

horse of the USA and red horse of Russia along with all their coalitions during the Ezekiel war is combined and absorbed creating the great military power of the Leopard in Daniels's dream, Dan 7:3-7. The white horse of Rev 6:1 has now become the Leopard of Daniel's 3rd Beast that had the wounded head but did live. We must note that the wounded head is not of a man but of nations of great political and military intrigue. We must also note that the Ezekiel 38&39 war created the Black horse of great worldwide economic failure initiating poverty and the Pale horse of world famine and starvation. Through political and military strategy by world political powers designed by Satan as the Anti-Christ comes to full power during the 1st half of the Tribulation. All the armies of the world combined to create the last and final 4th Beast of Daniel's dream called the "Beast with iron teeth" of great military power, Rev 13:4, **"who is able to make war with him"**.

Rev 13:3 Describes one of the heads of the Beast being killed as explained in the note above. This event takes place in Rev 6:1-4 during the Ezekiel 38 War and verse 3 states, **"and I saw one of its heads as it were wounded to death; and his deadly wound was healed"**. This deadly wound is the head of NATO of the White Horse in Rev 6:1-2 where the Red Horse killed it in battle in Rev 6:3-4 before Red Russia was destroyed. This event is mentioned in Daniel's dream as the Lion in Dan 7:4 where it's **"wings therefore were plucked"**, as recorded in Rev 13:3 and 13:12 where its head was killed but did live. Verse 4 gives this wounded Beast great power for being revived from death.

Rev 13:5-10 Describes this Beast that was killed but came back alive as the Anti-Christ Beast System for it states in verses 5 thru 9:

a. Power was given him to speak great blasphemies to continue **"forth and two months"** or 3½ years during the last half of the seven-year Tribulation.

b. It was given unto him to make war with the Saints and to overcome them and power was given him over all kindreds, tongues and nations.

c. All on earth were to worship him that was not written in the book of life that love Jesus from the foundations of the world.

Main Event: Satan the Devil called the Anti-Christ or Beast is now in full power given to him by the people of the world in Rev 13:5 allowed by God, "and power was given unto him to continue forty and two months", which is 3½ years of the last half of the Trib.

Important Note: There are two distinct and different Beast Systems mentioned in the Old and New Testaments that we must separate and divide:

God's Kingdom as the four Beast System
Righteous Church

Rev 4:6-7, Ezek 1:5,10,15&10:14 as a "wheel"
the Cherub/calf, man, lion and eagle are the four
brigades of the twelve tribes of Israel as the
Church the lost sheep in Matt 10:6, 15:24, Ezek 3:1-5
And Acts 10:36 which is the 5th Stone Kingdom
mentioned in Dan 2:32-35&44-45 as the Church
destroys Satan's four world kingdoms of Babylon,
Med-Persian, Greek and Roman empires as stated in
Dan 2:44-45 and Matt 21:44.

The Four Brigades of Israel is Christ's Church as
stated above given the Gospel as the *roll* in Eze 3:1-5
and *the little book* in Rev 10:9-11 given to the
"shepherd, the stone of Israel" in Gen 49:24, only the
Lion/Christ the Lamb as the Church could open the
book in Rev 5:5.

Eze 1:10	Eze 10:14	Rev 4:5
Man	Cherub/Calf	Lion
Lion	Man	Calf
Ox	Lion	Man
Eagle	Eagle	Eagle

Note: the difference between the three verses in order
by name; Ox, Calf or Bull has the same meaning in
Hebrew, Cherub in Hebrew means imaginary figure
which is the calf of Manasseh in Duet 33:17, Gen 49:24
the stone Church as the house of Israel. The Lion is
Christ from the tribe of Judah as the Lamb which is
The Cornerstone of the Church.

Satan's three Beast System
Evil Mystery Babylon

The Anti-Christ, Beast and False Prophet
of Daniel's dream in Dan 7:3-7 of four
Beasts are the End Time Beast System

Four World Empires under Satan
Daniel's dream of the image in Dan 2:32
Head of Gold- **Babylonian** Empire
Breast & Arms of Silver- **Med-Persian**
Belly & Thighs of Brass- **Greek**
Legs of Iron and Feet of clay- **Rome**
Our modern system is still under
old Roman corporate law controlled by
the Roman Church that never died.

Beasts of Daniel's Dream in Dan 7:3-7
Lion having eagle's wings where his
wings are plucked or wounded in
Rev 13:3 & the White Horse of Rev 6:1
Bear with three ribs in the mouth
Leopard with four wings and four heads
Beast with great Iron Teeth having
Ten horns dreadful and terrible devoured
all.

Note: The White Horse in Rev 6:1-2 and
the Lion in Dan 7:4 is the same. The
Red Horse in Rev 6:3-4 and the Bear in
Dan 7:5 is the same creating a war
between red Russia and Mystery
Babylon.

132

This illustration are the symbols of the twelve tribes of Israel the four Brigades of 3 tribes each.

Compare the four Horses of Rev 6:1-8 to Daniel's four Beasts in Dan 7:3-7

Rev 6:1-8	Dan 7:3-7
1st Seal the **White Horse** is Mystery Babylon under UN control prior to its destruction.	Daniel's **Lion** is also Mystery Babylon where the Red Horse plucks its wings
2nd Seal the **Red Horse** is Red Russia making war with the white horse where Russia is destroyed in the valley of Hamon-gog.	Daniel's **Bear** is the red Bear of Russia having three ribs in its teeth rising up to make war and devour but it is destroyed.
3rd Seal the **Black Horse** came extreme economic destruction to the word created by the war between the white and red horses.	Daniel's **Leopard** became the aftermath of military and political structure of the Anti-Christ due to war of the red and white horses.
4th Seal the **Pale Horse** is destruction of the Economy creating great famine throughout the world bringing death and hell to kill 1/4th of the earth by the sword (war) hunger and disease.	Daniel's **Beast with Iron Teeth** having ten horns combining all nations and armies controlled by the Anti-Christ diverse from all the other beasts with great authority.

Rev 13:11 Describes another Beast that came up from the earth out of the bottomless pit in Rev 9:1 at the sounding of the 5th Trumpet. This Beast has two horns like a lamb and speak as a dragon. This verse indicate that he becomes the Anti-Christ Beast System. Note that the 5th Trumpet occurs at the two-year mark of the 1st half of the Tribulation where it takes him 1 and ½ years to come to full power where he has 42 months in the last half in Rev 13:5 & Dan 7:25. Rev 13:12 This Beast **"exerciseth all the power of the first beast"**. Who is the 1st Beast? It is referring to the first Beast of Daniel's dream in Dan 7:4 as the Lion which is compared to the Lion of Judah in Rev 4:7 which is considered a righteous Beast. Satan is emulating Christ's Church of the Lamb or Lion of Judah (Christ) to his Lion as his Beast System creating a world religion for the world to follow, **"and causeth the earth and them which dwell therein to worship the first beast"**. It states in verse 11,**"and he had horns like a lamb, and he spake as a dragon"**. Satan is imitating the Lamb of God for his one world religion, the False Prophet. This verse goes on to say,

"the first beast, whose deadly wound was healed". This verse explains in how the head or crown of the white horse (Babylon or NATO of the UN) in the 1ˢᵗ Seal was killed in this verse and confirmed in Rev 13:14 and plucked in Dan 7:4. This is where the Red Horse or red Bear of Russia kills the head of the white horse but the white horse of Rev 6:1-2 survives and its head or "deadly wound was healed" becoming the powerful Anti-Christ Beast System under the Dragon, Satan from the Bottomless Pit. Study the beast systems listed in the illustrations above.

Rev 13:13-17 Describes the power of the surviving white horse and the lion of Daniel's dream as the Dragon's Beast System:
He makes fire come down form heaven in front of the world.

He deceives all the world by miracles from his given power.

He made an image of the beast **"which had the wound by a sword, and did live"** giving life to the image (White Horse and the Beast Lion) for it to speak political intrigue for the world to follow as a military and political New World Order.

He killed every person on earth that did not worship the image which is the leader of the New One World Beast System as the Anti-Christ or the Apotheosis, man god.

"He causeth all, both small and great, rich and poor, free and bond, to receive a mark in their right hand, or in their foreheads".

"no man might buy or sell, save he that had the mark, or the name of the beast, or the number of his name".

Rev 13:18 Gives wisdom for the Church to better understand the coming of the Beast System in the last days. The number of the Beast System is **"Six hundred threescore and six"** or 666.

Revelation Chapter 14 John's Commentary of the prior Sealed 144000 standing on Mount Sion with Jesus the Lamb at the middle of the Tribulation after the blowing of the 7ᵗʰ Trumpet and before the pouring of the 1ˢᵗ Vial.

Rev 14:1-6 (opened by the voice of the Lamb Jesus Christ) Describes a Lamb, **"lo, a Lamb stood on the mount Sion and with him an hundred forth and four thousand having his Father's name written in their foreheads"**. This verse is speaking of Christ sealing his 144,000 Saints for his father's name (God) was written on their foreheads. Christ is standing on mount Sion representing his Church and New Jerusalem for the Greek meaning of Sion in Ref#4622 of the Strong's Concordance, *a hill of Jerusalem* and *the Church*. Question? If the Church was present on earth at this time, why would the 144,000 Sealed Christians represent Sion as the Church? The reason is simple, the Church was taken or Raptured at the beginning of the seven-year Tribulation meaning that the Sealed Saints took the place of the Church to rule in the Millennial Reign just as Noah were to repopulated the earth! The two witnesses in the first half represent the Church with each having a candlestick and the 144,000 Saints represent the Church body. The 144,000 Sealed at the opening of the 6th Seal in Rev 6:12 marks the one year and one month point in the first half of the Trib. This is when the Lamb as the Church sealed them at the opening of the 6th Seal. We must also note the similarities between the 144,000 Sealed and the two Witnesses. The Church is called a *virgin bride* and the sealed 144,000 are called *virgins* with a song from God representing the absent Church. Rev 11:4 describes the two Witnesses as two olive trees having a candlestick each. Throughout the Old and New Testaments, an olive tree represents God's Temple or Christ's Church. Rev 1:20 clearly state that a candlestick is the Church. If the Church was present during the first or last half of the seven years of Tribulation, the 144,000 and the two witnesses would not be necessary for the Church is the salt of the earth for it has been taken prior to wrath in Rev 6:17.

Rev 14:1-5 A loud voice from Heaven sounded as if it were a great thunder and voices of harpers with harps singing a new song before the throne. The four Beasts representing the lion, calf, man and eagle and the elders, where no one knew the song except the redeemed *virgins* [represents the Church] of the 144,000. They were not defiled by women that follow the Lamb being the "first fruits" without fault before God. These 144,000 were saved during the opening of the first five Seals.

Rev 14:6-13 (1st Angel) List six consecutive Angels flying in Heaven maintaining a constant timeline after the Lamb speaks:

The 1st Angel occurs at the very beginning of the Tribulation where man is saved in the first half for the Gospel is finished in the middle in Rev 10:7, 11:7 and Dan 12:7. The 6th Angel occurs in the middle of the Trib. when the Anti-Christ kills all that refuse the Mark except the Sealed 144,000. No one is saved in the last half for all are killed that do not take the Mark except for the Sealed 144,000 as stated in Rev 13:15. When the Anti-Christ kills the two Witnesses after finishing their Gospel in Rev 11:7, all Christians on earth are killed by the 1st Sickle which is a mercy death by Christ himself. The "finished" Gospel by the two Witnesses and the Gospel being "finished" in Rev 10:7 and Dan 12:7 at the blowing of the 7th Trumpet, clearly indicate that the Gospel on earth is completely finished. We know that the number 7 is God's number of completion so, notice that this event occurred at the 7th Trumpet in the middle of the Trib. and each of these three verses happens in the 7th verse, the Gospel is complete.

Rev 14:6 - 1st Angel, flying in Heaven having the everlasting Gospel **"and**

I saw another angel in the midst of heaven" preaching to every nation kindred, tongue and people warning of judgment that follows, **"for the hour of his judgment is come"** beginning of wrath as first recorded in Rev 6:17 when Babylon falls.

The fall of Babylon takes place at the opening of the 6th Seal at the one year, one month mark of the first half of the Tribulation as explained by Commentary in Rev 14:8, 17:1-18 and 18:1-24.

Rev 14:8 - 2nd Angel, saying, **"Babylon is fallen, is fallen, that great city, because she made all nations drink of the wine of the wrath of her fornication"**. This event occurred at the opening of the 6th Seal where wrath began in Rev 6:17.

The 3rd Angel occurs in the middle of the Tribulation when the Gospel is finished and hard WRATH begins.

Rev 14:9-13 - 3rd Angel with a loud voice warning man that if any man worships the beast and his image or receive his Mark in the forehead or hand, he shall receive WRATH of God. The smoke of their torment will ascend up for ever and ever with no rest day nor night that worship the beast and image or take his mark.

John's commentary in the next few verses explains a very controversial subject in how God preserves his Saints from the WRATH that he brings upon ungodly men.

Authors commentary: Other Biblical verses that prove God always allows his righteous to escape from judgment as the following verses clearly state: I Thess 1:10**, "delivered us from the wrath to come"**, 5:9, **"For God hath not appointed us to wrath"**, Rom 5:9, **"we shall be saved from wrath through him"**, Matt 24:13, **"But he that shall endure unto the end, the same shall be saved"**, Dan 12:1, **"and there shall be a time of trouble, such as never was"** & **"and at that time thy people shall be delivered everyone that shall be found written in the book"**. Clearly by these Scriptures and Dan 12:1, all righteous people will be saved from enduring the seven years of Great Tribulation called the Time of Trouble. The following verses further proves this fact.

Clearly in Jasher 5:1-22 God saved all his righteous people through death prior to the wrath of the Flood, for it states in verse 21, **"And all the sons of men who knew the Lord, died in that year before the Lord brought evil upon them [the Flood]; for the Lord willed them to die, so as not to behold the evil that God would bring upon their brothers and relatives, as he had so declared to do"**. God gave the book of Jasher as a record to the Holy

Scriptures recorded in Joshua 10:13 and II Sam 1:18 proving it's truth.

God saved Noah, his family and two of each animal from the wrath of the flood in Gen chapters 7&8.

God saved Lot and his family from the wrath and total destruction of Sodom and Gomorrah in Genesis chapter 19 where in verse 17 the word **"Escape for thy life; look not behind thee, neither stay thou in all the plain; escape to the mountain, lest thou be consumed"** for the word escape is used in regard to wrath of destruction used to save Lot's family. The word "escape" is used in Luke 21:36 also in respect of escaping the Tribulations period mentioned in all of chapter 21, **"that ye may be accounted worthy to escape all these things that shall come to pass"**. Daniel 12:1 says that we are to be delivered from the time of trouble which is the Tribulation period in the book of Revelation.

Now we come to Rev 14:12-16 where all righteous people are taken through a mercy death prior to God bringing great wrath upon ungodly men in Matt 24:9 & Rev 13:15. We know that the Christians killed in these verses are taken through a mercy death for verses 12-13 proves this fact. All faithful were taken just as in Jasher 5:5&21 prior to the Flood explains. Closely study these verses.

Rev 14:12-16 - the 4th Angel is reaping by the 1st Sickle which is Christ himself sitting on a cloud with a golden crown as the son of man having a sharp sickle. The people reaped in these verses are people of God for verse 12-13 state that they are **"the patience of the saints"** and **"they that keep the commandments of God, and the faith of Jesus"**, **"Blessed are the dead which die in the Lord from henceforth"** that **"they may rest from their labors; and their works do follow them"**. The Angel that sat on the cloud (Christ) thrust in his Sickle and the earth was reaped. Clearly by these two verses, all people killed henceforth through verses 14-16 are Christian Saints through a mercy death in peace just as the thousands or millions of Gods faithful in Jasher 5:1-22 prior to the wrath of the flood as stated above.

Rev 14:17 - the 5th Angel has the 2nd Sickle and came out of the Temple in Heaven having a sickle of DEATH and Hell giving the Anti-Christ the authority to kill all that refuse his mark in Matt 24:9 and Rev 13:15. God's Angel has the sickle but the Anti-Christ does the killing.

Rev 14:18-20 - the 6th Angel came out from the Alter having power over fire and cried to the 5th Angel having the 2nd Sickle to thrust in and reap the clusters of the vine for her grapes are ripe **"and cast it into the great winepress of the wrath of God"**. Verse 20 gives the reader a clear view of this earthly slaughter of blood for it states, **"blood came out of the winepress, even unto the horse bridles by the space of a thousand and six hundred furlongs"**. We must note that the people killed by the Angel with the 2nd Sickle which is the Anti-Christ in Rev 13:15 are not Christian but all unsaved people that refused to take the Mark of the Beast. Their reason could be due to morals, political reasons, patriots or non-Christian religious beliefs such as Muslim, Hindu or any other religion. There will be many people that refuse the Mark that are not Christian.

Revelation Chapter 15 This chapter occurs in the middle of the Trib. immediately after the 7th Trumpet is blown in Rev 10:7 & 11:15. Note that the 7th Trumpet is mentioned twice illustrating in how time reverts back and forth in Commentary but the timeline never changes.

Rev 15:1 A great marvelous sigh in Heaven showing seven Angels having the seven last plagues **"the wrath of God"**. This chapter prepares for the pouring of the seven Vials of WRATH. Note that the word **"wrath of God"** is mentioned twice, in Rev 15:1&7 and again in Rev 16:1 indicating a special kind of WRATH on ungodly man. We must also note that verse one indicates that the 1st and 2nd half of the seven-years of Tribulation is considered WRATH for it states, **"seven angels having the seven last plagues; for in them is filled up the wrath of God"**. According to this verse, if the seven Vials are wrath, then, the seven Seals and Trumpets are also **"the wrath of God"**. This verse clearly describes the seven Seals, Trumpets and Vials as Gods wrath upon the nations that cover seven years. The 1st half is vengeance upon the nations of the world with Seals and Trumpets and the last half is wrath of Vials on godless men that takes the Mark of the Beast.

Rev 15:2-4 describe the Saints standing on a sea of glass mingled with fire claiming victory that were killed by the Beast during the first half of the Tribulation. These Saints sang a song of Moses giving glory to God.

Rev 15:5-8 the temple of the tabernacle of the testimony in Heaven was opened where the seven Angels having the seven plagues came out and one of the four beasts (Lion the Lamb of God Jesus) gave the seven angels seven golden vials full of the **"wrath of God"**. The temple was filled with smoke from God's glory and power and no man could enter till the seven plagues of the seven angels were fulfilled.

John's commentary in the next few verses explains a very controversial subject in how God preserves his Saints from the WRATH that he brings upon ungodly men.

Rev 16:1 A great voice out of the Temple saying to the seven Angels, go your ways and pour out the vials of the **"Wrath of God"** upon the earth.

Rev 16:2 the pouring of the 1st Vial - there fell a noisome and grievous sore upon the men which had the mark of the beast, and upon them which worshipped his image.

Rev 16:3 the pouring of the 2nd Vial - upon the sea and it became as the blood of a dead man and every living soul died in the sea.

Rev 16:4-7 the pouring of the 3rd Vial - upon the rivers and fountains of waters and they became blood. The Lord which **"art"** (Present) and **"wast"** (Past) and **"shall be"** (Future) brings righteous judgment upon the people that killed the Saints and Prophets.

Rev 16:8-9 the pouring of the 4th Vial - upon the sun and power was given unto him to scorch men with fire and great heat that blasphemed the name of God and they repented not to give him glory.

<u>Rev 16:10-11</u> the pouring of the 5<u>th</u> Vial - upon the seat of the beast and his kingdom was full of darkness. They gnawed their tongues for pain and blasphemed the God of Heaven because of their pains and sores and repented not of the sins.

<u>Rev 16:12-14&16</u> the pouring of the 6<u>th</u> Vial - upon the great river Euphrates and the water dried up for the way of the kings of the east (China) might be prepared. Verse 13 speak of the **Dragon** (Satan as the Anti-Christ) **the Beast** (Military and Political System) and **the False Prophet** (World Religious System) where an unclean spirits like frogs come out each of their mouths. These Spirits are devils working miracles which go forth unto the kings of the world to gather themselves to the battle of Armageddon mentioned in verse 16. This verse speaks of a subject that very few Christians understand. Most Christians think that this battle is between the armies of the world but if we closely study this verse, all the kings of the world come together to do battle with God and Christ for the three spirits of the three frogs lead them to face God in the air when he comes back at the very end of the Tribulation. This is clearly a war between God and Man. Satan knows almost to the day of Christ's return in Rev 19:11-19, Rev 1:7 and II Thess 1:7-10, for the kings of the world to prepare for this event called Armageddon. In Rev 16:16 in Greek #717 it means, *a symbol name for* #2022, *to pour upon*, 1909, *superimposition of time, place, and order*, 4023, *astonished*, 4012, *used in various application*. Zondervan's Bible Dictionary copyright 1967 says that Armageddon in Hebrew means "Mount Megiddo", a final battleground between the forces of good and evil. The word Armageddon is mentioned only once in the Bible in Rev 16:16 and note that chapter and verse ends with a six, man's number "It is done" at the pouring of the 7th Vial.

<u>Rev 16:15</u> This verse is completely out of context of this chapter for it is a WARNING to the current Church to be explained below.

Author's Commentary Note: there is a strange thing with Rev 16:15 for it is totally out of context. John is giving a Commentary WARNING to all the Church from the time of Acts 2 up to the taking or Rapture of the Church for it states, **"Behold, I come as a thief, Blessed is he that watcheth and keepeth his garments, lest he walk naked, and they see his shame"**. This is almost the same warning that God gave to the Church in Rev 3:1-5, verse 2, **"Be watchful"**, verse 3, **"received and heard, and hold fast, and repent. If therefore thou shalt not watch I will come on thee as a thief"**, verse 4, **"which have not defiled their garments"**, verse 5, **"He that overcometh, the same shall be clothed in white raiment; and I will not blot out his name out of the book of life"**. There are five words in these verses that are critical in keeping our Salvation by not being blotted out or removed from the book of life. They are, come as a thief, he that <u>watch</u>, and <u>keep our garment clean</u>.

Other key words in how to "<u>overcome</u>" by not defiling our garments in this world is by <u>hearing</u>, <u>receiving</u>, <u>hold fast</u> God's Word, <u>repenting</u> of our sins and always be <u>watchful</u> for his coming. The word thief or "come as a thief" is also critical for a thief always come in the night at an unknown and unpredictable time to kill and destroy, Luke 12:39, *"broken through"* John 10:10 to *"steal"*, *"kill"* and *"destroy"*, I Thess 5:4 *"darkness"*, and II Peter 3:10, *"the day of the Lord will come as a thief in the night"*. Christians are to always watch and be ready for Christ's coming for his Church.

Rev 16:17-21 the pouring of the 7<u>th</u> Vial - upon the air and there came a great voice out of the Temple of Heaven from the Throne saying, **"it is done"**. The Great Tribulation of WRATH is complete and God's plan of his Gospel with sinful man is "done". This verse also fulfills Daniel's 70th week for Dan 9:24 states, **"to finish the transgression, and to make an end of sins, and to make reconciliations for iniquity, and to bring in everlasting righteousness, and to seal up the vision and prophecy, and to anoint the most Holy"**. IT IS DONE. Verse 18&19, in Heaven there were voices, thunders, lightnings and a great earthquake, the greatest of all times dividing Jerusalem into three parts, all cities of the nations fell, and remembrance of Great Babylon of the fierceness of his wrath. Verse 20, every island fled away and the mountains were not found, verse 21, great hail out of Heaven about the weight of a talent fell upon man and they blasphemed God because of the plague of the hale being exceedingly great.

Revelation Chapter 17 John's Commentary of the Judgment of the Great Whore of Babylon that took place at the opening of the 6th Seal at the one year and one month mark of the first half of the Trib.

<u>Important Note</u>: Destruction of Babylon is mentioned in Rev 14:3-8, 16:19, 17:1-18, 18:1-24 and Rev 19:1-3, all occurring at the moment of the opening of the 6th Seal making it the most important and talked about subject in the book of Revelation. Mystery Babylon is our current Deep State, Economic, Religious, Banking, Military and Political system under the Democratically controlled NATO, UN, One World political system. Babylon takes us into the seven-year Tribulation Period as the White Horse of Rev 6:1-2 with the opening of the 1st Seal that eventually becomes the Anti-Christ Beast System of great power. Chapter 17 can relate in how Babylon as the Roman Catholic/Jewish Cabbala system has persecuted and killed the fundamental Christian Church for the past 1500 years. Compare this chapter to the book Foxe's Christian Martyrs of the World written by John Foxe of the Moody Press in Chicago. Rev 17:6 clarifies this fact, **"And I saw the woman drunken with the blood of the saints, and with the blood of the martyrs of Jesus: and when I saw her, I wondered with great admiration"**. Clearly by this one Scripture, the Babylon system was the organization that killed Jesus and his Saints from the time Christ established his Church till the fulfillment of these Scriptures.

Rev 17:1-2 Identifies one of the Angels having the seven Vials of wrath came and talked to John saying, **"I will shew unto thee the judgment of the great whore that sitteth upon many waters** [Nations]**"** with whom the kings of the earth have committed fornication and made drunk with the wine of her fornication. This gives us an idea in how America has polluted and forced the world to accept, sex, pornography, drug trade, same sex marriage, LGBT, Adrenochrome production, Hollywood, pedophilia and all the other corruptible vices of the world. Her judgment has come!

Rev 17:3-6 The Angel carried John away in the spirit into the wilderness where he showed him a woman sit upon a scarlet-colored beast full of names of blasphemy having seven heads and ten horns. Verse 4 describes the woman being arrayed in purple and scarlet decked with gold and precious stones with pearls having a golden cup in her hand full of abominations and filthiness of her fornication. This surely describes the wickedness of America today. Verse 5 describes a name written on her forehead, **"MYSTERY, BABYLON THE GREAT THE MOTHER OF HARLOTS AND ABOMINATIONS OF THE EARTH"**. This describes the Roman Catholic Church very well for only a little study will show how the Vatican controls the World Banking System thru "Vatican City" in Rome, "District of Columbia" in Washington DC and "City of London" in England all Sovereign Cities free from federal jurisdiction. They are controllers of the Vatican Bank through the Black Nobility of the Masonic/Illuminati organizations which is Mystery Babylon which includes the Jewish Cabala. Verse 6 describes her spirituality as quoted in the note above as being in a horrible condition that forces its evil ideologies upon the nations of the world. This verse describes the Anti-Christ Beast System of the Dragon, Beast and False Prophet in Rev 16:13. We must NOTE at this point, when Mystery Babylon is destroyed in Rev 14:8 and judgment comes in Rev 17:1, its political ideology and military remnant became the New World Order as the end time Beast System of the Anti-Christ called a *"woman"*, **"I will tell thee the mystery of the woman, and of the beast that carrieth her"**. Mystery Babylon is now called the Anti-Christ Beast System that creates the Mark of the Beast of Satan worship.

Rev 17:7-18 Tells us the mysteries of the women and the beast that carries her that has the seven heads and ten horn which are the nations of the world that has merged with the Anti-Christ Beast System. The MYSTERY is the shifting of world power from Mystery Babylon at its destruction where all of its military and political assets merge to become the Anti-Christ Beast System. The following are its mysteries:

The Seven Mysteries of the Beast

1st Mystery: verse 8, describes a Beast **"that was, and is not and yet to come"** comes out of the **"bottomless pit"** and goes into **"perdition"** where all that is not written in the book of life will follow after him. This verse is speaking of Satan as the Anti-Christ spoken of in II Thess 2:3, **"and that man of sin be revealed, the son of perdition"**. Let's note the phrase *"that was and is not and yet to come"* means that the world thinks that Satan don't exist. This has been his great lie from the beginning of man for he has convinced the world, for the most part, that he does not exist as a spiritual power but only a fable or fairytale. Satan deceives the whole world, Rev 12:9&13:14. In reality he does exist "that was" but as a fable he as the term "and is not" don't exist thru deceit but also in reality is "yet to come" to fulfill prophecy. What a concept!

2nd Mystery: verse 9-10, here is wisdom, the seven heads are seven mountains [nations], on which the woman sits upon. Verse 10, of the seven kings five has fallen and one is, and the other is not yet come; and he comes only for a short time. This is speaking of Satan as the Anti-Christ Beast System for he knows he has only a "short time", Rev 12:12 **"he knoweth that he hath but a short time"** and 17:10 **"he must continue a short time"**. Again, Satan "was", "is not" and "yet to come", a mystery.

3rd Mystery: verses 11-12, Again the mystery of the Beast that was and is not is the eighth head of the Beast being of the seven that goes into "perdition'. This verse shows us the political intrigue of how the head of the White Horse of the 1st Seal is merged with Dan 7:3-8 four Beasts as the Lion, Bear, Leopard and Beast with iron teeth that become one organization as the Anti-Christ Beast System. Verse 12 somewhat explains this for the ten horns are ten kings having received no power as kingdoms but receive their power as kingdoms one hour with the Beast. In other words, these kingdoms only have power through the authority of the Anti-Christ, power not of themselves.

4th Mystery: verse 13 explains verse 12 for these kingdoms [the Beast System] have one mind, and shall give their power and strength unto the beast. This explains how all the military and political power of the white horse [NATO/UN of America and England] as the Lion of Dan 7:4 and the red horse which is also the red Russian Bear of Dan 7:5, all merge into the end time Anti-Christ Beast System. The only great nation left is China and they come into play to fight with the Anti-Christ against God in Rev 9:14-16 and 16:12-16 at the battle of Armageddon.

5th Mystery: verse 14, these ten kingdoms make war with the Lamb and the Lamb [Christ from the Lion of Judah Israel] shall overcome them as Lord of Lords and King of Kings. Note that in this verse the Anti-Christ in not fighting Saints of the earth but Jesus from Heaven with all his Saints for all have been killed. The 144,000 Sealed Saints are all that is left on earth that did not take the Mark and Satan knows that he cannot kill them for they are protected by

God, therefore, he fights Christ the Lamb coming with fire from Heaven.

6ᵗʰ Mystery: verse 15-17 the Angel speaks to John saying, the waters which you saw where the whore sits are peoples, multitudes, nations and tongues that give the Anti-Christ his power in Rev 13:5. Verse 16 says these are the ten horns which you saw upon the Beast System (Anti-Christ) that hate the whore (Babylon of the Roman Vatican City) and shall make her desolate and naked, and shall eat her flesh and burn her with fire. We must note that the Anti-Christ cannot become god as the Apotheoses till the Masonic/Illuminati Roman Babylonian Corporation **"whore that sitteth upon many waters"** in Rev 17:1 is destroyed. This battel is the destruction of the Old-World System and given to the Anti-Christ's New World Order. Verse 17, for God hath put in their hearts to fulfil his will and give their kingdom (Old Babylon the whore) to the Anti-Christ Beast for the words of God shall be fulfilled.

7ᵗʰ Mystery: verse 18, the Angel says to John, the woman which you saw is the great city which reigns over the kings of the earth. This verse is truly a Mystery for most Christians fail to see or refuse to understand where God has placed the Church into a state of delusion for their failure to want to see. The **"great city which reigeth over the kings of the earth"** is the Masonic Order headquartered out of Rome where Mystery Babylon controls the world military, economic, religious and political world system through three Sovern cities free from federal jurisdiction which are Rome in Vatican City, the District City of London in England and District of Columbia in Washington DC. Vatican City, DC and District of London all has their own government and police forces for they are Sovern nations within themselves.

Revelation Chapter 18 Commentary by John in continuing the destruction of Mystery Babylon, Timeline is unbroken.

Note: another Angel came down from Heaven saying, **"after these things"**. The term *after these things* is key in understanding the timeline for it indicates that all the events listed above occurred in a constant unbroken period of time. John's commentaries seem to be out of sequence but in reality, can be placed somewhere within the ongoing sequential timeline that range over almost two thousand years. The verses within this chapter reverts back to the full reign of the old Mystery Babylon hundreds of years ago.

Rev 18:1-3 the Angel that came down from Heaving saying, "after these things", had great power lighting the earth with his glory crying with a mighty voice saying, **"Babylon the great is fallen, is fallen"** becoming the habitation of devils, every foul spirit and cage of every unclean and hateful bird. Verse 3 states in how all nations have drunk of the wine of the wrath of her fornication along with the kings of the earth committed fornication with her and the merchants of the earth waxed rich through the abundance of her delicacies. This verse is speaking of our current world economic and trade system reaching to

143

every sea port and airport in the world creating great wealth called Mystery Babylon controlled from Wall Street in NY City, London, Rome and all the other major Stock Exchanges throughout the world.

Rev 18:4 Another voice from Heaven saying, **"Come out of her, my people that ye be not partakers of her sins, and that ye receive not of her plagues"**. Let's pause and identify "come out of her" and "my people" which is speaking of Babylon and Christ's Church and all the Saints that were saved in the first half of the Tribulation period. We know that the Church was taken into Heaven at the beginning of the Tribulation so this verse has to be speaking prior to that time or the ones during the first half. The Church is confirmed in Rev 18:23-24 being within Mystery Babylon for it clearly states, **"And the light of a candle shall shine no more at all in thee; and the voice of the bridegroom and of the bride shall be heard no more at all in thee for thy merchants were the great men of the earth"**. This is Mystery Babylon and God told his people, the Church, to come out of her which is the polluted Laodicean Roman Corporate 501C3 Churches in the last days. According to this verse, *"the light of the candle shall shine no more at all in thee"* indicate that the candle or Church has been taken away at the writing of this verse. The following verses describe the condition of Babylon and the people that are within her:
Rev 18: 5 Her sins have reached unto Heaven and God hath remembered her iniquities.

Rev 18:6 God will reward her as she rewarded you (the nations) double unto her double according to her works into the cup which she has filled to her double. Babylon is to be double plagued including the nations that fornicate with her.
Rev 18:7 Babylon glorified herself and lived deliciously and for this will receive so much torment and sorrow for she in her heart sits as a queen not a widow but will see sorrow.
Rev 18:8 Because of her sins, her plagues will come in one day, death and mourning, famine, be utterly burned with fire for strong is the Lord God who judge her.
Rev 18:9-10 The kings of the earth who committed fornication and lived deliciously with her shall bewail her and lament for her when they shall see the smoke of her burning standing far off for the fear of her torment. They shall say "alas, alas" that great city Babylon that mighty city for in one hour is the judgment come.
Rev 18:11-14 **"And the merchants of the earth shall weep and morn over her; for no man buyeth their merchandise any more"**. Her gold, silver, precious stones, pearls, fine linen, purple, sild, scarlet, precious wood, vessels of ivory, brass, iron, marble, cinnamon, odors, ointments, frankincense, wine, oil, flour, wheat, beast of sheep and horses, chariots (cars & trucks), slaves and souls of men (sex and pedophile rings) and all the fruits that the soul lust after

departed from her.

Rev 18:15-19 The merchants of which were made rich by her shall stand afar off for the fear of her torment weeping and wailing. They are saying alas, alas that great city that was clothed in fine linen and purple decked with precious stones, **"For in one hour so great riches is come to naught. And every shipmaster and all the company in ships, and sailors, and as many as trade by sea, stood afar off"**. They cried when they saw the smoke of her burning saying what city is like unto this great city of Babylon? They cast dust on their heads and cried weeping and wailing.

Rev 18:20 **"Rejoice over her, thou heaven, and ye holy apostles and prophets; for God hath avenged you on her"**. This verse is in reference to Rev 1:7 where Babylon pierced Jesus on the cross **"and they also which pierced him: and all kindreds of the earth shall wail because of him"** and all generations of the men of Babylon (the western Christian Culture) will see her destruction to include all the killed Saints, Apostles and Prophets. This vengeance covers thousands of years of the timeline from ancient Israel to the modern house of Israel as the Church, Matt 10:6, 15:24 and Act 10:36.

Rev 18:21 Describes a mighty Angel casting a great millstone into the sea causing a great title wave of water violently destroying that great city Babylon. This verse sure sounds like Russia's new 100meg nuke torpedo that is fired from a submarine off the coast that creates title waves. This is a highly talked about technology that the Russians now have in their Navy. Research this subject for yourselves.

Rev 18:22 Babylon is destroyed for the voice of harpers, musicians, pipers, trumpeters shall be heard no more in her and no craftsman will be found in her and no sound of a millstone shall be heard no more in her. The word "millstone" is referring to technical machinery such as manufacturing plants etc., its economy is dead. An ancient millstone is a mechanical stone gear that crush when it rotates.

Rev 18:23-24 These verses are critical in understanding, therefore, will be fully quoted; **"And the light of a candle shall shine no more at all in thee; and the voice of the bridegroom and of the bride shall be heard no more at all in thee: for thy merchants were the great men of the earth; for by thy sorceries were all nations deceived"** and **"And in her was found the blood of prophets, and of saints, and of all that were slain upon the earth"**. These verses speak for themselves for clearly the Church as Christ's Bride was at one time a part of or within Mystery Babylon. By this Scripture, the Church has been taken out or raptured. This would mean that the western Christian Culture of America, Europe, England, Austria and all the other Christian nations were once a part of the Mystery Babylon system.

145

Revelation Chapter 19 John's Commentary is a major link in understanding the consecutive timeline where the first two events occur immediately after each other at the opening of the 6th Seal and the last three events occur also in sequential order at the end of the Tribulation.

Note: Five major events occur in this chapter, the first two at the opening of the 6th Seal confirmed in Rev 6:12&7:3-8 and 14:1-5&8 the sealing of the 144,000, fall of Babylon and Marriage Supper happens in sequential order. All these verses are linked together.
Judgment of the great Whore of Babylon where Babylon falls.
Immediately after Babylon falls the Marriage Supper of the Lamb takes place in Rev 19:7-9.

John's Commentary at the end of the Trib.

Jesus comes back in power and glory on a white horse with his Saints and Angels.
The Battle of Armageddon where the nations gather together to do battle with Jesus on the white horse.
The Beast and false Prophet is cast into the lake of fire and the "remnant" that took the Mark was killed by him that sat on the white horse **"and all the fowls were filled with their flesh"**.

Rev 19:1-3 And another great voice from much people in Heaven saying "after these things" meaning that it is in sequential order. This Author believes that "much people" is all the Saints from Adam till when this verse takes place, all Saints in Heaven, give glory, honor and power to our Lord God in Heaven. The Saints say for true and righteous are his judgments upon Babylon for he hath judged the "great whore" which did corrupt the earth with her fornication and avenged the blood of his servants at her hand. Again, they praised God and said "Alleluia" for her smoke rose up for ever and ever.
Rev 19:4-6 The four and twenty elders and the four "beasts" which is the house of Israel fell down and worshiped God. The Elders are all the great patriarchs chosen by God to be the elders of Israel from its beginning. The four Beast is the four brigades of the house of Israel as the Lion, Calf/Ox, Man and Eagle as Christ's Church proven in Matt 10:3, 15:24, Act 10:36, Eze 3:1-5 and Rev 10:9-10 as Christ's Gospel called the "roll" and "book". All stand before God in Heaven as he sat on his throne singing **"Alleluia"**. Verse 5&6 says a voice came out of the Throne saying, "Praise our God, all ye his servants, and ye that fear him, both small and great". John heard a voice of a great multitude of many waters (nations of people) as a voice of mighty thundering say "Alleluia" for the Lord God omnipotent reigns.

Marriage Supper of the Lamb takes place

<u>Rev 19:7-10</u> John says, **"Let us be glad and rejoice, and give honour to him; for the marriage of the Lamb is come and his wife hath made herself ready"**. She was arrayed in fine linen clean and white for fine linen is the righteousness of Saints. The voice of the Angel told John to write, **"Blessed are they which are called unto the Marriage supper of the Lamb"** for these are the true sayings of God. In verse 10 John fell before the Angel to worship him but the Angel told him no but to worship God for the testimony of Jesus is the spirit of prophecy.

<u>Rev 19:11</u>- John saw Heaven open and a white horse and he that sat upon him was called Faithful and True (Jesus the Lamb) and in righteousness he judges and makes war. This verse is speaking of Christ's Church going into the world to preach and teach as a nation having a great army to battle for his Gospel. This war is the power behind the Western Christian Culture during the Church Age such as England, Spain, France and America projecting the Gospel backed by their armies and navies worldwide.

Note: The 1st War is between Satan and the Church as the Saint's on earth spreading the Gospel stated in Rev 2:26-27 and 12:5. This is the war against Satan where the Church rules with a **"rod of iron"** making Christ's Christian's **"Kings and priests"** in Rev 1:6 to rule the earth as the Church. This is King David's throne in England proven in Jerm 23:3-6 **"I will raise unto David a righteous Branch, and a King shall reign and prosper"**. This is the 1st War spoken of in these verses. The 2nd War is when God comes to rules with **"a rod of Iron"** in Rev 18:15 when he comes with smoke and fiery clouds.

<u>Rev 19:12</u> The 2nd War is between God and Satan when Christ comes riding on a White Horse with Power and Glory. This verse tells us that when Heaven opened and beheld the white horse, he that sat upon him was called **"Faithful and True, and in righteousness he doth judge and make war"**. This verse is speaking of a different war not by the Church Age but when he comes in power and glory at the end of the age. Verse 13 says that Jesus was clothed with a vesture dipped in blood and his name is called the **"Word of God"**. The blood of his Saints that were killed for preaching the Word of Christ as his Church throughout time and Babylon the Great was the world's religious system that had Christ and is Servants killed in the 1st War. It is now time for the 2nd WAR of vengeance on Mystery Babylon.

<u>Rev 19:14-16</u> The war begins when the armies which were in heaven followed Jesus on the white horse having their own white horses clothed in fine linen white and clean. This is the battle of **"Armageddon"** in Rev 16:16 bringing vengeance. Verse 15 says and out of his mouth goes a sharp sword to smite the nations to rule over them with **"a rod of Irion"** where he treads the winepress of the fierceness and wrath of Almighty God. We must note that the Church was given the task to rule the earth with the rod of iron called the Gospel but

now God has taken that responsibility for the Church is in Heaven. Verse 16 has his name written on his vesture and thigh called **"KING OF KINGS, AND LORD OF LORDS"**.

Rev 19:17-18 John saw an Angel standing in the sun crying with a loud voice saying to all the fowls that fly in the midst of heaven (the firmament or sky), come and gather yourselves together unto the supper of the great God that they may eat the flesh of kings, captains, flesh of mighty men, flesh of horses and their riders and the flesh of all men both small and great. This is all the flesh killed from the great battle of Armageddon. Verse 19 reverts back till prior to the battle and where John says, and I saw the beast and kings of the earth and their armies gather together to make war against him that sat on the white horse and against his army or Saints.

Rev 19:20-21 Describes in how the Beast and False Prophet that wrought miracles deceiving the world to receive the Mark of the Beast and to worship his image, both were cast alive into a lake of fire burning with brimstone. Verse 21 goes on to say the remnant were slain with the sword of him that sat upon the horse which sword proceeded out of his mouth fulfilling verses 17 and 18 where all the fowls were filled with their flesh.

Revelation Chapter 20 John's Commentary in how Satan the old Dragon that old Serpent the Devil is cast into the Bottomless Pit during the millennial reign Judgment of Man and Satan has come.

Rev 20:1 John saw an Angel come down from Heaven having the key of the bottomless pit with a great chain in his hand.

Rev 20:2-3 And he laid hold on the Dragon the old Serpent the Devil called the Anti-Christ and bound him a thousand years till the end of the millennial reign. The Angel cast him into the bottomless pit and shut him up with a seal upon him that he should not deceive the nations till the thousand years should be fulfilled and then he was to be loosed for a little season.

Rev 20:4-6 John **"saw thrones, and they sat upon them and judgment was given unto them"** and the souls of them that were killed for the witness of Jesus for the Word of God that did not take the Mark of the Beast during the last half of the Tribulation. They lived and reigned with Christ a thousand years. Matt 19:28 tells us that **"That ye which have followed me, in the regeneration when the Son of man shall sit in the throne of his glory, ye also shall sit upon twelve thrones, judging the twelve tribes of Israel"**. According to this verse, not only the twelve Apostles will rule on twelve thrones but *"ye which have followed me, in the regeneration"* will have a throne. These Saints will rule and reign with Jesus for a thousand years. Verse 5 tells us that the rest of the dead did not live until the thousand years were finished called the first resurrection. Verse 6, blessed and holy is he that has part in the first resurrection where the second death has no power, for they shall be priest of God and Christ and reign with him a thousand years just as Matt 19:28 state.

Rev 20:7-9 says that when the thousand years have finished, Satan shall be loosed out of his prison and verse 8 says he shall go out to deceive the nations which are in the earth where Gog and Magog are located. They shall gather themselves together to battle for the number of them is as the sand of the seas. Verse 9 says, and they went up on the breadth of the earth and compassed the camp of the saints and the beloved city (Jerusalem) and fire came down from God out of heaven devouring them. Who is Gog and Magog in this verse if God and Magog is Russia in the book of Revelation? In Greek the word Gog in ref #1136 means, *a symbolic name for some future Antichrist*. In Greek the word Magog in ref #3098 means, *a nation that is Antichristian party*. In other words, Gog and Magog in this verse simply means a nation that has fallen away from God and became Antichristian which is an Antichrist that hates God the Almighty. Satan again deceived them for the last time.

Rev 20:10 **Satan's Judgment**. The Devil that deceived them was cast into the Lake of Fire and Brimstone, where the Beast and the False Prophet are and shall be tormented day and night for ever and ever.

Rev 20:11-15 **Man's Judgment**. John saw a Great White Throne and him (God) sat on it from whose face the earth and the heaven fled away and there was no place for them. Verse 12, John saw the dead small and great stand before God and the books were opened. And another book was opened which is the Book of Life and the dead were judged out of those things which were written in the books according to their works. Verse 13, the sea gave up the dead, dead and Hell delivered up the dead which were in them and they (God and Christ) judged every man according to their works. Verse 14 says that Death and Hell were cast into the Lake of Fire which is the second Death. Verse 15 clearly state that whosoever was not found written in the book of Life was cast into the Lake of fire along with Satan, the Beast and the False Prophet. These dead people were once living that rejected Christ and God or at one time a believer that refused to repent to keep their robs clean and were blotted out of the Book of Life found in Exo 32:32-33, Deut 9:14&29:20 and confirmed in Rev 3:1-5. Yes, we can be blotted out of the Book of Life if our garments become spotted due to daily sin. We must repent often in Heb 9:25-26 to keep from being blotted out just as the man in Christ's parable in Matt 22:1-14 where once he was a faithful Servant cast into outer darkness with weeping and gnashing of teeth. Clearly by Scripture, we can lose our Salvation.

Revelation Chapter 21 John's Commentary of the New Heaven & New Earth coming down from God with no Sea and the descending of New Jerusalem from Heaven. These events fall within the Timeline after the Millennial Reign and destruction of Old Heaven & Earth.

Rev 21:1-2 John saw a New Heaven and a New Earth for the first Heaven and the first Earth were passed away and there was no sea. Why would God destroy the Old Heaven and Earth? The answer is simple, Satan was in the old earth and old Heaven where he corrupted it with evil, therefore, it has to be destroyed. Verse 2, John saw the holy City New Jerusalem coming down from God out of Heaven prepared as a Bride adorned for her husband.

Note: This is a very important verse for all Christians to understand. Many believers are either ignorant or refuse to see that Jerusalem and Israel was one of the names of Christ's Church. This chapter proves the Church is Jerusalem or New Jerusalem which is the Capital City of the house of Israel, his lost sheep.

Rev 21:3-4 John heard a great voice out of heaven saying, behold the Tabernacle of God is with men and he will dwell with them and they shall be his people. God himself shall be with them and he shall be their God. Verse 4 God shall wipe away all tears from their eyes and there shall be no more death neither sorrow or crying, neither shall there be any more pain for the former things is passed away.

Rev 21:5 And he that sat upon the throne (Jesus) said, behold, I make all things new and he said unto me, write for these words are true and faithful.

Rev 21:6-8 The Angel told John, **"It is done. I am Alpha and omega, the beginning and the end. I will give unto him that is arthirst** (*to thirst*) **of the fountain of the water of life freely"**. Verse 7 He that overcome shall inherit all things and I will be his God and he shall be my son. The word overcometh in Greek means, 3528, *to subdue, conquer, overcome, prevail* and *get the victory*. Key words to overcome in victory is directly related to Rev 3:1-5 in being "watchful", "receiving", "hearing", "holding fast" and "repenting" often of our sins in Heb 9:25-26. If we fail in maintaining these key words to keep our garments clean, we are no longer in a perfect spiritual state as stated in Heb 6:1&2-6. We will be blotted out just as Rev 3:5 states. If we fail to overcome, we fail to drink "of the fountain of the water of life" and will receive the 2nd Death. Verse 8 But the fearful, unbelieving, abominable, murders, whoremongers, sorcerers, idolaters and liars shall have their part in the lake which burns with fire and brimstone which is the second death. The words listed above is not what sends us to Hell, it's the failure to maintain an "often" repentance, the phrase "once saved always saved" is not true but a Satanic Lie.

Rev 21:9 One of the seven Angels that had the seven Vials full of the seven last plagues came and talked to John. He said, come hither, I will shew thee the bride, the Lamb's wife. Verse 10 takes John away in the spirit to a great and high mountain and shewed him that great city, the Holy Jerusalem descending out of Heaven from God. Verse 11 having the glory of God and her light was like unto a stone mount precious even like a jasper stone, clear as crystal.

Rev 21:12 the City Jerusalem had four walls great and high with twelve gates and at the gates twelve Angels with their twelve names written which are the twelve tribes of Israel as the children of Israel. Verse 13 On the east three gates, on the north three gates, on the south three gates and on the west three gates. Verse 14 And the wall of the city had twelve foundations and in them the names of the twelve Apostles of the Lamb as his Church. According to Rev 5:5-6, the Lion of the tribe of Judah, the slain Lamb and the seven spirits sent into all the earth is the Church which is Christ himself. He was the only one authorized to open the Seals, Trumpets and Vials of wrath.

Note: Clearly the wall and foundation of the walls were built upon the twelve tribes, three tribes or gate to each wall is the Beast in Rev 4:7 as the four brigades of the twelve tribes or lost sheep of the house of Israel as the Lion, Calf, Man and Eagle. These four brigades are proven in Numbers chapter two and Ezk 1:10&15, 10:14-16 as a wheel traveling to spread the Gospel. They are Christ's Church in Matt 10:6, 15:24, Act 10:36 and Ezk 3:1-5. We must note that the house of Israel as the ten northern tribes, not including the house of Judah, is called the children of Israel in I Kings 12:24&19-24. The ten northern tribes are the lost sheep of the house of Israel in Matt 10:6, 15:24 where Christ himself gave them his Church. The Church is called the children of Israel in Act 10:36 and Rev 2:14. These verses clearly state that the name of Christ's Church is called Jerusalem the adorned Bride in Rev 21:9, the children of Israel where Christ sent his twelve Apostles only to the lost sheep of the house of Israel to teach his Gospel. We know the Church was to rule the world in Christ's absence so let's see the meaning of Israel, Strong's Concordance, in Hebrew #3478, *he will rule as God*, 8280, *to prevail, have power as a prince* and Israelites in Greek 2475, Israelite, 2474, *Israel, the adopted name of Jacob and his descendants*. These definitions are speaking of the Church. The Church is called Israel with its Capital City Jerusalem to rule as God as a Prince.

Rev 21:15-17 The Angel that talked with John had a reed to measure the city, gates and the walls. Verse 16 The city lieth four-square, the length is as large as the breadth measuring the city with the reed twelve thousand furlongs with the length and the breadth and height are equal. Verse 17 And he measured the wall a hundred forty and four cubits according to the measure of a man that is of the Angel. Verse 18 And the building of the wall was of jasper and the city was pure gold like unto clear glass. Verse 19 And the foundations of the wall of the city were garnished with all manner of precious stones. The first foundation was jasper, the second sapphire, the third a chalcedony, the fourth an emerald. Verse 20 The fifth a sardonyx, the sixth a sardius, the seventh a chrysolite, the eighth a beryl, the ninth a topaz, the tenth a chrysoprase's, the eleventh a jacinth and the twelfth an amethyst. Verse 21 And the twelve gates were twelve pearls, every gate was of one pearl and the street of the city was pure gold as it were transparent glass. Verse 22 And I saw no temple therein for the Lord God Almighty and the lamb are the temple of it.

Rev 21:23 And the city had no need of the sun neither of the moon to shine in it for the glory of God did lighten it and the Lamb is the light thereof. Verse 24 And the nations of them which are saved shall walk in the light of it and the kings of the earth do bring their glory and honor into it. Verse 25 And the gates of it shall not be shut at all by day for there shall be no night there'. Verse 26 And they shall bring the glory and honor of the nations into it. Verse 27 An there shall in no wise enter into it any thing that defile, neither whatsoever worketh abomination or make a lie but they which are written in the Lamb's book of life.

Revelation Chapter 22 John's Commentary continues in describing the New Heaven and Jerusalem descending down from God.

Rev 22:1-5 The Angel shows John a pure river of water of life clear as crystal proceeding out of the throne of God and of the Lamb. Verse 2 In the midst of the street of it and on either side of the river, was there the tree of life which bare twelve manner of fruits and yielded her fruit every month and the leaves of the tree were for the healing of the nations. Verse 3 And there shall be no more curse but the throne of God and of the Lamb shall be in it and his servants shall serve him. Verse 4 And they shall see his face and his name shall be in their foreheads. Verse 5 And there shall be no night there and they need no candle neither light of the sun for the Lord God giveth them light and they shall reign for ever and ever.

Rev 22:6 And the Angel said to John, these sayings are faithful and true and the Lord God of the holy prophets sent his angel to shew unto his servants the things which must shortly be done. This verse is telling John to write these things to the Church for the End of Days.
Rev 22:7 Behold I come quickly: blessed is he that keep the sayings of the prophecy of this book. God is telling John that the Christians that read and study the book of Revelation to include all Biblical Scripture, will receive a very special blessing. Do not listen to the Pastors that teach that Prophecy and the Scripture is not to be believed or studied for it is a Satanic lie.

Rev 22:8-16 John heard and saw these things and fell down to worship before the feet of the angel which shewed me these things. Verse 9 The Angel said to John, do it not for I am thy fellow servant and of the brethren and prophets and of them which keep the sayings of this book: worship God. Verse 10 The Angel told John, seal not the sayings of the prophecy of this book: for the times at hand. Verse 11 He that is unjust let him be unjust still and he which is filthy let him be filthy still and he that is righteous let him be righteous still and he that is holy let him be holy still. Verse 12 And behold, I come quickly and my reward is with me to give every man according as his work shall be. Verse 13 I am Alpha and Omega the beginning and the end, the first and the last. Verse 14 Blessed are they that do his commandments, that they may have right to the tree of life, and may enter in through the gates into the city. Speaking of New Jerusalem. Verse 15 For without are dogs, sorcerers, whoremongers, murderers, idolaters and whosoever loveth and makes a lie.

Verse 16 I Jesus have sent mine Angel to testify unto you these things in the Churches. I am the root and the offspring of David and the bright and morning star. This verse is very important for Jesus himself is speaking and telling John to teach the Churches in what he saw in Heaven. Note that he calls them Churches indicating that they are seven individual Churches representing seven separate periods of time as this Author has shown within this book.

Rev 22:17 And the Spirit and the Bride say, come and let him that heareth and thirst come. Whosoever will let him take the water of life freely. This verse is speaking to all humanity, to anyone that is willing to drink of the water of life is welcome into New Jerusalem and to set with God on his Throne.

A WARNING is given in Rev 22:18-19

Rev 22:18-19 **"For I testify unto every man that heareth the words of the prophecy of this book, If any man shall add unto these things, God shall add unto him the plagues that are written in this book"**. Verse 19 **"And if any man shall take away from the words of the book of this prophecy, God shall take away his part out of the book of life, and out of the holy city, and from the things which are written in this book"**. These two verses terrify this Author, for if I change the meaning of any portion of these Scriptures, I shall burn in Hell just as anyone that does these things. Each time I set down to write, I pray for guidance of the Holy Spirit for wisdom and knowledge to maintain the integrity of these Prophecies.

Rev 22:20-21 **"He which testifieth these things saith, Surely I come quickly. Amen. Even so, come, Lord Jesus. The grace of our Lord Jesus Christ be with you all. A-men"**.

Chapter 7

WW III Muslim Jihad (Holy War) of Russia/BRICS and the Western nations of NATO America/British (Deep State)

The following information within this lesson is based upon the date of 31 Aug 2023 to date, world events are currently occurring extremely quickly. In light of what is happening within daily events, it is clear that a war between the Russian/Muslim BRICS (Brizal, Russia, India, China, S. Africa) nations with a world currency backed by gold is inevitable. By 1 Jan 2024, BRICS will be up to approx. 14 nations that will controls 42% of world population and 27% of world GWP (Global Product) which is critical in destroying the Dollar. Twenty-eight other nations are waiting to join BRICS. The western Christian nations of NATO cannot allow the Dollar to be destroyed by a new world currency which will eventually be digital. The Dollar is currently king by simply printing paper creating mountains of debt backed by nothing. The world is tired of the American world reserve currency based on a debt-based system simply by printing money backed by no tangible assets. There will be a world war that is inescapable spoken of in Ezekiel chapter 38 and 39. This will be an economic and political war for the control of oil and world economics of all mining materials over the battle of the Dollar. As of the date above, there has been four African nations that has had military coups to shake off the American and French shackles, NATO, controlling their natural resources of oil, diamonds and other valuable mining medals. The western influence that controls the natural resources of third world countries does not help the people but go into the pockets of international bankers with NATO as their military arm of control. The new BRICS nations, in the very near future, will control most of the world's oil reserves causing the west to have to formulate a world war. We can clearly see that the world is rebelling against the West and gravitating to the BRICS coalition that promise wealth and prosperity to the people not controlled by criminals. WWIII is quickly coming and documented very well within the Scriptures. The battle of Jehoshaphat is recorded in Joel 3:2, Ezekiel 38:1-11 and Isaiah 34:6-7 as the bull (United States) and unicorn (Great Britain) and is the battle that takes place in the valley of Hamon-Gog in Ezekiel 39:11. It will also be fought in almost every nation in the world either economically or physically. This war is mentioned all through the book of Isaiah referring to World War III at the beginning of the seven-year Tribulation Period of Judgment. This war strictly deals with judgment on the house of Israel (western nations NATO) and Judah (Isa 11:14, 13:4) which is Mystery Babylon during the 1st half of the Trib. This book has proven that the Ezekiel 38 and 39 war occurs at the beginning of the Tribulation of seven years at the opening of the 2nd Seal when the red horse battles the white horse. Eze 38:16 states that this war occurs **"in the latter days"** and Eze 39:9 clearly state that it takes seven years to burn all their weapons proving that the Tribulation Period last for seven years. Armageddon is the last battle at the end of the seven-year period of Wrath that judges the Anti-Christ and his followers. The 1st half of the Trib is wrath on the western nations of Babylon the Great and the last half is wrath upon ungodly man and the Anti-Christ Beast System. The war in the valley of Haman-Gog recorded in Ezekiel 39:11 is the same war in Micah 5:1 and 7-15 that occur at the beginning of the Tribulation.

Who starts WWIII?

According to Eze 38:2, Russa which is Gog leader of the BRICS nations, the land of Magog, the chief prince of Meshech and Tubal with a confederate group of nations listing Persia (Iran, Syria), Ethiopia, Libya, Gomer (Germany) and Togarmah (Turkey) as listed in verses 5-6. With Russia as their leader verse 2 states, **"And I will turn thee back, and put hooks into thy jaws and I will bring thee forth, and all thine army, horses and horsemen, all of them clothed with all sorts of armour, even a great company with bucklers and shields, all of them handling swords"**. This Scripture does not list North Korea and China from the East. An unknown major world event causes Russia to be hooked or dragged into a war with the West. At this very moment in time, America, England and NATO are purposely provoking Russia to attack NATO due to the Ukrainian war. The American and world economy is on the verge of total failure and the Western nations need a war to divert attention. War is coming quickly and the people of the west is not being told by the international media in what is truly happening with the Ukraine war or world economy due to media blackout.

The current Palestinian and Israeli issue in the Middle East over the west bank and Gaza strip could be one of many flash points and the Bible calls the modern Palestinian's, Palestina, Philista and Philistine. In Hebrew, the word Palestina means, *the west coast of Canaan, rolling, migratory, a region of Syria, to roll in dust and roll (wallow) self*. Philista or Palestine means, *land of the Philistia and Philistine means, an inhabitant of Philistia*. The Palestinian problem dates back thousands of years and deep rooted in extreme hatred between Ishmael and Isaac which are the two sons of Abraham. The war between Iran and Iraq stems from the Palestinian terrorist problem in the Middle East. The story is recorded in Genesis chapter sixteen and seventeen. We must note that Egypt, Iran, Saudi Arabia and UAE are scheduled to be admitted into the BRICS coalition on 1 Jan 2024. The Mideastern nations of Kuwait and Palestine along with Venezuela have already applied for BRICS. Afghanistan, Pakistan, Sudan and Syria are potential members to join BRICS. Russia, Venezuela, Kuwait, Saudia Arabia, UAE, Afghanistan, Syria, Iran and Egypt are some of the most oil producing nations in the world and all of them are soon to join BRICS. Many of these oil rich nations are aligned in the Ezekiel War listed in Eze 38:1-6 and could very well start WWIII. The following Scriptures are just a few that mention this up-coming war called WWIII or the battle of Hamon-gog in Eze 39:11:

Joel 3:2- **"I will also gather all nations, and will bring them down into the valley of Jehoshafhat and will plead with them there for my people and for my heritage Israel, whom they have scattered among the nations, and parted my land"**.

Eze 38:8- **"After many days thou shalt be visited: in the latter years thou shalt come into the land that is brought back from the sword** [England, America, Austria etc]**, and is gathered out of many people, against the mountains of Israel** [the Western Christian nation called Babylon]**, which have been always waste: but it is brought forth out of the nations, and they shall dwell safely all of them"**.

Eze 39:11- **"And it shall come to pass in that day, that I will give unto Gog a place there of graves in Israel, the valley of the passengers on the east of the sea: and it shall stop the noses of the passengers: and there shall they bury Gog and all his multitude: and they shall call it the valley of Hamon-gog"**.

Isa 34:1-10- (Nuclear wasteland) These verses is speaking of WW III that occurs at the beginning of the Trib. as the Magog war in Ezekiel 38 and 39 and in verse two states, **"For the indignation of the Lord is upon all nations, and his fury upon on all nations"**, **"he hath delivered them to the slaughter"**, verse 4, **"the heavens shall be rolled together as a scroll"**, verse 5, **"for the Lord hath a sacrifice in Bozrah, and a great slaughter in the land of Idumea"** which is Russia. Verse 6, **"The sword of the Lord is filled with blood, it is made fat with fatness, and with the blood of lambs** [civilian people] **and goats** [military soldiers]**, with the fat of the kidneys or rams** [military leaders and politicians]**: for the Lord hath a sacrifice in Bozrah, and a great slaughter in the land of Idumea** [Russia]**. And the unicorns** [England/America] **shall come down with them, and the bullocks with the bulls** [again England/America listed in Duet 33:17]**; and their land shall be soaked with blood, and their dust made fat with fatness. For it is the day of the Lord's vengeance, and the year of recompences for the controversy of Zion** [House of Israel the Church Matt 10:6&15:24]**. And the streams thereof shall be turned into pitch, and the dust thereof into brimstone, and the land thereof shall become burning pitch** [nuclear war]**. It shall not be quenched night nor day; the smoke thereof shall go up for ever: from generation to generation it shall lie waste; none shall pass through it for ever and ever"**. All of these verses are speaking of WWIII that could happen at anytime.

The United States is determined to finish the war on terrorism in Iraq/ Afghanistan and the Middle East in an effort to promote Democracy that could very well trigger the Palestinian war mentioned above. All the verses relating to God gathering and planting his people in the wilderness within a safe peaceful land can in no way be speaking of the promised land of Canaan due to all the hatred that has been documented in the past 3500 years surrounding Palestine. This peaceful dwelling place can be found in Jeremiah 23:6, 32:37, 33:16, Ezekiel 28:26, 34:25&28, 38:8,11&14, and 39:26. These verses can only be speaking of the western Christian Culture lead by England and America that settled the wilderness of the west as cattle ranchers as the bull and unicorn in Duet 33:17. The Scriptures are clear that Isaac was to receive the great blessing of receiving the promised land Hebrew, not Ishmael as Muslim (Gen 16:11-16, 17:19-22) and Isaac were to be the covenant people of God for their name is to be called after their seed of Isaac's sons meaning Saxon (Gen 21:12, Heb 11:18) not Jewish. Satan has emulated the Muslim Religion to counteract Gods Covenant with Israel allowing this problem to occur in the last days just as the Bible has foretold. The Muslim Religion and the ideology of Communism created by Jewish Secret Societies (The Red Horse) were developed in the last days to destroy Christianity and establish Lucifer's world system. The Jewish Rabbinical System hates Christianity for it almost destroyed their wealthy system of power, therefore, they rejected Christ and had him killed. In the last days the Jews used the Jewish Caballa to created Communism for the purpose of destroying Christianity. The Jews has an extreme hatred for Christianity due to the fact that the Church destroyed their established system of wealth and political power within the nations of the world. Since the destruction of the Temple in Jerusalem in 70AD, the Jew has been persecuted and kicked out of almost every nation in the world for the hatred they have for the Gentiles/ Christian. The German Jewish Holocaust of WWII is only one example.

There are two distinct major wars recorded to take place during the Tribulation Period. The first battle takes place at the beginning of this seven-year period in the valley of Hamon-Gog (Ezekiel chapter 38 and 39 and Dan 11:40-45). The purpose of this war is to bring judgment upon the nations of the house of Israel and Judah called the Great Whore of Babylon due to national sin of Baal worship. There are several wars that occur within the seven Seals and Trumpets during the first half of the Tribulation. These wars establish the Anti-Christ into power and destroys the Palestinian Arab and Russian coalition along with the fallen away western Christian culture. The first war occurs due to religious hatreds between Christianity, Islam, atheist and nihilism with the purpose of establishing a one world religion/god as the Anti-Christ.

This war causes so much destruction creating an extreme distain for organized religion that the world leader is able to change age old traditions of times and laws (Dan 7:25). The changing of these laws creates a great religious void and allows the Anti-Christ to step in and proclaim himself to be god, the Apotheosis in the middle of the seven-year period. This battle occurs at the beginning of the Tribulation period for it takes the Israelites, as the house of Israel, seven years to burn their weapons (Eze 39:9). The battle of Hamon-Gog could very well be the war against terrorism where the West invaded the Middle-east and in time triggers the war where God destroys the nations of the house of Israel and their cities (Mic 5:14). This war is a punishment for falling away from his Christian commandments. The event of 911 in New York City could very well be the precursor of World War III. The next major war is the Battle of Armageddon that occurs seven years later at the end of the period of Wrath and is the war of all wars, (Rev 16:16) where man gathers to fight God/Christ and his Angels when he comes in power and glory with fire. This war is against ungodly man that has the mark of the beast and to bring final judgment upon the wicked people of the world. It takes place at the end of the seven-year Tribulation just prior to the return of Christ in power claiming his throne in Jerusalem.

The Old Testament prophetic books are laced with warnings of destruction to the cities of the house of Israel in the last days (Isa 24:12, Jerm 4:29, 15:8, Mic 5:14 and II Esdras 15:15-19 "Apocrypha "). First, we must understand the division of Israel in our present day to know the identification of the true Israel. This war could very well be the Judgment of the destruction of our cities due to present day immoralities mentioned in the previous segment. According to Genesis 48:16-22, the name Israel was given only to Ephraim and Manasseh, Joseph's two sons as the Bull and Unicorn. They are clearly called the house of Israel which is modern day England and the United States. The family name blessing was not given to the Jews as confirmed in I Chron 5:1-2. The cities of Israel being destroyed would be the cities of the western culture, the Common Wealth of Great Britain and the United States. This war is recorded in Isaiah 34:6-10 where Britain is the unicorns and the United States the bullocks. Bozrah, Seir and Idumea are the Communist Bloc nations of Eastern Europe as outlined within this book by tracing ancient names of the house of Israel. Isaiah 34:9-10 describes the nuclear war that destroys our western cities to include England.

The Scriptures are clear on an end time war that destroys Israel's cities (western nations) prior to Christ's 3rd coming in power and glory. To better understand why this occurs, we must read and study Leviticus chapter 26 and Deuteronomy 28 for why God brings punishment to his nations for disobedience of his laws. We must also remember that modern day Israel is the house of Judah and not the whole house of Israel. The inheritance blessing under the primogeniture law gave Ephraim (Ephratah Mic 5:2 and I Kings 11:26&28, 12:20-21&24) the leadership of the house of Israel (ten northern tribes) and received the family name Israel above Judah, the Jews. It is recorded in Micah 5:1-2 placing

Ephratah (Ephraim) above Judah as leader of the troops as nations which is Gods battle ax and army as in Jeremiah 51:19-20. The house of Israel is King of all Israel proven in I Kings 12:21&24 (children of Israel) and Matt 10:6 and 15:24 as his lost sheep where Christ himself gave them the Church in the last days in Gen 49:1.

Because of Gods inheritance law (Gen 48:16, I Chron 5:1-2) the cities of Israel that is destroyed during the upcoming war of Jacobs trouble would be the cities of the house of Israel in the wilderness (US and GB), not Jerusalem of modern Israel as we all think. God would never nuke Jerusalem! Why would Satan want to destroy Jerusalem for that is where he plans to establish his earthly Headquarters and throne? When you study where the nuclear missiles of China and Russia are pointed, it is not toward modern Israel but the United States and Great Britain. We as the house of Israel (Gods Battle Ax) are his main threat, not the small nation of Israel. This answers a lot of Scriptural questions.

According to Chronicles 5:1-3, the firstborn or the chosen inheritance was to receive his kingdom; therefore, Ephraim and Manasseh became leader of the largest part of Gods kingdom receiving the double portion. They received the total kingdom when Jesus rebuked the Jews in Matthew 21:43, giving the complete kingdom to the house of Israel to be led by Ephraim and Manasseh as the Bull and Unicorn of England as recorded in Duet 33:17. They were given the responsibility of maintaining the family name of Israel as recorded in Genesis 48:16 and the kingdom in I Kings 11:11-13 in approx. 992 BC to be completely overturned in Matthew 21:43, approx. 30AD, to Ephraim and Manasseh. King David's throne was overturned to England in Eze 21:25-27, 17:21-24.

Who is the Outcast, Isa 56:8, Young Lions, 38:13 and Hidden Ones, Ps 83:3?

The Scriptures clearly identify by name the collation of nations within the Gog and Magog group found in Eze 39:2&5 but secretly hides the identity of the western NATO nations. Why? God for some reason wants to keep it a hidden secret! It is this Authors belief that if God had maintained all twelve tribes under Judaism and the law of Moses of blood sacrifice in Jerusalem, all Israel would have rejected the Messiah at his coming. Therefore, God divided the twelve tribes of Israel into two houses or kingdoms. The two southern tribes of Benjamin and Judah became the house of Judah in Jerusalem of Judia and the northern kingdom of ten tribes to the house of Israel as recorded in I Kings 11:25-43&12:19-24. God chose to separate the northern kingdom called the house of Israel as the children of Israel in I Kings 12:20&24. In Matt 10:6, 15:24, Acts 10:36, Rev 2:14 and Eze 3:1-5, the Church is called **"lost sheep"**, **"children of Israel"** and **"the house of Israel"** where Christ sent his Apostles

160

to teach only the lost sheep of the house of Israel. Note that lost sheep is directly related to hidden or secret meaning they had to lose their language, identity and history of being under Judaism if they were to accept Christ's Gospel when it came. This means, they had to be hidden as a secret and could not be under the Law of Moses. They became lost sheep as scattered strangers where James and Peter sent their Epistles in James 1:1 **"twelve tribes which are scattered abroad"**, I Peter 1:1 **"to the strangers scattered throughout"** and Jerm 50:17 **"Israel is a scattered sheep"**. The Scriptures call the house of Israel by different names which are **"the hidden ones"** in Ps 83:3, Hosea 5:14 calls them Ephraim **"For I will be unto Ephraim as a lion, and as a young lion to the house of Judah"** and Micah 5:8 **"as a young lion among the flocks of sheep"**. All through the New Testament sheep is directly associated with the Church, therefore, if they are among the sheep, they have to be the Church. They are called **"mine outcast"** in Isa 16:4 where they dwell with Moab. In the Scriptures above the house of Israel also called the children of Israel and identified as, scattered strangers abroad, the hidden ones, Ephraim a young lion and outcast in Isa 11:2.

The word secret is also associated with the house of Israel as the young lions in Ps 91:1 and Lamentations 3:10 for chapters two and three is speaking directly to the daughter of Zion being in secret places. The house of Israel received the Church in Matt 10:6, 15:24, Heb 8:8-10 and Jerm 31:31-33 for Zion/Sion is the Church as the New Covenant. These Scriptures place the house of Israel in a secret place or land called Zion in Isa 18:7 (America) that is spoiled with great rivers of a nation scattered, meted and peeled in Isa 18:2&7. Meted in Hebrew means surveyed by string. The thirteen original American Colonies were the first nation in history to be surveyed at its official founding. As we go deeper into the Old Testament, we can further identify ancient nations of the house of Israel that were associated with these names such as Moab in Isa 16:4, Elem in Jerm 49:36 and Egypt in Isa 56:8. The house of Israel is Moab, Elem and Egypt. Both houses of Israel were scattered abroad throughout the world as the lost sheep of Gods chosen people, the peculiar ones to be Christ's Church as named in I Peter 2:9. James 1:1 clearly state that all twelve tribes of Israel were scattered abroad and called strangers. The word abroad in Greek means #1290, *Israelite resident in Gentile countries which are scattered abroad.* James and Peter are speaking of the lost tribes of Israel being scattered abroad throughout the world. After the ten northern tribes were released from their Assyrian captivity, they never returned to the Promised Land and migrated into the wilderness across the Euphrates River recorded in II Esdras 13:40-46. Only a remnant of Jews returned to Judia according to Jerm 40:11 to fulfill Daniel's 70th Week Prophecy in Dan 9:24-27. According to James, all twelve tribes were scattered into the wilderness of the world as Christ's lost sheep to be hidden as a secret for to hide something is a secret. The Young Lions, the Outcast Israelites and the Hidden Ones as Israelite Hebrews are the lost secret hidden sheep of the house of Israel that were commanded by Jesus in the last days to be his Church proven in Matt 10:6 and 15:24.

After reviewing all the nations listed above, the house of Israel called the mountains of Israel as many nations are the Young Lions, the Outcast and Hidden Ones in Eze 38:8 identified in Eze 39:13 as Sheba, Dedan, Tarshish, Moab, Elem and Egypt. These nations are the Western Christian Confederation of NATO that fights Magog in the Ezekiel 38 and 39 war. Many Scriptures in the Old Testament, Egypt is referred to as being leader of the world in ancient times for Israel and other nations always used Egypt as their protecter and to escape famine and war. Joseph was the second most powerful man under Pharoah and considered king of Egypt. Egypt was the leader of all the world in ancient Biblical days prior to Assyria and Babylon.

Now let's review Scripture that documents the soon coming Magog war of Ezekiel 38. First, we must identify the difference between the battle of Jehoshaphat mentioned in Joel 3:2, the battle in the valley of Hamon-Gog (Eze 39:11&15) and the battle of Armageddon (Rev 16:16).

The battle of Jehoshaphat and Hamon-Gog are the same war that brings Gods judgment upon the house of Israel and Judah which is the Great Whore of Babylon. This war occurs at the beginning of Daniel's 70th week or seven-year prophecy for Ezekiel 39:9 states that it takes the people of the cities seven years to burn their weapons. This indicates that it begins at the beginning of Daniel's seven-year prophecy. The Hebrew word Jehoshaphat means; *a place of Judgment*. There is no ancient Biblical record of the valley of Jehoshaphat for in the 4th century AD it was named after the Kidron Valley. Jehoshaphat is believed to be a symbolic valley where all the nations of Israel is gathered by Jehovah for judgment. The Hebrew meaning of Armageddon means *to pluck or to gather* and this is the gathering of all heathen nations for Gods judgment at the end of the seven-years of Tribulation.

The war that takes place in the valley of Hamon Gog occurs at the very beginning of Daniel's seven-year prophecy for two main reasons. The first is to punish the house of Israel (Christian nations) for their falling away from Gods covenant (the Church). The second is to show the world that he is God the Almighty and for his people to accept his truth (Eze 39:22&28). The Church will be taken away (I Thes 4:14-17) prior to the nuclear war and the beginning of Wrath for I Thessalonians 1:10 and 5:9 clearly states that his Church will not see his Wrath on the wicked, **"even Jesus, which delivered us from the wrath to come."** and **"For God hath not appointed us to wrath but to obtain salvation"**. Couple these verses with Jasher 5:5 where God took all that followed him before the flood, **"And all who followed the Lord died in those days, before they saw the evil which God declared to do upon earth."** God will not allow his people (the Church) to see the Wrath he brings upon the wicked in the last days of Tribulation. Another aspect to consider is why 12,000 from each tribe of Israel is sealed in Revelation 7:5-8 if the Church is still present on the earth. It makes no sense for all Christians in the Church already has the seal of the Holy Spirit. We must understand that the Holy Spirit is not taken off earth at the taking of the Church at the beginning of the Trib for it has to remain so that millions of people can be saved during the 1st half of the Tribulation under the preaching of the two Witnesses for 3½ years or 1260 days just as Rev 11:3 states. The 144,000 are saved during the first half of the Trib.

Exactly three and half years later they are killed in the middle of the Trib and immediately the Anti-Christ take power. The Holy Spirit is not taken till the Gospel is finished in Rev 11:7 when the two witnesses are killed and the Gospel is finished. The Beast or Anti-Christ has no power to kill till the Holy Spirit is taken away. The 144,000 Hebrews and Jews are sealed because the protection of the Church has been taken for the Anti-Christ cannot be revealed and receive power till the Holy Spirit is also taken in II Thessalonians 2:7 and Rev 11:7. The Church age of the house of Israel and Daniel's 70th week or seven-year period of the house of Judah cannot overlap for it would interfere with Gods prophetic plans. The key is the removal of the Holy Spirit under the New Covenant and is why the 144,000 have to be sealed prior to the middle of the seven-year period. If the Church or any Christians are present during the last half of the Tribulation, they would be killed for Rev 13:15 clearly states that all would be killed by the Anti-Christ if they fail to take his mark and worship the image of the Beast. Rev 13:15 takes place at the middle of the Tribulation for the seven Vials has not been fulfilled in Revelation chapter sixteen.

The Hebrew meaning of Gog and Hamon-Gog is the same; *a place East of the Dead Sea, the multitude of Gog, the fanciful name of an emblematic (symbolic) place in Palestine, a noise, tumult, crowd, wealth, abundance, company, rumbling, make a loud noise, to rage war, moan, clamor, consume, crush, to trouble and to vex.* It is believed that the nation of Gog or Magog is the old Russian and Communist (Anti-Christian) bloc coalition gathered against the house of Israel in the valley of Hamon-Gog. The ancient name of Meschech found in Ezekiel 38:3 is believed to be modern Moscow in Russia. Hamon-Gog is a place east of the Dead Sea and interesting to see that the tribe of Reuben (Modern France) and Moab is located due east of the Dead Sea as indicated on Biblical maps in ancient times. Ancient Reuben located east of the Dead Sea was a part of the lost tribes of the house of Israel that settled Europe and is now modern France that created Communism. The Arab and Communist nations are called Edom (Russia) in Ezekiel 25:12-16 where they have troubled Israel and Judah during the last days. We must note that Saudi Arabia in the last few years has turned to the Russian bloc nations fulfilling prophecy. The philosophy of

Communism (Godless Religion) came from Reuben that is modern France and implemented by the nations of Edom, the Arab and Eastern European nations. This fulfills the Prophecy of the war mentioned in Ezekiel 38 and 39 and the firstborn inheritance feud between Ishmael (Islamic), Esau (Communism) and Jacob (Christian) culminating into the end time wars. We must also note that Russia and its allies are more Democratic today than America and England. The west has adopted a form of Communism in the last days during its turning away from God becoming the daughter and spirit of Babylon.

How does this war begin? I Thessalonians 5:3 tells us that, **"For when they shall say, Peace and safety; then sudden destruction cometh upon them,"**. This cannot be speaking of modern Israel (the house of Judah) for they are constantly vigilant against terrorism and war. This verse is speaking to the house of Israel (US and GB) for it perfectly matches the present state of the American and British people. We are at rest and ease that dwell safely (Eze 38:8&11) in un-walled cities for we believe our nation cannot be destroyed. We are being lied to by the Main-Stream Media. Verse 8 speaks of the mountains or nations of Israel that was carved out from the wilderness of the world such as America, Australia, New Zealand and all the other colonization under the British Empire. In Hebrew, Abraham means High Father or colonizer indicating that we are the birthright tribes of Abraham's descent as world colonizers. The un-walled cities are the Christian nations in the world living in peace that dwell in safety on foreign continents across the vast oceans (Isa 16:8, Eze 27:4&24 and PS 80:11). We are presently at war with Russia through Ukraine and the world is quickly aligning against us.

Something drastically changes in world politics with Russia and their coalition for Ezekiel 38:4 states, **"And I will turn thee back, and put hooks into thy jaws, and I will bring thee forth, and all thine army, horses and horsemen, all of them clothed with all sorts of armor, even a great company with bucklers and shields, all of them handling swords;"**. For an unspecified reason, Gog or Russia is quickly drawn into a mighty war according to this verse. The next verse aligns Gog or Russia (Eastern bloc nations) with Persia (Arab nations), Ethiopia and Libya, which is the present coalition against Israel and the US in the Middle East of today.

This verse is being fulfilled at this very moment. The above verse states that Gog, Magog and Tubal (Eastern Communist nations) will have hooks put into their jaw to cause them to go to war with the house of Israel (Christian Nations of NATO). This writer believes that the hook in their jaw is either a Nuclear incident or oil and gas to include economic trade sanctions between Russia and the Arab nations forcing them to go to war for Ezekiel 38:4 indicates a reluctance. WW II with Japan started over oil and trade embargos. The Hebrew word hooks mean, *to have a ring for the nose and a way of guiding a domestic farm animal.* For some reason, Russia is drawn into this war due to politics along with their Arab coalition. The American proxy war with Russia through Ukraine could be the hook in the jaw of Gog and Magog, the catalyst for war. Russia supplies a vast amount of technical and military aid to Iran and Syria and could be a conduit to war for NATO through Turkey is stealing millions of dollars of oil each month. Therefore, America's proxy war and economic sanctions with Russia could very well trigger a massive confrontation with Russia/China/North Korea and all the Arab nations as foretold in Ezekiel chapter 38 and 39.

The falling of Babylon mentioned in Revelation 18:2 with the destruction of her cities is the same war that destroys the cities of the house of Israel (western culture of NATO) in Ezekiel 38 and 39. The Babylon of Revelation chapter 18 is simply a symbolic BAAL name for it represents the same scale of idolatry and wealth from the time of the Tower of Babel to King Nebuchadnezzar in ancient Babylon. The Kings of Babylon controlled most of the wealth of the known ancient world just as the United States and NATO today through world banking and trade as the "rich men of the world".

It is very important to have a full understanding of the identity of Mystery Babylon in the book of Revelation for it is a key in comprehending end time prophecy. Like many other Hebrew words, its identity lies within deep-rooted cross references found within the Strong's Concordance. This segment will change your perspective of Babylon's true identity. The Greek meaning comes from Revelation 18:2, (897) *the capital of Chaldaea and literal or figurative as a type of tyranny.* It is crossed referenced to (894) which means, *wormwood as a type of bitterness or calamity (indicating war)* and (895) Ezra 5:12, *as being, lifeless, inanimate or mechanical without life.* From (895) Babylon is crossed referenced to the most important in reference numbers (5590) indicating Babylon being spiritual for its meaning is; *breath by implying a spirit, abstract or concretely from reference* (4151) *the rational and immortal soul; reference* (5592 and 5594) indicate *a coolness, cold or chill referring to wax cold* (Matt 24:12) and (4151) *a current of air, breath or a breeze, by analog or figurative a spirit of the human rational soul and implied as a superhuman, an angel, demon, divine God, Christ's Spirit and Holy Spirit.* It is also crossed referenced to (2222) which means; *life as living literal or figurative.* Reference number (5590) also cross-reference to the Hebrew meaning given in (5315) *"a breathing creature", ghost, mortally, soul,* (7307) *"breath" implying a spirit* and (2416) *"alive" a living thing.* The words figurative, Spirit, wax cold, vex, Christ's Spirit and the Holy Spirit connects Babylon as a figurative ghostly spirit of the Church and America. The Spirit of the Church and the western nations have waxed cold and lifeless as foretold in II Thessalonians 2:3 just prior to its removal in Revelation 18:23-24.

The Hebrew meaning of Babylon is found in reference (894) meaning; *confusion; Babel (Babylon) including the empire*. It is then crossed referenced to (1101) meaning; *primitive root; to overflow with oil; implies to mix, to fodder, anoint, confound, mingle and temper*. It is then crossed referenced to (1098) which means *feed for cattle, corn and fodder*.

After a close study of all the above definitions and cross-reference, we come up with at least two main aspects of Babylon. One coming from the Hebrew meaning as being the physical city or empire representing the spirit of man under one single government and a polytheistic religion controlled by great wealth. Babylon is a symbol of great wealth from the nations of the earth and Spiritualism under Baal worship of many gods. This same religion can be seen in the World Council of Churches of today where all religions of many gods fall under one god that will culminate into Lucifer becoming god as the Apotheosis called the Anti-Christ for 42 months in Rev 13:5-8.

The other aspect can be seen in the Greek definitions as being a symbolic meaning representing the modern spirit of man again indicating the Baal worship of ancient Babylon, worship other than the true God of Jehovah. Baal worship has been passed from generation to generation never changing. By definition, Babylon is a spirit, breath, breeze, tyranny, immortal soul, coolness, wax cold, vex, angel or demon, divine Spirit of God and a living thing or soul. It is a spiritual religion through secret societies such as Free Masonry and Illuminism (Illuminati). These definitions indicate how man's spirit will be manipulated by Satan called the angel of light and his demons to implement his final New World Order as Babylon, the world's economic system. All these aspects of the spirit of Babylon can be seen in our New Age Religions and Liberal Agenda promoted by the wealthy nations of the world just as in ancient days. By definition, the Whore of Mystery Babylon the Great in the book of Revelation is a religious spirit controlled by America and England through Wall Street of New York City, London and Rome. The ideology and spirit of Babylon is slowly culminating into a one world government and religion just as the Tower of Babel almost 6000 years ago. It is a Satanic worship of Lucifer the Devil through secret societies. History is repeating itself just as the Bible predicts.

There is another aspect that we need to consider. God brought judgment upon the people of Mesopotamia due to their pride by eliminating God for they wanted to build a stairway to heaven without including God. God brought judgment by confusing their language (Babel). Today this same ideology that man can become god himself is the same as ancient Babylon. The term Babylon is simply a symbolic name of an age-old religion. God is going to bring judgment upon this organized religion (Liberalism) just as in ancient days but this time it is going to burn as recorded in Revelation chapter 18. Key

Words within the definition such as, wormwood, calamity, vex and tyranny indicate a great war where God brings judgment as recorded throughout the Bible. Revelation 18:23 states that the spirit of the light of a candle and the Bride of Christ which is the Church was no more in Babylon indicating that Babylon has to be the wealthy Christian nations of the west, United States and the British Empire. The Spirit of the Church as indicated in Rev 18:23 was at one time within Babylon, **"And the light of a candle shall shine no more at all in thee; and the voice of the bridegroom** [Christ] **and of the bride** [Church] **shall be heard no more at all in the: for thy merchants were the great men of the earth; for by thy sorceries were all nations deceived"**. Clearly by this Scripture, the Bride of Christ was at one time a part of Babylon but due to the Western Christian nations falling away from Grace, the Church was raptured/taken from her to keep the Church from being killed. Rev 18:4 proves this fact by stating, **"And I heard another voice from heaven saying, Come out of her** [mystery Babylon]**, by people** [the Church]**, that ye be not partakers of her sins, and that ye receive not of her plagues"**. This verse is a warning to all Church members to get out of the Laodicean 501C3 tax exempt Church's to a fundamental Church that teach the true Gospel. The definition of Babylon recorded above is a divine Satanic Spirit controlled by the Roman Catholic Church. That divine Spirit was taken over by a demonic spirit when the Church was removed in Revelation 18:23, therefore, Lucifer declares himself as god in the middle of the Tribulation Period.

Let's make a simple deduction. What single modern city controls most of the world's wealth of our modern time? What stock market manipulates every stock market in the world, therefore, controlling all the wealth of the world? It is the New York City Stock Exchange, the Bull of Wall Street controlled by the United State, Manasseh as the Bull (Duet 33:17). This can be proven by Revelation 18:23-24 as quoted above. According to this verse, Babylon at one time possessed the Church, the voice (Holy Spirit) candlestick and Bride of Christ, but before Babylon was destroyed in Rev 14:8, 18:17 and 19:2, the Church and Spirit was taken. Babylon is the house of Israel possessing great wealth that the Church is in but fell form Gods Covenant and grace, the great falling away, bringing judgment. Babylon represents the political and financial institutions of the world that is presently destroying the Church through Liberalism and is not of God. The term, **"for thy merchants were the great men of the earth"**, indicate that Babylon symbolize the Capitalistic System of the free world controlled by Ephraim and Manasseh as the Birthright tribes. The great wealth of the United States and Great Britain was Christian at one time but the power of Lucifer the Devil infiltrated our system by turning it into the evil spirit of Babylon through Liberal Socialist Communism, Political Correctness and has totally corrupted our Christian institutions and nation.

The atheistic Communist nations of Eastern Europe, the oriental nations of

Buda, the Eastern Mystic nations of India and the growing religion of Islam controlled by the Arab nations make up the majority of the nations of the earth. None of these nations has embraced or practiced Christ's Gospel of his true Church for his Spirit to be in them. The Babylon of Revelation 18:23 can only be the wealthy Christian nations of the west for this verse specifically states that Gods Spirit of the Church was in it before he destroyed its system.

The people of the house of Israel and other nations were deceived by sorceries of Satan's human agents where they penetrated government through the massive wealth of huge Corporations. We must understand that God blessed the United States as a people first and then as a nation because of our righteousness. The government is not necessarily the will of the people for the nihilist has taken over our government. Note in Revelation 18:23 that when this war occurs, the candle and Bridegroom is gone from Babylon or Gods righteous people (the Church) has been taken out or ruptured. Many Christians do not believe there is going to be Rapture at the beginning or in the middle of the seven-year period of John and Daniel's seven-year prophecy of Tribulation. They simply do not understand the time periods as a sequential timeline outlined within this segment and Revelation.

Two thousand years ago when Satan realized he could not stop the coming of the Messiah, he then tried to destroy the Church and Gods Battle Ax (the house of Israel Jeremiah 51:19-20), as his inherited birthright tribes of Ephraim and Manasseh. Satan also knew that he could not physically destroy either but could slowly tear down by infiltrating from within using Secret Societies and organizations. All of ancient and modern history is nothing more than the fight between God and Satan, good and evil and light and darkness, a world war between Christianity and Liberalism which means *change*. The establishing of Secret Societies, philosophies, Religion and evil governments within nations has all but completed his task. The term Babylon is used to indicate the same ancient sorceries used to destroy Babylon that is used to destroy and deceive nations of modern times as Revelation 18:23 states. Huge Corporations controlled by just a few families within the world have implemented Satan's agenda through the accumulation of great wealth. These families worship Lucifer as their Religion with a final goal to place Lucifer (Satan) into power as the Apotheosis under a single world government, the New World Order. They truly believe that Lucifer, the Angel of Light, is the true god and savior, not Satan or Christ but Lucifer. Their infiltration can be seen on the back of the American one-dollar bill (Babylon of the all-seeing eye) by the Latin term, "Novus Ordo Seclorum", New World Order written at the base of the Pyramid under the observance of Lucifer's all-seeing eye. Their intent is to use the One Dollar bill to create a tax base financed by the American people so they can bankroll their one world system. When they have used Babylon (Capitalism) to establish their system, it will no longer be needed and its destruction is necessary just as Revelation chapter 18 predicts. The new world economic system will be implemented through the United Nations paid for by the American Tax Payer, the One Dollar bill "Novus Ordo Seclorum".

There is one more aspect that we need to consider in light of Lucifer (Satan) becoming the world leader and proclaiming himself as god. Understand that Satan has been planning this event for approx. 6000 years and has laid out a brilliant plan channeled to his human children or agents. We must understand that Satan wants to be called Lucifer for the name Lucifer was given to him by God when he was an angel in Heaven as the angel of Light. God changed his name to Satan that means "advisory" after he rebelled in Heaven, therefore, he wants to be called Lucifer after his Heavenly name. For Satan to claim himself as world leader, he has to destroy the current world powers that are the American, Russian and China coalitions through great wars. To proclaim himself as god the Apotheosis, he has to destroy fundamental religions such as Christianity, Atheism, Buda, Judaism and Islam. All the other passive and progressive religions will conform to his new Religious System due to massive death and destruction created by World Wars. These wars have multiple purposes for Lucifer to be placed into power. Ezekiel 38 and 39 says that the Russian coalition destroys the house of Israel but in turn, Russia and their coalition is destroyed with secret weapon the Deep State possess. It is this Author's belief that the Deep State has secrets weapons that the world knows nothing about (space based weapon DEW) and they allow Russia to destroy America before they release their weapons destroying the Russian coalition just as Eze 39 states. For the benefit of the Anti-Christ, this destroys the American coalition of Christianity/Judaism, the Arab nations of the Islamic Religion and the Russian coalition of Atheism, eliminating the world's major fundamental Religions.

The war that occurs in the valley of Jehoshaphat and Hamongon eliminates the world-class powers of America, Britain, Arab and Russian coalitions along with the influence of Christianity, Islam and Atheism. This first war of approx. three wars allows the Anti-Christ to take power for the Spirit of the Church and the strength of Christianity is taken away (Ruptured) just prior to this Great War.

To sum up this segment, there are a few dynamic chapters in Ezekiel that should be considered. The whole book of Ezekiel deserves to be closely studied for it is a progression of how God established the nation of Israel in the wilderness of their own land and overturned his throne from Jerusalem to the house of Israel within the wilderness. This can be seen in chapter 17 through 22. Chapters 34 through 39 is a walk-through time concerning the prophecies of Israel from the time they became a nation in ancient times till the last days of the time of Tribulation. This is the war of their judgment due to breaking of

Gods two Covenants, ancient Old Covenant under Judaism and modern New Covenant Church. Ezekiel 34:23 explains how the house of Israel is scattered into the wilderness to establish Christ's Church and states, **"And I will set up one shepherd over them, and he shall feed them, even my servant David; he shall fed them and he shall be their shepherd"**. This verse places King David's throne in the wilderness under Gods New Covenant of the Church spoken of in Hebrew 8:8 and Jeremiah 31:31 where the throne was overturned to England in Ezekiel 21:25-27. Chapter 35 is the warning to the mountains or nations of Seir that is a region south of the Dead Sea called Idumaea and its aboriginal occupants. It is this writer's belief through study that Idumaea is the descendants of Esau (the Red Baby) of Edom that became the Communist bloc nations of Russia (Red Communism of the Red Horse Rev 6:4). They call their elective legislative assembly of the lower house of parliament the Duma indicating their connection to Idumaea. This chapter is a warning of their Godless evilness and soon coming destruction as predicted in Ezekiel chapter 38 and 39.

Chapter 36 is the warning to the mountains or nations of the house of Israel (Ephraim GB and Manasseh USA) of their soon coming judgment and destruction. Verse 8 speaks of how Israel will shoot forth branches and be fruitful (Christian) to be tilled and sown and verse 17 says that they shall dwell in their own land where they defile and pollute, turn against Gods Covenant. Eze 36:24-27 establishes the Church in the wilderness where the house of Israel is gathered into their own land from all countries of the world. They are given a new heart and Spirit where Gods Spirit is given them so they can keep his statutes and judgments. This can only be Christ's Gospel and Church. These verses are not speaking to the Jews of modern Israel but the Christian nations of the world. Eze 36:33-34 states how the house of Israel will be given their own land and cities to dwell and how they came from the land that lay desolate and became as the Garden of Eden. This is their colonization of the desolate continents of the world given to the house of Israel to fulfill the promise of greatness to be nations and kingdoms given as a firstborn birthright inheritance to Ephraim and Manasseh in Gen 48:16-22. Just look at the great wealth that the desolate continents have produced in the past 300 years and most of these lands are Christian, fulfilling Gods promise of greatness to a multitude of nations as Gen 48:19, **"and his seed shall become a multitude of nations"**. Verse 38 calls these waste cities in the wilderness Jerusalem just as it has a duel meaning. Jerusalem is filled with flocks of men that know the Lord. In no way can this verse be speaking of the modern city of Jerusalem as the Jews for they still reject Christ their Savior.

When WW III begins, the Church will have been taken away by Christ so the Marriage Supper of the Lamb can take place in Heaven and the war of Ezekiel chapter 38 and 39 begins. This war is the judgment of the wicked physical house of Israel and Judah that is not a part of Christ's spiritual Church for the Church will clearly not see WRATH according to I Thess 1:10, 5:9, Dan 12:1 and worthy to escape wrath in Luke 21:36. According to Rev 6:16 Gods wrath does not occur till the opening of the 6th Seal at approx. the 11th month of the 1st half of the Trib. If we meet the criteria of Rev 3:1-5, <u>receive,</u> <u>hear,</u> <u>hold fast,</u> <u>repent</u> and <u>watch</u> for the Gospel, we will escape and be taken away by the Rapture. Read and study these two chapters for details of the soon coming Magog war that is on the verge of occurring. If we apply all the information given above to the following Scriptures below, it will give us a clear picture of historical facts that has taken place in the last two-thousands years identifying Gods people and his Church.

<u>World War III</u>

<u>Ezekeal 38-39 speaks of a limited nuclear war</u> called the battle of Hamon-Gog where the bodies of Magog are buried. This war was a mid-east war where their nuclear missiles came to Europe and America: Nuclear missiles came to the "isles" as "wormwood" in Jerm 9:15 during the 2nd Seal. Rev 6:12-17 *"as a scroll"*, Rev 8:11 at the 3rd Trumpet *"called wormwood"* and Isa 34:4 also *"as a scroll"*. According to these Scriptures, there are at least three nuclear wars. <u>One</u> at the beginning of the Trib where Damascus and Ephriam is destroyed in the Eze 38 war which takes place in Rev 6:3-4 where the Red Horse has **"a great sword"** of war. The <u>2nd</u> in Rev 8:10-11 at the 3rd Trumpet a falling star called "wormwood" and the <u>3rd</u> in Rev 6:12-17 at the opening of the 6th Seal for verse 14 says **"and the heaven departed as a scroll when it is rolled together"** indicating a nuclear blast. This same war is recorded in Isa 34:1-10 **"and the heavens shall be rolled together as a scroll"** bringing judgement to the nations in the 1st half of the Tribulation.

The first war is where Ephraim (America as leader sitting on the White Horse 1st Seal), Russia and Damascus are destroyed by nuclear weapons in Isa 17:1-3 and Amos 1:1-5. Russia loses 5/6th of their army according to Eze 39:2 **"and leave but the sixth part"**, verse 6, **"And I will send a fire on Magog, and among them that dwell carelessly in the isles"**, those that dwell in the isles are the 46 nations of the Commonwealth of England that are mostly islands and America where they are nuked and destroyed. Eze 39:11&15 clearly speak of **"the valley of Hamon-God"** where Russia and 5/6th of their coalition is buried. Note that Eze 39:6 speak of Magog and those that *"dwell carelessly in the isles"* are destroyed. All through the Old and New Testaments, when referring to the "isles", it is speaking of Ephraim and Manasseh in where they migrated after the Assyrian and Babylonian captivities. They are the "Scottish children" spoken of in Jerm 4:22 as the Outcast Ps 147:2, Hidden Ones Ps 83:3, Young Lions Eze 38:13 and scattered strangers in I Peter 1:1 and James 1:1. They are the lost sheep of the house of Israel in Matt 10:6 and 15:24 which

171

is Christ's Church of England and America. A biblical fact is that the Scottish Bag Pipe derived from the flute which was a part of the Hebrew culture from Israel as a musical instrument used within the Temple and when rejoicing. The pipe or flute is mentioned in I Sam 10:5, Isa 5:12, Isa 30:29 and I Cor 14:7. In Hebrew pipe means, #2485, Isa 30:29, *a flute as perorated*, 2490, *to play the flute*, 2470, *to be rubbed or worn* , Greek in I Cor 14:7, #836, *a flute as blown, pipe*, 109, *to breath unconsciously, respire, to blow air*, 5594, *to breath voluntarily but gently*, 4154, *denotes a forcible respiration*. The flute was an instrument invented by the Scottish that could be blown into and be rubbed or worn as a musical instrument as related to the "Sottish children" in Jerm 4:22.

Important Note: Many Christians do not believe that the Tribulation last for seven-years and broken into two 3½ year periods. Those that do, do not believe that the first half is of wrath. Joel 2:1-3 gives a dire WARNING and proves differently just as Rev 6:16-17 calls it "wrath is come". Many of the following Scriptures describes war at the beginning of the seven-year Trib that catapults the Anti-Christ into power at the middle of the Trib. Joel 2:1 state, **"Blow ye the trumpet in Zion** [the Church]**, and sound an alarm in my holy mountain** [house of Israel]**: let all the inhabitants of the land tremble: for the day of the Lord cometh, for it is nigh a hand:"**. Verse 3 states, **"A fire devoureth before them; and behind them a flame burneth: the land is as the garden of Eden before them, and behind them a desolate wilderness; yes, and nothing shall escape them"**. This verse calls this land the garden of Eden for it is a righteous wealthy plush nation as Christ's lost sheep, Matt 10:6 and 15:24.

The following verses describes a war that destroys Jerusalem or Israel as God's people that disobey his commandments bringing judgment in ancient (twelve tribe of Israel) verses modern times (the lost sheep of the house of Israel). These Scriptures explains the Gaza war and the up-coming Ezekiel 38 war to include the following wars during the first half of the Tribulation:

Note: We must remember the mirror effect of Prophecy when it comes to God's WRATH for what happened in ancient days will also occur in the end time wars of the last days. We must understand that all the Prophetic books of the Bible were written directly to the Church in the last days just as Gen 49:1 and Isa 2:2 state. This one verse speaks directly to the blessings given to all twelve tribes of Israel as separate nations to take place in the last days, **"that I may tell you that which shall befall you in the last days"**. We are now in the "last days" and these prophetic wars are on the edge of fulfilment.

The Gaza Strip war that is currently occurring (started on 10/08/2023)

The Bible is accurate and truthful in describing the war between Israel and

Gaza not only in ancient times but in our current time period. Prophecy is a mirror in time. This Author believes the Gaza war is the beginning of the Ezekiel 38 & 39 war that kicks off the seven-year period of the Tribulation. Zephaniah 2:1-7 clearly lays out the Gaza situation where Zeph 1:14-15 give the time frame in **"The great day of the Lord"** and verse 15 calls it **"That day is a day of wrath, a day of trouble and distress"**. Daniel 12:1 calls the Tribulation a **"time of trouble"**, Jerm 30:7 **"for that day is great, so that none is like it: it is even the time of Jacob's trouble"** and II Thess 1:6 even calls it **"tribulation to whom that trouble you"**. Clearly in Scripture, when ever the term **"in the day of visitation"** in Isa 10:3, **"day of the Lord"** in Isa 13:6, **"in that day"** in Isa 2:20, **"Day of trouble"** in Isa 22:5, **"until this day"** in Isa 39:6, **"day of vengeance of our God"** in Isa 61:2 for all of these verses came out of the book of Isaiah that was to take place in **"the last days"** according to Isa 2:2. With all these Scripture in mind, the Israeli Gaza war in Zeph 2:1-7 was to take place in the last days which is our current time period.

Brief History of Gaza

Modern Palestine are the Palestinians presently located in the Gaza Strip, the area of the ancient Philistines in 2000BC to approx. 500BC

Zeph 2:1-7: Now let's break down Zeph 2:1-7 verse by verse to identify the war that is currently taking place. Verse 1-3 calls these people **"gather together, O nation not desired"** and to **"seek ye the Lord"**, **"before the day of the Lord's anger"**. Verse four identifies these people, **"For Gaza shall be forsaken and Ashkelon a desolation: they shall drive out Ashdod at the noon day, and Ekron shall be rooted up"**. According to this verse, Ashkelon, Ashdod and Ekron are cities just north of the Gaza Strip on the coast of Israel soon to be destroyed. These people are Palestinians that no country in the world wants not even the Arab countries for they are hate filled self-destructive evil murderous people where God warns them to seek meekness and righteousness before the day of his judgment.

The following verses ties in with the war between the red and white horse in the 1st and 2nd Seals which are the Lion of Judah as the house of Israel, UK & America, the Bear of Russia in Dan 7:5, and Ezekiel chapters 38-39, they are the same war.

Jeremiah, Ezekiel, Isaiah and Daniel were written to the Church to take place in the Last Days.

Jerm 8:19&9:13-19: Is speaking to "the daughter of my people" which is Israel as the Church for Jerm 8:19 calls them **"Is not the Lord in Zion? Is not her king in her?"**. We know that Zion is Christ's Church for chapter eight and nine is talking directly to "the daughter of my people" in 9:1-2 being scattered in the "wilderness". Jerm 9:13-15 states, **"Therefore thus saith the Lord of hosts, the God of Israel; Behold, I will feed them even this people, with wormwood, and give them water of gall to drink"**. This Godly judgment occurs in the 2rd Seal of Rev 6:3-4 as a limited nuclear war between the Red and White horses of NATO with America at its head and the Red Russian bear. The head of NATO which is America is destroyed by Russa but before the war is complete, Russia is destroyed by the remaining NATO forces as stated in Eze 25:12-16 for verse clearly states, **"And I will lay my vengeance upon Edom** [Russia] **by the hand of my people Israel** [England/America as the house of Israel]**; and they shall do in Edom according to mine anger"**. NATO survives and becomes a great army of the 4th Beast with iron teeth for the Anti-Christ in Dan 7:7.

Jerm 10:15-25 – remember the mirror effect of prophecy what happened in the past with Israel is going to happen in the last days Gen 49:1. Verse 15 **"their visitation they shall perish"** verse 17, **"gather up thy wares out of the land, O inhabitant of the fortress"** Babylon and America with UK, verse 21 **"for the pastors are become brutish, and have not sought the Lord."** The Church of the house of Israel is the USA & UK, Matt 10:6, 15:24 and Acts 10:36, verse 25 **"made his habitation desolate"**. God destroys America as the head of NATO that created the antichrist beast with the wounded head that occurred in the Ezekial 38 war. The 1st and 2nd Beast in Dan 7:3-5 is the NATO war with the Red Bear of Russian in Daniel's dream. This great limited nuclear war clips the wings of the Lion which is the head of the White Horse in the 1st and 2nd Seal. The wounded head of the white horse is spoken of in Rev 13:3&12-14, 6:3-4 where its deadly wound was healed. There are several wars that occur between the 3nd Seal and the 7th Trumpet in the 1st half of the Tribulation. All military armies and equipment during these wars are rebuilt into the Anti-Christ's army to include the 3rd Beast of Daniel's dream. The deadly wound that was healed are the revived armies that became the 4th Beast with iron teeth as the great military power of the Anti-Christ.

Note: Jeremiah 2:4 tells us to whom the book of Jeremiah is written, **"Hear ye the word of the Lord, O house of Jacob, and all the families of the house of Israel"**. We must note that this verse is speaking of many nations as families for Jacob has twelve sons and each as a family were an individual nation according to II Kings 17:26 and Gen 48:19. Jerm 3:18 gives us a time period in when this book takes place, **"In those days the house of Judah shall walk with the house of Israel, and they shall come together out of the land of the north to the land that I have given for an inheritance unto your father"**. When you see the term "in those days" it is speaking of the **"that which shall befall you in the last days"** as Gen 49:1 state when it comes to inheritance of Israel's twelve tribes. According to Jerm 3:18, Israel came from the land of the north for the north is where the house of Israel went after their Assyrian captivity. We must note that in II Kings 17:23 the ten northern tribes of the house of Israel are called only Israel for it states, **"Untill the Lord removed Israel out of his sight, as he had said by all his servants the prophets. So was Israel carried away out of their own land to Assyria unto this day"**.

Clearly the house of Judah and house of Israel are two separate nations of people. After their captivity to Assyria, the house of Israel departed to the north into Europe according to II Esdras 13:40-46 into the land of Arsareth and in Hebrew means *a far-away land beyond the Euphrates River*. By Scripture, Israel was many nations when they were taken captive into the northern wilderness to never return to the Promised Land of Cannan. Where are they today? They are under the throne of King David in England according to Jerm 23:3-6, **"that I will raise unto David a righteous Branch, and a King shall reign and prosper, and shall execute judgment and justice in the earth"**. The term "justice in the earth" is speaking of the Gospel of the Church for Judaism was never in the whole earth.

Jerm 4:22&29: Israel is called "Sottish children" in Jerm 4:22, **"For my people is foolish, they have not known me; they are sottish children, and they have none understanding: they are wise to do evil, but to do good they have no knowledge"**, for they are foolish and silly. Verse 29, **"The whole city shall flee for the noise of the horsemen** [the Red horse] **and bowmen; they shall go into thickets, and climb up upon the rocks: every city shall be forsaken, and not a man dwell therein"**. In verse 16 of this chapter, it explains to whom this verse is speaking and it is **"watchers come from a far country, and give out their voice against the cities of Judah"**. Who are these *"watchers from a far country"*? Watcher in Hebrew, Jerm 4:16, ref #5341, *to guard in a good sense to protect, maintain, obey or **a bad one to conceal**, besieged, **hidden thing**, keeper, monument, observe, preserver, subtil*. According to this definition, these watchers were to be concealed and hidden as a people just as the Hidden Ones of the lost tribes of Israel spoken of in Ps 83:3. The house of Israel as "Sottish children" migrated into Ireland, Scottland and England where God hid them in the wilderness. The term "sottish" in Hebrew means, ref. #5530, *silly or foolish*, 5528, *to be silly, do play that turns into foolishness*. They mingled with the Gentiles of Europe losing their Hebrew language and identity where they were divorced from God due to Idolatry in Jerm 3:8, **"And I saw, when for all the causes whereby backsliding Israel committed adultery, I had put her away, and given her a bill of divorce"**.

God sent them into the wilderness of Europe to wait for the coming of Christ and his Gospel to be his Church where they were remarried in Hos 2:19 **"And I will betroth thee unto me for ever; yea, I will betroth thee unto me in righteousness, and in judgment, an in lovingkindness, and in mercies"**. It

175

is uncanny that the word Scottish people and the Sottish Children are almost identical. In the time of Jeremiah approx. 519BC, according to the historian Sir. Henry Rawlinson, hordes of Scythian Barbarians swarmed into Southwest Asia through the passes of the Caucasus Mountains. They massacred everything as they went and weakened the Assyrian Empire. We know through ancient English historical writers, the early Israelites were called Sakasuni, Saki, Guti, Getai, Sak-Goleths, Skuthai, Skoloti and Scythians, "Tracing Our Ancestors" by Frederick Haberman page 130. The ancient historian Ptolemy calls the Scythians a race that sprung from the Sakai called Saxons. According to these ancient writers, the Scythians were of Hebrew descent for during the Assyrian captivity of the ten northern tribes, they deported many Hebrew people of the tribes of Israel into Spain and other parts of Europe to include Scottland (Sottish Children), Ireland and England. We also know through the study of ancient history, many Hebrew people of the twelve tribes of Jacob, especially Dan, was of ships (Judges 5:17 **"why did Dan remain in ships"**) departed Egypt due to enslavement by Pharoah. Also, a portion of the Tribes did not depart Egypt with Moses at the Exodus but departed by ship into Europe for many Hebrews were both sea and Nial river mariners for the Egyptians. The name British in Hebrew means *"covenant of man"* and the Galic language is based upon Hebrew letters. This is why Ephraim and Manasseh, the two sons of Joseph, carry the symbols of the Unicorn of England and the Bull of Wall Street in Duet 33:17. They are the *"Sottish children"* and *"watchers come from a far country"* in Jerm 4:16&22. This is just a few facts on English/Hebrew if you are willing to research ancient British history. The reason Jeremiah said these things about the Hebrew people being unwise or foolish as being sottish or evil is that these invading forces were of Hebrew descent as Scottish/British children that lost the Hebrew faith of God's righteous commandments.

Jerm 15:8 – This verse is in direct reference to Jerm 4:22&29 above where Gods people as a nation are judged, **"I have brought upon them against the mother of the young men a spoller at noonday; I have caused him to fall upon it suddenly, and terrors upon the city"**. Read verses 1-7 to understand to whom and why God brought judgment against his people. They were judged by God through their own Hebrew ancestors that migrated into Europe centuries prior to this war by watchers from a far country. They were called the "Sottish children" possibly as Scottish tribes of people.

Jerm 49:13: The destruction of Russia is recorded in this verse, **"For I have sworn by myself, saith the Lord, that Bozrah** [modern Russia] **shall become a desolation, a reproach, a waste, and a curse and all the cities thereof shall be perpetual wastes"**. Perpetual waste indicates a nuclear war producing a wasteland. Bozrah is Edom a town in modern Lebanon but was part of Israel during the time of King David and Solomon. We know that Edom or Idumea is Russa for the Russian parliament is called the Duma and Meshech, lineage of

Shem in I Chron 1:17. In Eze 38:2 this alinement is called Moscow of modern Russia as Magog. Meshech dwells in the tent of Kadar, Ps 120:5 meaning the Russians were of Arab descent.

The book of Isaiah in Isa 1:2 is written to all Israelites of Judah and Jerusalem in the last days, **"I have nourished and brought up children, and they have rebelled against me"** and in verse 8 called them **"the daughter of Zion"** offspring or daughter of the house of Israel. Isa 2:2 places the time to occur, **"And it shall come to pass in the last days"** just as Gen 49:1 says. Isaiah brings judgment upon rebellious children and ungodly man!

The book of Isaiah is a dire WARNING to the Church and the Whole World for Isa 6:11-12 state **"Then said I, Lord, how long? And he answered, Until the cities be wasted without inhabitant, and the houses without man, and the land be utterly desolate, And the Lord have removed men far away, an there be a great forsaking in the midst of the land"**. According to Isa 66:1 and Acts 7:49, *"my throne, and the earth is my footstool"*, therefore, the term "in the midst of the land" has to be speaking to all the earth just as Christ sent his Apostles and Church to teach all the earth his Gospel.

Isa 17:1-5 Describes total nuclear destruction of Damascus Syria. Isa 17:1-3, **"The burden of Damascus, Behold, Damascus is taken away from being a city, and it shall be a ruinous heap** [nuclear war]**. The cities of Aroer are forsaken: they shall be for flocks, which shall lie down, and none shall make them afraid. The fortress also shall cease from Ephraim** [Young Bulls as Outcast and Hidden Ones of USA/UK]**, and the kingdom from Damascus, and the remnant of Syria: they shall be as the glory of the children of Israel, saith the Lord of hosts"**. This verse is speaking of a future war for as of September 2023 history proves that Damascus was one of the first ancients cites of the world and has never been destroyed. During this same future war, Ephraim is also destroyed and we know that Ephraim was given the firstborn birthright to be many nations in Gen 49:16-22 as the lost sheep of the house of Israel given Christ's Church as unicorns and bulls as the stone of Israel in Gen 49:24, Duet 33:17 and Matt 10:6, 15:24. This Isa 17:1 war is found in Zephaniah 2:11-13 for verse 11 state, **"The Lord will be terrible unto them"** **"even all the isles of the heathern** [speaking of the English Isles]**"**, verse 12-13, **"Ye Ethiopians also, ye shall be slain by my sword. And he will stretch out his hand against the north, and destroy Assyria; and will make Nineveh a desolation, and dry like a wilderness"**. Amos 1:4-5 below goes into more detail.

Amos 1:4-5, This is the same war as in Isa 17:1-5, **"But I will send a fire into the house of Hazael, which shall devour the places of Benhadad. I will break also the bar of Damascus, and cut off the inhabitant from the plain**

of Aven, and him that holdeth the scepter [Throne of England] **from the house of Eden** [the Church of Ephriam in Isa 17:3 is England and America]: **and the people of Syria shall go into captivity unto Kir, saith the Lord".** Verse 12, **"But I will send a fire upon Teman** [a race and district of Edom Russia]**, which shall devour the places of Bozrah".** This verse speaks of a war that destroys Christian NATO countries and cities along with Russia.

Hazael: (Syria) I Kings 19:15 a King over Syria,
Benhadad: (Syria) II Chron 16:2 also a King of Syria
Damascus: (Syria/Russia) (II Sam 8:6 Capital of Syria coalition of Russia)
Aven: (BAAL Religion) a symbol of BAAL Worship, Gen 41:45 dedicated to the sun, modern city of Heliopolis eight miles from Cairo called "City of the Sun" BAAL as worship of the sun.
Eden: (England/America) Amos 1:5 Joel 2:3, *"the house of Eden"*, Hebrew 5731, *the region of Adam's home*, 5730, *pleasure, delicate, delight*, 5727, *to be soft or pleasant, to live voluptuously, delight-self.* Eden is the righteous Christian nations of the house of Israel prior to their falling away for Eden is Zion in the wilderness given to the lost sheep in Isa 51:3, **"For the Lord shall comfort Zion: he will comfort all her waste places; and he will make her wilderness like Eden".** Isa 51:5 says the people in the wilderness as God's people will wait for Christ's Gospel for it states, **"My righteousness is near; my salvation is gone forth, and mine arms shall judge the people; the isles shall wait upon me, and on mine arm shall they trust".**
Teman: (Russia) Amos 1:12, Hebrew 8487, *the name of two Edomites of the region and descendants of one of them on the south side, 8486, the sough as being on the right hand of a person facing the east, south side-ward, wind, 3225, the right hand or side, leg, eye of a person or other object as the stronger and more dexterous, locally the south side.*
Bozrah: (Russia) Hebrew in Mic 2:1, Amos 1:12, 1224, *a place in Edom,* 1223, *an enclosure or sheep fold,* 1219, *to gather grapes, to be isolated or inaccessible by hight or fortification, wall up,* 1210, *the grape crop or vintage.*
Edom: (Russia) Joel 3:19, Edom *"a desolate wilderness"*, Amos 1:6-11, 123, Hebrew, *red, elder twin brother of Jacob, the region of Idumea,* 122, *rosy red or ruddy,* 119 *show blood in the face, flush red.* They are Edomites of Edom descendants of Esau that migrated into southern Europe and becoming the Russian people as Red Russia.
Kir: in Hebrew means *an enclosure wall, or prison*, a place to which the Assyrians carried the inhabitants of Damascus captive in II Kings 16:9 and Amos 1:5. May not be a true proper name at all but an enclosure where prisoners were dept.

Isa 63:1-8 Verse 2, **"Where art thou red in thine apparel, and thy garments like him that treadeth in the winefat?"** indicating Red Russia, verse 4, **"day of vengeance is in mine heart, and the year of my redeemed is come"**, they

178

fell into sin and iniquity so he redeemed his righteous. Verses 7-8 explains how the Lord has bestowed goodness on the house of Israel his mercies for they are his people and children being their Savior. Big problem, they fell away into sin so he brought vengeance upon them using Russia with war!

The war that destroyed the Great Whore of Babylon in Rev 6:12 at the 6ᵗʰ Seal

11ᵗʰ month mark of the first half of the Trib

Jerm 50:1-46, Chapters 50 and 51 take place in the **"later days"** according to Jerm 49:39 and speaking directly to Babylon for 50:1 state, **"The word that the Lord spake against Babylon and against the land of the Chaldeans by Jeremiah the Prophet"**. The house of Israel has become Babylon of the Chaldeans and both chapters are a treasure trove of information in identifying this fact so carefully study both chapters. Jerm 50:1 speak directly to Babylon as Israel, **"The word that the Lord spake against Babylon and against the land [Israel] of the Chaldeans by Jeremiah the prophet"**. Verse 4, **"In those days, and in that time, saith the Lord, the children of Israel shall come"** and verse 6, **"My people hath been lost sheep: their shepherds have caused them to go astray"** and verse 17, **"Israel is a scattered sheep the lions have driven him away"**. The "lost sheep" and "scattered sheep" in these two verses confirmed in I Peter 1:1 and James 1:1 as "scattered strangers abroad" where James 1:1 directly identifies them as **"the twelve tribes"** of Israel. By these Scriptures, Babylon is the lost sheep of the house of Israel as Christ's Church proven in Matt 10:6 and 15:24. Verse 9 speak of Russia coming against Babylon America, **"For, lo, I will raise and cause to come up against Babylon an assembly of great nations from the north country:"** which is Russia during the 2ⁿᵈ Seal of the Red horse of the Ezekiel 38 war. Verses 15 and 28 calls this war vengeance not wrath. Verse 33 calls this nation of people the **"children of Israel and the children of Judah"** as being one. Verse 34-38 brings a sword upon her wealth, upon her liars, upon her mighty men and a drought upon her waters.

Jerm 51:1-64: War against Babylon called the house of Israel. We must note that Jerm 3:6-8 speak of the houses of Judah and Israel as **"Backsliding Israel committed adultery I had put her away, and given her a bill of divorce: yet her treacherous sister Judah feared not, but went and played the harlot also"**. These verses are referring to ancient and modern times for now the Church has fallen away just as Rev 3:14-19 is fulfilled and spiritually has become Babylon the Whore.

Verse 1, **"Thus saith the Lord; Behold, I will raise up against Babylon and against them that dwell in the midst of them that raise up against me, a**

destroying wind:".

Destruction of Damascus in Eze 38 War or WWIII

Nahum 2:1-9 Jacob and the house of Israel fall from God's grace due to wickedness and verse 13 burn her chariots in the smoke and devour the young lions, the house of Israel, and the voice of her messenger herd no more.

Zephaniah 1:14-15 verse 14, **"The great day of the Lord is near"**, verse 15, **"That day is a day of wrath, a day of trouble and distress, a day of wasteness and desolation, a day of darkness and gloominess, a day of clouds and thick darkness"**. These two verses describe most of the seven Seals and Trumpets as wrath, trouble, distress, wasteness, desolation, gloominess and clouds of think darkness. The first 3½ years of the seven-year Tribulation where Daniel calls it the time of Trouble in Dan 12:1 is nothing but war one after another. Let's do a quick break-down of the first and second halves of the Tribulation by the seven Seals, Trumpets and Vials:
Zach 14:12- **"flesh and eye sockets melt" WWIII**

Warning of Sudden Destruction and Power source of the Deep State

There is a WARNING that should be mentioned in reference to what some Authors and talk show host are currently talking about. There is a belief that President Trump is going to return and clean out the DC swamp. We are going to get our country back and have a strong prosperous economy with great peace. That is just not true if we follow the Scriptures, for I Peter 5:8 clearly state that in the last days evil men will only become more seductive, devouring and this evil world will wax worse and worse. Ephesians 6:12 proves this point for it states, **"For we wrestle not against flesh and blood, but against principalities, against powers, against the rulers of the darkness of this world against spiritual wickedness in high *places"***. According to this verse, Satan which is the Deep State, has control of this country and will only get worse, not better, just as the Scripture state. The Satanic Liberal Communist has a moto, *if needed, take one step back to take two steps forward*. Trump, being out of office, is fighting the greatest power ever devised by evil men and their power comes direct from Lucifer the Devil, the principalities of darkness. Can Trump win the next election, I do not think so, if there is an election, for sudden destruction will come for 1 Thessalonians 5:3 tells the facts, **"For when they shall say, Peace and safety; then sudden destruction cometh upon them"**. It is this Authors belief that we are now currently within this time period for many Christians have given up the fight for they believe Trump is going to bring Peace. We may think President Trump is going to be reelected and clean up Washington and we are going to go into a peaceful time period but be WARNED, according to Scripture, sudden destruction occurs. An unexpected event transpires that cause Gog, believed to be Russia, to ignite WWIII as Ezekiel 38:4 states, **"And I will turn thee back, and put hooks into thy jaws, and I will bring thee forth, and all thine army, horses and horsemen, all of them clothed with all sorts of armor, even a great company"**. This verse is speaking of WWIII with their coalition of nations in the Middle East just as they are aligned today as listed in Eze 38:5-6, **"Persia, Ethiopia, and Libya with them; all of them with shield and helmet: Gomer, and all his bands; the house of Togarmah of the north quarters, and all his bands: and many people with thee"**. These are the same nations aligned with Russia today. Trump had the power as president to drain the swamp but he failed for he did not place the right people into the important positions prior, so, the election was taken from him. Now, the Deep State controlled by the Liberal Democrats that worship Lucifer the Devil could possibly force Russia into war and the beginning of the Tribulation. Peace is not going to happen for we are at the door and where Satan is striving to form his godless New World Order and it will be on schedule according to Scripture. The current political, military, international debt crises and economic situation of the world is extremely dire and could explode at any moment. When the markets crash, the world always goes to war.

Brief overview of the seven Seals, Trumpets and Vials in 1st and 2nd Half of Tribulation bringing VENGEANCE & WRATH

Events of the 1st 3½ years or 1260 days by each Seal and Trumpet:
Time period is for the two Witnesses
The first Five Seals are Vengeance upon the nations

1st Seal- The first five Seals are Vengeance upon the nations of man and Babylon. White Horse, noise and thunder of conquering and to conquer, WAR!
2nd Seal- Red Horse, power to take peace from the earth given a great sword to kill WAR!
3rd Seal- Black Horse, having a pair of balances, world economic collapse.
4th Seal- Pale Horse named Death and Hell power given to kill with sword and hunger, world famine and WAR!
5th Seal- Saints under the Alter **"crying how long O Lord, holy and true, dost thou not judge and avenge our blood"** indicating that WRATH and judgment has not come at this Seal.

WRATH upon the nations begins in the 6th Seal

6th Seal- Great earthquake, sun black as sackcloth of hair, moon became as blood, heaven departed as a scroll (Nuke WAR) where every mountain and island moved out of its place and "wrath is come". WAR! Six major events occurred at the 6th Seal. 1st. Rev 6:12 Souls under the Alter released, 2nd.

144,000 Saints Sealed 3rd. Rev 7:4, 14:3, Fall of Babylon 4th. Rev 14:3-8 & Ch 17&18, 5th. Marriage Supper of the Lamb Rev 19:9, WRATH begins Rev 6:17, 6th. 2nd Nuclear War Heaven scrolls in Rev 6:14 and Isa 34:1-10 indicating a nuclear blast.

7th Seal- Silance in Heaven for ½ hour silent prayer for the Saints under the alter up to God, seven angels prepare to blow the seven Trumpets.

1st Trumpet- Fire mingled with blood cast upon the earth with 1/3 of trees, and grass was burnt up. WAR!

2nd Trumpet-Great Mountain burning with fire cast into the sea, 1/3 of sea became blood, 1/3 of creatures in the sea died, 1/3 of ships destroyed. War!

3rd Trumpet- Great star burning as a lamp (Nuke missile) fell upon 1/3 of rivers and fountains of waters called Wormwood (bitter as radiation poison) made bitter and many men died.

4th Trumpet- 1/3 part of sun, moon and stars were darkened for 1/3 of day and night not shine. WAR!

5th Trumpet- **Proceeds for 5 months**, a Star (angel) fell from Heaven on to earth having the key to the bottomless pit where the sun and the air were darkened by reason of the smoke of the pit. Locusts came out of the smoke having a king called Abaddon in Hebrew and Apollyon in Greek which is Satan or the Anti-Christ. They were commanded to not hurt grass of the earth or any green thing **"but only those men which have not the seal of God in their foreheads"** (Rev 9:4) to not kill but to torment for 5 months. Note, this indicate that the MARK of the Beast has not occurred but takes place at the blowing of the 7th Trump. This is the 1st WOE which is Wrath of dark smoke WAR!

Beginning of God's wrath and judgment

6th Trumpet- **Proceeds for 13 months** (Rev 9:13), The four angels of the Euphrates River released **"for an hour, and a day, and a month, and a year, for to slay the third part of men"** to dry it up so the armies of the kings (China and N. Korea) of the east could cross to do battle with two million soldiers. Total WAR!

7th Trumpet- Rev 10:7&11:15, The angel shouted, **"the mystery [Gospel] of God shall be finished"**, meaning the Gospel of Jesus is complete and confirmed when the two witnesses are killed in Rev 11:7, **"And when they shall have finished their testimony"** and also confirmed in Dan 12:7, **"when he says that it shall be for a time, times and an half [1260 days]; and when he shall have accomplished to scatter the power of the holy people, all these things shall be finished"**. The holy people are the sealed 144,000 Saints that depart into the wilderness to escape the Anti-Christ in Rev 12:14 for 1260 days during the last half of the Tribulation. This occurs approx. 30 days prior to the Anti-Christ receiving his power for 42 months in Rev 13:5 where he

KILLS all that do not take the Mark in Rev 13:15. Note, the Saints escaped into the wilderness for 1260 days or 3½ years and the Anti-Christ was given 42 months or 3½ years to rule. There are no humans left to be saved during the last half of the Trib for all have been killed that were not Sealed by God or that have taken the MARK of the Beast. The last half of the Trib is pure wrath upon man that has the Mark!

Important Note: If the 5th Trump lasted 5 months and the 6th Trump lasted 13 months, the 5th Trump had to be blown at the two-year mark of the first half of the Tribulation placing the 7th Trump at the middle of the seven years. This means each half-lasted 3½ years for a total of 7 years or 2520 days representing Gods number of punishment.

Middle of the Tribulation

Events of the 2nd Half 3½ years or 42 months or 1260 days of seven Vials. Time period for Satan or Anti-Christ to Rule. The seven Vials are wrath upon ungodly man.

1st Vial- poured upon the earth a noisome grievous sore upon men that had the mark of the beast that worshiped the Beast.

2nd Vial- poured upon the sea that became as blood of dead man and living died in the sea.

3rd Vial- poured upon the rivers and fountains of waters becoming blood and another angel shouted that Gods judgment was right and just.

4th Vial- poured upon the sun to scorch men with fire and heat and man repented not.

5th Vial- poured upon the seat of the beast and his kingdom was full of darkness they gnawed their tongues for pain, man blasphemed God and they repented not for their deeds.

6th Vial- poured upon the great river Euphrates and water dried up of the kings of the east to prepare for the Armageddon War. Three unclean spirits like frogs came out of the mouth of the dragon, beast and false prophet as spirits of devils working miracles that was sent to the Kings of the Earth to battle Almighty God to a placed called Armageddon.

7th Vial- poured upon the air and a great voice came out of the Temple in Heaven from the Throne saying **"It is done"** the Tribulation is complete! A great earthquake occurred dividing Jerusalem into three parts and all cities of the earth fell, God remembered Babylon the Great to give unto her the cup of the wine of the fierceness of his "wrath" that took place in the opening of the 6th Seal. The battle of Armageddon is described very well in Zach 14:12 where it is clearly WRATH, **"And this shall be the plague wherewith the Lord will smite all the people that have fought against Jerusalem; Their flesh shall consume away while they stand upon their feet, and their eyes shall consume away in their holes, and their tongue shall consume away in their**

mouth". This verse does not describe a nuclear war but the fire from Heaven by Christ and his Angels along with all of his Saints. All were riding horses caring flames of fire and Zach 14:12, Rev 1:7 & 19:11-21 gives a good account of the battle of Armageddon.

Note: all the Vials were to pour God's WRATH upon ungodly men and the only war taking place was in the 6th Vial for man to battle against God, not each other for all kings and nations are aligned with the Anti-Christ. This WAR is the war of all wars, judgment and final WRATH upon godless men and the Beast Kingdom, the battle of Armageddon.

-Piece together the wars in Eze, Jerm, Dan into the timeline Damascus war

-the Trib. is wrath Zech 1:15, Zech 1:8-10 is Russia

     -Isa 6:11 "cities be wasted"

     -Daughter of Babylon means offspring

Bible references referring to WWIII

All Bible references came out of the King James Authorized 1611 Version Bible. Ps 46, Eze 35, mount Seir- descendants of Edom or Esau the land of Seir or Edom Gen 14:6, Duet 2:1, 12, Josuah 15:1, Judges 11:17-18, I Kg 9:26. Connection to Palestinian and communist Edom, Isaiah 17:1 Damascus destroyed along with cities of Aroer Moabites. II Esdras 8:50&56 and 15:15-19.

Signs from Heaven	I Thes 5:3
Matt 16:1-3 signs of the times	Isa 13:6-9
Dan 12:1-3 time of Trouble	23:1-14, 24:6
Jude saving of all Israel	Cities Destroyed
Dan 12:4 signs travel, knowledge	Isa 24:1-&12
Matt 24:6-7 Wars and rumors of war	Jerm 4:29, 15:8
21:22 then great tribulation	Eze 9:4-9 destruction
Rev 6:3-4	of people in cities
Comfort from desolation Pro 3:25-26	26:18-19
WW III Ex 15:14, Isa 14:29 and 31	Isa 34:6-7
Philista - land of the Philistia	Eze 38:1-11
Ps 60:8, 87:4, 108:9	

The Simple Plan of Salvation

The terms Eternal or Eternity are the prime objective of God's creation of Man in his Spirit and Image. God created man to live forever with an eternal Spirit. Every man from creation is given a prime decision at some point in their lives to either accept or deny Gods son as the only true Christ. Man has an inherent desire to believe in God for he placed that need in all of us when Adam was kicked out of the Garden. God truly loves his creation of man and gave each person a drawing to him and free will in each of us to seek him. Satan's serpent causing Eve to partake in sin created a rift and void between God and man leaving man with a choice of free will to choose between good or evil. The following verses and reference numbers give us a good idea in the meaning of "ever" in the light of eternal salvation and a glimpse of eternity in reference to our souls. Do we want to be with our Lord and Savior in Heaven or Lucifer the Devil called Satan burning in the pit of Hell and Fire? The choice is only ours to make as individual souls!

Jesus tells us in Matt 16:26, **"For what is a man profited, if he shall gain the whole world, and lose his own soul?"** Place Eternity into this equation and determine if the timing of a blinking of an eye equates to the pleasures of this earth. Is it worth it! Look around at the beauty and intricate creation of this earth and truly say to yourself that God did not create this wonderful world, you only fool yourself. With that in mind, what does it take to go to Heaven. The Apostle Luke gives a very good example in what it takes for us to enter heaven for Luke 23:39-43 tells a wonderful story that explains salvation very clearly. The thieves on the cross on either side of Jesus, prior to his death, spoke and one said, **"If thou be Christ, save thyself and us"** and the other thief rebuked him and said **"we received the due reward of our deeds: but this man hath done nothing amiss"**. When Jesus heard this, he said, **"And Jesus said unto him, Verily I say unto thee, today shalt thou be with me in paradise"**. This thief never went to Church, tithed his money or did good deeds for the Jewish faith or for the poor but he went to Paradise and later to Heaven with Jesus. There are only two factors in entering Heaven according to this verse and that is believe that you are a sinner and <u>repent</u> and <u>believe in Jesus that he shed his blood on the cross for our sins</u>. The thief on the cross meet both of these categories for he recognized his sins by repenting to Christ and personally saw Christ die on the cross for Jesus died first. Works do not get us to Heaven but by a simple Faith in Jesus as the Messiah. The following Scripture prove this point:

<u>Rom 10:13</u> **"For whosoever shall call upon the name of the Lord shall be saved"**
<u>Rom 10:9</u> **"That if thou shalt confess with thy mouth the Lord Jesus, and shalt believe in thine heart that God hath raised him from the dead, thou shalt be saved"**
<u>Act 4:12</u> **"Neither is there salvation in any other: for there is none other name under heaven given among men, whereby we must be saved"** This verse makes Masonry, Allah, Buda, Illuminism, secret societies and all the other religious gods null and void if we want to go to Heaven. Only Jesus is the answer. John 14:6 **"Jesus saith unto him, I am the way, the truth, and the life: no man cometh unto the Father, but by me"**
<u>Luke 13:3</u> **"I tell you, Nay; but except ye repent, ye shall all likewise perish"**. This verse is speaking to non-Christians and the born-again for we must maintain

an "often" repentance as stated in Heb 9:25-26 to Jesus as our High Priest.

John 3:16 a most simple verse, **"For God so loved the world, that he gave his only begotten Son, that whosoever believeth in him should not perish, but have everlasting life"**. Knowing that you have sinned and believing in Jesus asking for salvation with a repenting heart, you will be saved.

Romans 5:12 **"and so death passed upon all men, for that all have sinned"** and Rom 6:23, **"For the wages of sin is death; but the gift of God is eternal life through Jesus Christ our Lord"**. According to these verses, knowing that you have sinned and repenting ("often") and believing in Jesus are the two factors in going to Heaven.

Romans 13:1 **"Let every soul be subject unto the higher powers, For there is no power but of God: the powers that be are ordained of God"**. There is a great deception today for many people mistake the spirit of Satan and his demons called Lucifer, illuminism or knowledge, as being the real god of this world. Satan's spirit is the second most powerful force in the universe and can be easily mistaken for the Spirit of Christ. Be very careful for these spirits can be conjured through drugs, sex, occults, secret organizations and many pleasurable vices within this world, I Peter 5:8 **"Be sober, be vigilant; because your adversary the devil, as a roaring lion, walketh about, seeking whom he may devour"**. This verse is speaking of both Christian and non-Christian.

Rom 6:3 **"Know ye not, that so many of us as were baptized into Jesus Christ were baptized into his death?"** The term Christian means Christ like, Christ was baptized with water and Spirit so shall we, Christ died and his body rose from the grave so shall we, Christ ascended into the clouds so shall his Church at their taking or rapture. Everything that Christ did so shall we as Christians.

Eph 2:8-9 **"For by grace are ye saved through faith; and that not of yourselves: it is the gift of God: Not of works, lest any man should boast"** Luke 13:3 **"I tell you, Nay; but except ye repent, ye shall all likewise perish"**.

Romans 13:1 **"Let every soul be subject unto the higher powers, For there is no power but of God: the powers that be are ordained of God"**.

Important Note: With all these Scriptures in mind, we can lose our state of Spiritual perfection Eph 6:1 and lose our Salvation if we fail one thing! We willfully return to our sins (vomit) and fail to repent, II Peter 2:20-22, **"For if after they have escaped the pollutions of the world through the knowledge of the Lord and Savior Jesus Christ, they are again entangled therein, and overcome, the latter end is worse with them than the beginning. For it had been better for them not to have known the way of righteousness, than after they have known it, to turn from the holy commandment delivered unto them. But it is happened unto them according to the true proverb, The dog is turned to his own vomit again; and the sow that was washed to her wallowing in the mire"**. If the righteous man returns to his sin (vomit), his robs become dirty and spotted and he will be blotted out of the book of life as clearly stated in Rev 3:5, **"He that overcometh, the same shall be clothed in white raiment; and I will not blot out his name out of the book of life, but I confess his name before my Father, and before his angels"**. All these Scriptures are based on an often repentance as stated in Heb 9:25-26, **"Nor yet that he should offer himself often, as the high priest entereth into the holy place every year with blood of other; For then must he often have suffered since the foundation of the world: but now once in the end of the world hath he appeared to put away sin by the sacrifice of himself"**.

If you truly believe in the need of salvation from the depth of your heart, simply say the following prayer: *"Dear Jesus, I am a sinner and ask that you forgive me of my sins that you wash away my sins by your shed blood on the Cross by dying for me that I may be with you in Heaven. Thank You Jesus, Amen"*. If you ask this simple prayer in total sincerity, you meet the requirements of salvation just as the thief on the cross and you will be saved. The most important decision any person can make in their lifetime is to accept Jesus as your personal Savior. If you fail to make this one simple decision, you will lose your soul for eternity just as Matt 16:26 states. What did Jesus say to the prostitute that the Priests were going to stone in John 8:11, Jesus forgave her but she had to pay a price for her sins, **"and Jesus said unto her, Neither do I condemn thee: go and sin no more"**. It is very simple but hard, after we repent of our sins and gain eternal salvation, Christ expect us to "sin no more". The Holy Bible is the most sold and proven book on earth so what do you believe, the decision is yours?

With eternal salvation in mind as these verses quote, read the Biblical Definitions of Ever, Eternity and Eternal for better understanding, our souls are endangered for Eternity/Forever.

Eternal Duet 33:27, 6924 Hebrew, *the front, of place absolutely the fore part, the East or time antiquity, before anciently, eastward, aforetime, ancient time, before, east end part, side ware, eternal or ever-lasting, old, past 6923, to project one self, precede, to anticipate, hasten, meet for help, come or go before, disappoint, meet, prevent. 6926, the forward part or East on the east or in front of eastward.*

Isa 60:15, 5769, Hebrew, *the vanishing point, time out of mind past or future, eternity, always, ancient time, continuance, ever-lasting, of old, long or old time, perpetual, beginning of the world without end.*

Matt 19:16, 166, Greek, *perpetual as used in past time or past and future, eternal, for-ever, everlasting, world began.*

Eph 3:11, 165, an age, perpetuity past, the world, a Messianic period present or future, age, course, eternal, forever more, the world began without end.

Eternity Isa 57:15, 5703, Hebrew, *termins as in duration, perpetuity, eternity, ever-lasting-more, old, perpetually, world without end.*

Ever Gen 3:22, 5769, Hebrew, *concealed, i.e. the vanishing point, time out of mind past or future, eternity, always, ancient time, any more continuance, eternal, ever-lasting-more, perpetual, beginning of the world without end.* Gen 43:9, Hebrew meaning of "ever", 3605, *the whole or whosoever,* 3117, *unused root word to be host, a day as the warm hours, a space of time associated term, age, always, chronicles, continually-ance, daily, elder, end evening, for everlasting, process of time, space, in trouble, whole age, full year-ly, younger.*

Can we lose our Salvation?

Once a person is born into God's family through the Lord Jesus Christ, can we lose out salvation? Yes, and it is clear in the Scriptures. It is **most Important to understand** the following verses. Heb 6:1-6 tells a true statement but it comes in two parts. This is a very controversial subject and for many years I truly believed that it is impossible to lose your salvation once born again as Christ's child. To understand this subject, we really need to closely study exact verses within the Scriptures. The Bible clearly states in Heb 6:4, **"for it is impossible"** to lose your salvation when you are born again and Christ would have to be retried and crucified if that were to happen. Because of this one verse, Christians fail to understand other important Scriptures that clearly state, you can and will lose your salvation by being blotted out due to self-refusal of an "often" repentance by falling from grace and not found worthy to overcome or endure till the end. The following Scripture clearly state that a born-again Christian that has tasted the wonderful gift can lose their salvation just as half of the Church, only five of the ten Virgin Brides (Born again Christians) went into the marriage supper in Matt 25:1-12 where Christ said **"I know you not"**. They believed once saved always saved and failed to repent often. Do the Scriptures contradict itself? No, it does not and I will clearly explain. A Christian can only live his life in one of two spiritual categories just as there is either light or darkness, salt or pepper and good or evil. These two spiritual conditions are, **(1)** Heb 6:1, being in a state of **"perfection"**: related words as Rev 3:4, **they are worthy**, Rev 3:5, **overcometh**, Matt 24:13, **endure to the end**, Duet 6:25, **righteousness** with the award of entry into God's Kingdom. Titus 3:5 clearly state the Holy Spirit has to be renewed through repentance, **"by the washing [repent] of regeneration, and renewing of the Holy Ghost"**. All these Scripture is based upon an **"often"** repentance in Heb 9:25-26 by our High Priest Jesus Christ. The other spiritual status; **(2)** in a "fallen" state, Galatians 5:4, **"ye are fallen from grace"**: Related words such as Rev 2:5 **"from whence thou art fallen and repent"**, Rev 3:5, **blotted out of the lamb's book**, I Cor 6:9-10, **unrighteous** with the punishment to not see God's Kingdom but be cast into outer darkness with gnashing of teeth as explained in Matt 22:13 for they are not welcome into the Marriage Supper of the King. All these verses are speaking directly to Church members as Christians that fail to repent often. Read all of Christ's parables in how he cast his unfaithful servants that refused to repent into outer darkness!

Heb 6:1-6 is the most important verse to understand for most Christians do not comprehend. They leave out the 1st part. There is a saying, *"once saved always saved"* which is not true if you properly read the Scriptures. 1st Part is in verse one and it states **"let us go on unto perfection: not laying again the foundation of repentance from dead works"**. Two key words in this verse, perfection and repentance, meaning, as long as we have repented of our sins "often", we are in a state of perfection. 2nd Part in verse four states, **"For it is impossible for those who were once enlightened, and have tasted of the heavenly gift, and were made partakers of the Holy Ghost, and have tasted the good word of God, and the power of the world to come, If they shall fall away, to renew them again unto repentance; seeing they crucify to themselves the Son of God afresh, and put him to a open shame"**. A fact, if we maintain perfection thru repentance, we cannot lose our Salvation but if we fail to maintain an often repentance, we will lose our salvation by being blotted out of the book of Life as stated in the Scripture below. Hebrew 9:25-26 explains these verses by saying that under the Old Covenant a believer had to repent once a year by blood sacrifice thru the High Prist put under the New Covenant of the Church a Christian must repent "often" under the blood of Jesus Christ. This verse kills the term "once saved always" for we must often or frequently repent of our daily sins or be blotted out.

The following verses list the word Blot, Blotted, Blotting in the Old and New Testament: Study each of these verses for they are based upon sin against God and failure to repent.

Note: If we fail to repent of our sins often, we will be blotted out of the Lamb's Book of Life just as Rev 3:5 state. According to the New Strong's Exhaustive Concordance, the word "blot" is mentioned thirteen times in the Scriptures, twelve in the Old Testament and once in the New. The word "blotted" is listed six times, five in the Old and once in the New Testament.

Rev 3:1-5 The most important verses to understand as Christians for John is speaking directly to the Church as a WARNING, **"He that overcometh, the same shall be clothed in white raiment; and I will not blot out his name out of the book of life, but I will confess his name before my Father, and before his angels"**. Verses 1-4 list key words to be saved and maintain that Salvation, "be watchful", receive, heard, hold fast, and repent. This verse is a direct reference to the Church and as a member if you fail to overcome by not repenting you will be blotted out of Christ's book of life and lose your Salvation. Rev 2:5 is also a WARNING that relates to this verse and it states, **"repent, and do the first works; or else I will come unto thee quickly, and will remove thy candlestick out of his place, except thou repent"**. As these two verses state, if we as Church members (born-again) fail to repent, Christ

189

will remove our candlestick as a Church and as individuals will be blotted out of the book of Life. The following Scriptures list the word blot.

Exo 32:32-33 verse 32, **"Yet now, if thou wilt forgive their sin; and if not, blot me, I pray thee, out of thy book which thou hast written"** verse 33, **"And the Lord said unto Moses, Whosoever hath sinned against me** [without repentance], **him will I blot out against me, him will I blot out of my book"**

Num 5:23, **"And the priest shall write these curses in a book, and he shall blot them out with the bitter water:"** People or nations are cursed when they fail to repent of their sins.

Duet 9:13-14, **"Furthermore the Lord spake unto me, saying, I have seen this people, and, behold, it is a stiffnecked people: Let me alone that I may destroy them, and blot out their name from under heaven: and I will make of thee a nation mightier that they."** Gods people were stiff-necked because they failed to repent, therefore, they were blotted out of God's book. You must be written in as a servant of God before you can be blotted out.

Duet 29:20, **"The Lord will not spare him, but then the anger of the Lord and his jealousy shall smoke against that man, and all the curses that are written in this book shall lie upon him, and the Lord shall blot out his name from under heaven."** Blotted out due to not repenting.

II Kings 14:27, **"And the Lord said not that he would blot out the name of Israel from under heaven: but he saved them by the hand of Jeroboam the son of Joash."** God did not blot out Israel for disobedience because of their promised birthright inheritance for he knew that they would accept his Gospel in the future through the house of Jeroboam of Ephraim, I Kings 11:26-37. He is the house of Israel, his Church, Matt 10:6 and 15:24.

Ps 51:1 **"Have mercy upon me, O God, according to thy loveingkindness: according unto the multitude of thy tender mercies blot out my transgressions."** Asking for forgiveness through repentance.

Ps 51: 9 **"Hide thy face from my sins, and blot out all mine iniquities."** Not being blotted due to repentance.

Prov 9:7 **"He that reproveth a scorner getteth to himself shame: and he that rebuketh a wicked *man getteth* himself a blot"** In Hebrew rebuketh (3198) means, *to be right or correct, to argue, to decide, justify or convict.* By rebuking sin, you are not blotted out.

Jerm 18:23 **"Yet, Lord, thou knowest all their counsel against *me* to slay me: forgive not their iniquity, neither blot out their sin from thy sight, but let them be overthrown before thee; deal *thus* with them in the time of thine anger."** Again, the word blot is in reference to unforgiven sin.

Apply all the references to the word blot in the verse above in the Old Testament in reference to repentance or be blotted out of the Book of Life.

NOTE: When we identify the Greek and Hebrew meanings of words such as endure to the end, Overcome, and pray always to be found worthy to escape and <u>often,</u> they apply to the act of a frequent **repentance** through prayer. We can see a clear picture of why we are blotted out of the Book of Life simply for the failure to repent of our daily sins. The term *"once saved always saved"* is a lie for we can and will lose our Salvation if we fail to repent in a timely manner, "often" in Heb 9:25-26 as we stand before our God.

08/07/2018 11:18

About the Author

This Author has been a student of Biblical, Ancient and Secular history from the age of thirteen and drafted into the Army in 1970. Educated while in the Military and retired as Chief Warrant Officer Three (CW3) with 21 years of active-duty Army. Field of training in Data Communications holding a Top Secret Special Intelligence Compartmented (TSSCI) security clearance Military Intelligence in the Army Security Agency and Special Operations. Completed Army Flight School in 1978 and instructor course in 1985 as a helicopter flight instructor. Retired from the US Army in 1992 and Army Fleet Support (AFS) as a TH-67 Maintenance Test Pilot in 2014. Received the Defense Meritorious Service Medal to include many other awards and decorations. Deployed to five overseas assignments receiving the following combat citations, Joint Meritorious Unit Award, Southwest Asia Service Medal with 3 Bronze Service Stars and Kuwait Liberation Medal.

God has truly blessed me with a wonderful military and civilian flying career allowing me to amass a tremendous amount of military, historical and Biblical knowledge during my world travels. He has spiritually guided me and allowed me the ability to compile the material within this book through deep prayer, study and research. This Author is not affiliated with any Party, Denomination or Organization but simply have a great desire to tell America the truth of our national heritage as an old Soldier that loves and cherish our great nation and British brothers.